EPICU

HIS CONTINUING INFLUENCE
AND
CONTEMPORARY RELEVANCE

---

edited by
Dane R. Gordon
and
David B. Suits

RIT CARY GRAPHIC ARTS PRESS

2003

Epicurus: His Continuing Influence and Contemporary Relevance
Edited by Dane R. Gordon and David B. Suits

Published and distributed by
RIT Cary Graphic Arts Press
90 Lomb Memorial Drive
Rochester, New York 14623-5604
http://wally.rit.edu/cary/carypress.html

Inquiries about the content of this publication may be directed to the editors care of
Department of Philosophy
College of Liberal Arts
Rochester Institute of Technology
92 Lomb Memorial Drive
Rochester, New York 14623

Printed in the United States
ISBN 0-9713459-6-1

Cover: *Epicurus bust,* courtesy of Erik Anderson, *The Philosophy Garden.*
Papyrus image from the fifth book of Philodemus's treatise, *On Poems.* © Biblioteca Nazionale 'Vittorio Emanuele III' – Napoli and the Institute for the Study and Preservation of Ancient Religious Texts (ISPART) at Brigham Young University in Provo, Utah, USA, 2002. All rights reserved.

To
Judith Edwards Gordon
and
Christine Sage Suits

Epicurus: His Continuing Influence and Contemporary Relevance is the title of this book and the title of a conference held in April 2002 at Rochester Institute of Technology. It expresses what motivated both, namely, that the philosophy of Epicurus has been a quietly pervasive influence for more than two millennia. At present, when many long revered ideologies are proven empty, it is powerfully and refreshingly relevant.

The number of papers and books published, as well as conferences held in recent years, indicate a growing interest in Epicurean philosophy. Some of this addresses particular issues. Other work examines the connection between Epicurus and various thinkers, in this volume going back to Philodemus of the first century before the time of Christ, and forward to Sartre and de Beauvoir of the twentieth century after.

But much of the current interest in Epicurus has nothing to do with history. His philosophy offers a straightforward and courageous way of dealing with the imponderable, sometimes unbearable issues of life and death. Put simply, Epicurus taught that we can depend only on ourselves and on our friends. It is a simplicity of profundity, teaching that even if life at the end is like water draining into the ground from a broken pot, we do not have to grieve. We can take pleasure and pride in the fact that we lived life the best we could for as long as we could. That is an imperishable value even though we perish.

To Epicurus, friends are supremely important. Long after the *Analects* were written, he echoes Confucius's teaching about friendship, and long before the *New Testament* was written, he anticipates the second commandment. It is, in fact, the wisdom of the world. We need friends and they need us. At a time when nations are flexing their muscles in unilateral ways, that is important to remember. As Aristotle taught, we are social creatures. In the company of others we find our best strength and our greatest pleasure.

The chapters in this book provide a kaleidoscope of opinions about Epicurus's teaching through two thousand years. They tell us also about the discoveries in Oenoanda and Herculaneum that promise to augment the scant remains we have of Epicurus's own writing. This is truly exciting to those who value his teaching as a scholarly and personal resource for contemporary life.

Dane R. Gordon
David B. Suits

ACKNOWLEDGMENTS

We wish to acknowledge the financial support which the April, 2002 conference received from the Office of the Provost of R.I.T., from the College of Liberal Arts, from the Department of Philosophy, from the New York Council for the Humanities, and from the National Endowment for the Humanities.

CONTENTS

THE PHILOSOPHY OF EPICURUS:
IS IT AN OPTION FOR TODAY?

Dane R. Gordon

The continuing influence of Epicurus is discussed throughout this book. From Lactantius to Butler, Cicero to Gassendi, Augustine to Marx, Epicurean philosophy has been quietly pervasive. It flourished for about six centuries and then disappeared as an identifiable philosophic school. But it never ceased to attract persons for whom what Epicurus taught provides a thoughtful interpretation of the nature and conduct of life. My endeavor here is a personal estimate of that, an essay rather than a paper, to serve if it can as an appreciative context for the papers that follow.

The persistence of Epicureanism is somewhat remarkable given the way it has been parodied, misrepresented and trivialized, even during Epicurus's lifetime. My beginning students know little about philosophy, but they do know what (in their own view) Epicurus taught: eat, drink, and be merry, for tomorrow we die. When, on one occasion, I pointed out that that is quite wrong a student brought a philosophy text to class, published in 1973, which described Epicureanism as a "comic episode in philosophy". I was still not persuaded, but the student could have directed me to almost any English dictionary where typically "Epicurean" is defined in such terms as sensual, gluttonous, luxurious. Had he been unusually determined he might have discovered Zeller's harsh criticism, written at the end of the nineteenth century. He objected to Epicurus requiring his followers to learn his teaching by heart, the result being that unlike Stoicism and even Christianity Epicureanism did not change. This places its intellectual value, declared Zeller, "on the lowest level".[1]

Yet Zeller admitted, as a puzzling phenomenon, that the widespread and continuing interest in Epicureanism is out of all proportion to the judgments that can be brought against it. He would be puzzled now by the books and papers and translations being published, and conferences held more than a hundred years later. He would surely be intrigued, perhaps impressed by the excitement of philosophers, classicists, archeologists and others at the recovery of inscriptions from Oenoanda, and the restoration of texts from the hitherto almost indecipherable charred rolls found in Philodemus's house in Herculaneum.

The continuing influence of Epicurus is manifest. Does his philosophy

---

1 E. Zeller, *The Stoics, Epicureans and Skeptics*, trans. Rev Oswald J. Reichel, new and revised edition (London: Longmans, Green and Co., 1892), p. 420.

have contemporary relevance? Epicurus's teaching provided a philosophy of life for large numbers of people through six or seven hundred years. Could it provide a philosophy of life now?

History is both deceitful and encouraging, deceitful when we compare our own times with long ago and conclude, on the basis of apparent similarities, that they were just like us. The twelfth century Knight discovered in a bog in Britain some years ago, his body intact, looked as if he might be just like us. It is doubtful. He ate, he slept, and he experienced sensations like us. But he lived in a conceptual world that probably was not at all like ours. We have to be cautious when drawing historical parallels.

Yet history is encouraging. It invites us to consider the past, not as an utterly different realm, but rather as the earlier stage of a continuity of which we are a part. We can learn from it and be inspired by it, particularly with regard to literature and philosophy.

Menander was a contemporary of Epicurus. (I have described him to my students as the Neil Simon of the ancient world.) Close in age, they served in the Athenian army together. Many of his characters were foolish; so are we. Their children were irresponsible; parents still complain about that. They misunderstood one another and stumbled into needlessly complicated situations; so do we. A link exists between us and the past through our shared humanness.

Menander included little if any religious or philosophical reflection in his plays. His characters live for the present. They simply try to make the best of their lives, which is how most of us live and is consistent, even if he was not aware of it, with what Epicurus taught. Finally, Menander believed in happy endings. All his characters turn out to be friends (or at least not enemies). As the plots progress they find that they need one another, also an Epicurean teaching, so after all we might be encouraged to find some similarities between the present and the past, and as Epicurus's philosophy was meaningful to them it could, at least might, be relevant to us.

What people wanted most of all in the Hellenistic world was ataraxia, or peace of mind. Perhaps they got some of it from Menander's plays. Walking home after a performance they could believe, for a while anyway, that everything would be all right. But people were burdened with anxiety about the unpredictability of life which a play, however delightful, could not dispel. As one writer described it:

> tens of thousands of people were gripped by an unreasonable, dismal, desperate conviction that everything in the world was under the total control of Tyche and Fortune, Chance or Luck. There was a deep seated feeling that men and women were adrift in an uncaring universe, and that everything

was hazardous, beyond human control or understanding or prediction. And so the cult of chance swept conqueringly over the Mediterranean.[2]

"Take my word for it", wrote Meander, "every thought or word or action—sheer chance: we just append our signatures."[3] But people did not just append their signatures. They tried a variety of ways to escape from Tyche, to achieve peace of mind in spite of it. One way was by consulting the stars. People believed that if they knew what the stars foretold they could control and plan their lives.

Another was religion, particularly mystery cults that featured a divine Savior who could guide believers through this life and protect them from god's anger after they were dead.

But for some, neither astrology nor religion provided peace of mind. Among them were those who turned to philosophy, and one of the philosophic options they could choose was the teaching of Epicurus.

It is worth reflecting upon the boldness of what Epicurus proposed. He absolutely rejected astrology and religion. He was, in fact, particularly bitter about religion. Lucretius's description of Iphigenia's sacrificial death, at the beginning of *De Rerum Natura*, which, we can assume, represents closely Epicurus's own view of religion, is as harsh an attack on religion as one can find in literature. Epicurus was bold because what he rejected provided the major interest in life of most inhabitants of the Hellenistic world, it was their hope and consolation. Without it there was nothing to protect them (so they thought) from the utter arbitrariness of life. But Epicurus was bold in a special way. Unlike all the Hellenistic religions and some of the philosophies—for example, Stoicism—he did not attempt to challenge the arbitrariness of life, he accepted it.

"In supposing that the gods have arranged everything for the benefit of humanity these thinkers have obviously deviated far from the path of sound judgement."[4] As Lucretius records Epicurus's views, "Our world is the creation of nature, the atoms themselves collided spontaneously and fortuitously, clashing together blindly, unsuccessfully, and ineffectually in a multitude of ways...."[5]

Epicurus presented what the majority of those living in the Hellenistic world dreaded most and went to great lengths and cost to avoid, for them it was

2   Michael Grant, *From Alexander to Cleopatra: The Hellenistic World* (New York: Collier Books, Macmillan Publishing Co., 1982), p. 214.

3   *Menander: Plays and Fragments*, trans. with Introduction by Norma Miller (London: Penguin Books, 1987), p. 243.

4   Lucretius, *On the Nature of Things*, trans. with Introduction and Notes by Martin Ferguson Smith (Indianapolis: Hackett Publishing Co. Inc., 2001), p. 40.

5   Ibid., p. 62.

a worst case scenario. But for Epicurus it was not worst case, it was what is. The worst case is trying to avoid it through such delusions, as he regarded them, as astrology and religion. Superstition and supernaturalism were a disease to him, a burden that crippled life. His philosophy was a purgative. Accept it and the morbid fears that troubled men and women would disappear.

It was an uncompromising offer, a blood, sweat and tears operation, except that Epicurus demonstrated in his own life the attractiveness of such a philosophy. Perhaps blood and sweat, but not tears, because he offered people the greatest gift, the ability to be themselves and cultivate their own strength.

Centuries later, Simone de Beauvoir wrote in her *The Ethics of Ambiguity*

> if man is free to define for himself the conditions of a life which is valid in his own eyes, can he not choose whatever he likes and act however he likes? Dostoevsky asserted, "If God does not exist everything is permitted...." However, far from God's absence authorizing all license, the contrary is the case... man bears the responsibility for a world which is not the work of a strange power, but of himself, where his defeats are inscribed, and his victories as well.... One cannot start by saying that our earthly destiny has or has not importance, for it depends upon us to give it importance. It is up to man to make it important to be a man; he alone can feel his success or failure.[6]

It is another way of putting the existentialist maxim that we are the choices we make. We have no sign posts. We set our own agenda. We make our way in our own strength. That is what Epicurus taught, but the lesson has to be learned and learned again. If we study the Hellenistic age, the history of Europe, the history of this country in its early days and its society now we find a constant, urgent, never satisfied desire of people to unlock their hidden strength, to get in touch with their inner wisdom, to enlarge the possibilities of their lives. To accomplish this they turn to one religious, metaphysical, or psychological oracle after another, in more recent times Emmanuel Swedenborg, Franz Anton Mesmer, Ralph Waldo Emerson, Carl Rogers, Carl Jung, even contemporary witches.[7] Different as they were and are they share one belief; they are not alone in their endeavor. William James expressed it concisely, "we inhabit a wider spiritual environment as surely as we do our physical and social environment."[8]

---

6   Simone de Beauvoir, *The Ethics of Ambiguity*, trans. Bernard Prechtman (New York: Citadel Press, 1964), p. 15.

7   Robert C. Fuller, *Spiritual But Not Religious: Understanding Unchurched America* (Oxford and New York: Oxford University Press, 2001), p. 39ff, 96, 124ff.

8   Ibid., p. 132.

All this is completely alien to Epicurus, the anxious religious and metaphysical longing, the presumption of a spiritual reality. He puts it to us: These are delusions, foolishness, painful and unnecessary burdens that men and women need not have but bring upon themselves. Can we rid ourselves of these superstitious encumbrances? People did it then. Can we do it now?

Epicurus created a problem for his followers and prospective converts by the terms he used. "[P]leasure is the starting point and goal of living blessedly."[9] Realizing that this could be misunderstood (during his own life time it was), he explains what he means: "[W]hen we say that pleasure is the goal we do not mean the pleasures of the profligate or the pleasures of consumption.... For it is not drinking bouts and continuous partying and enjoying boys and women or consuming fish and other dainties of an extravagant table",[10] all of which were unashamedly enjoyed by Epicurus's Cyrenaic predecessor, Aristippus.

His manner of life was much more like that of an abstemious monk a thousand years later. His normal drink was water, although he enjoyed wine mixed with water. His normal food was bread, and vegetables from his garden. "Send me a little pot of cheese", wrote Epicurus to a friend, as recorded by Diogenes Laertius, "so that I can indulge in extravagance when I wish."[11]

Is this a philosophy for today? A recent issue of *Time* has a picture on its cover of a young woman with greedy eyes holding two plates, one with a large grilled steak, the other with pasta and red and green peppers. Inside, a box notes that 35% of Americans are overweight and an additional 26% are obese.[12] Some of the comments in the articles are not complimentary. "[S]edentary life styles and a cornucopia of food have transformed people into the equivalent of corn-fed cattle confined in pens. We have created the great American feed lot."[13] I did not find any references to Epicurus here. Is his philosophy relevant to that kind of society? I doubt it for the 61 percent.

Epicurus was not concerned primarily with food. His objective was to achieve ataraxia. He made himself more clear in the *Principal Doctrines*. "It is impossible to live pleasantly without living prudently, honorably, and justly and impossible to live prudently, honorably, and justly without living pleasantly."[14] Unfortunately many examples from history disprove that second statement, unless pleasantness can be achieved despite the slings and arrows. Epicurus's death is an example. He died from what must have been the prolonged and

---

9 "Letter to Menoeceus", in *The Epicurus Reader*, trans. and ed. Brad Inwood and L. P. Gerson, introduction by D. S. Hutchinson (Indianapolis: Hackett Publishing Co. Inc., 1994), p. 30.

10 Ibid., pp. 30–31.

11 *The Epicurus Reader*, p. 4.

12 *Time*, September 2, 2002, p. 51.

13 Ibid., p. 52.

14 *The Epicurus Reader*, p. 32.

---

extreme pain of an obstructed bladder, yet he died with courage and calmness. Was it pleasant? Can we dare to say it was? Physically, extremely unpleasant. Yet he was with friends comforting him and supporting him, however they could. Death comes to us all, we cannot avoid it, but we can hope that when it comes it will be in the presence of those we love. It is the best gift of friends to those who die. Diogenes Laertius notes that as Epicurus died he bade his friends to remember his teachings.[15]

Epicurus had many friends. According to Diogenes Laertius, "his friends were so numerous that they could not be counted by entire cities." He was "a friend to all mankind". No doubt his "unsurpassed acts of goodness" would account for much of that.[16] It could affect his puzzling comment that friendship "takes its origin from the benefits it confers on us".[17] What benefits might those be?

We can give reign to our suspicion that friendship to him was self-serving. But benefits can include having someone to love, to care for, to be a friend. And when he declares that nothing enhances our security as much as friendship,[18] he may mean physical safety, or he may mean that the possession of friendship provides a security greater than that provided by a strong arm or locked doors.

Epicurus's interest in friendship was not new in philosophy. Plato's *Symposium* and his *Lysis* are both about friendship. Books eight and nine of Aristotle's *Nicomachean Ethics* provide an analysis of different kinds of friends. But these, we might note, are descriptive accounts written somewhat impersonally (although if we go by his will Aristotle was a generous, heartfelt man). Epicurus wrote little about friendship, but he was a friend in the manner taught by another teacher three centuries later, in what is known as the second commandment. He was a friend as Gilgamesh was a friend, two thousand or so years earlier, to Enkidu whom he thought he could bring back to life by the depth of his grief. From Gilgamesh to now, friendship is relevant. To that extent so is Epicurus's philosophy.

Epicurus's teaching about death is presented as clearly as possible in his letter to Menoeceus. I quote a lengthy passage because it expresses his views so well.

> Get used to believing that death is nothing to us. For all
> good and bad consists in sense-experience, and death is the
> privation of sense-experience. Hence, a correct knowledge of

---

15 Ibid., p. 4.

16 Ibid., p. 3.

17 Ibid., p. 37.

18 Ibid., p. 34.

the fact that death is nothing to us makes the mortality of life a matter for contentment, not by adding a limitless time [to life] but by removing the longing for immortality. For there is nothing fearful in life for one who has grasped that there is nothing fearful in the absence of life. Thus, he is a fool who says that he fears death not because it will be painful when present but because it is painful when it is still to come. For that which while present causes no distress causes unnecessary pain when merely anticipated. So death, the most frightening of bad things, is nothing to us; since when we exist, death is not yet present, and when death is present, then we do not exist. Therefore, it is relevant neither to the living nor to the dead, since it does not affect the former, and the latter do not exist. But the many sometimes flee death as the greatest of bad things. And sometimes choose it as a relief from the bad things in life. But the wise man neither rejects life nor fears death. For living does not offend him, nor does he believe not living to be something bad.[19]

His argument about death is compelling. Yet, like his rejection of the supernatural, it is a bold step in the context of that world. South-east from Greece, across the Mediterranean, not a great distance, lay Egypt whose people were "deeply preoccupied with the problems of death".[20] Henri Frankfort explains, "Their belief in the continued existence of the dead is shown in a striking manner by the fact that in certain emergencies they addressed letters to dead relatives.... We may assume that in Egypt, as elsewhere, the continued significance of the dead in the emotional and intellectual life of their survivors established the reality of their after life beyond a doubt ... the survival of the dead belonged to the data of actual experience."[21]

This was overwhelmingly the view of Hellenistic society. Its people worshipped many deities; one of them was the gentle and compassionate figure of Isis. She came to people in dreams as in Apulius's story,[22] and she and her consort Osiris, worshipped by thousands of people in dramatic and emotional ceremonies, offered personal immortality.

Epicurus had no time for this. However out of step he may have been with prevailing belief he knew he had something to offer much better: the

---

19 Ibid., p. 29.

20 Henri Frankfort, *Ancient Egyptian Religion* (New York: Harper and Row Publishers, 1948, 1961), p. 88.

21 Ibid., p. 89.

22 Apulius, *The Golden Ass*, XI.6.15.

---

enjoyment of present life. Death is inevitable. But enjoy what you have; don't pine for what you cannot have. His sensible advice had been given centuries before by the alewife in the Mesopotamian Gilgamesh Epic.

> Gilgamesh, whither are you roaming?
> Life, [immortal life] which you look for, you shall never find.
> (For) when the gods created man, they set
> death as share for man, and life
> snatched away in their own hands.
> You, Gilgamesh, fill your belly,
> day and night make merry,
> daily hold a festival,
> dance and make music day and night.
> And wear fresh clothes,
> and wash your head and bathe.
> Look at the child that is holding your hand,
> and let your wife delight in your embrace.
> These things alone are the concern of man.[23]

Gilgamesh could not accept that advice. He continued his search. It continues still. Three centuries after Epicurus the Apostle Paul wrote about how the "last enemy" death had been defeated by the resurrection of Christ, an assertion that became the prevailing religious view in Europe for about sixteen hundred years. It remains so in the United States of America. Year after year Gallup polls report on the extremely high percentage of people in North America who believe in life after death.

In spite of it, do we take the position of Epicurus, or do we cling to belief of some kind to ameliorate our fears?

Yet putting the question this way does not take into account the profundity and mystery of the fact of death. Tomorrow (September 11, 2002) Mozart's *Requiem* will be sung by choirs all over the world to mark the first anniversary of the attack on the World Trade Center, in New York City, and the Pentagon in Washington, with terrible loss of life. In this writer's view the emotions involved are too deep to dismiss as superstition. The movement from life to death is a solemn moment, even for those used to it such as doctors, nurses, priests. The mind and heart are drawn almost inevitably to the unanswered question and the never quite dismissed hope that what those standing beside have just observed is not an end, not the flowing of water from a broken pot. But what else it might be is the question. Epicurus believed in his carefully

---

23 Thorkild Jacobsen, *The Treasures of Darkness* (New Haven: Yale University Press, 1976), p. 205.

constructed argument. He believed it took care of the issue. Perhaps it does, but he can be criticized for not recognizing that the often pathetic apprehensions of those he lived among required a more serous philosophical consideration than he gave them.

Mark Twain is remembered as a great American humorist. I have a small book entitled, *The Wit and Wisdom of Mark Twain,* filled with sharp, funny, thought provoking aphorisms. But the latter part of his life was darkened by tragedy, disappointment and an increasingly somber view of the nature of existence. His wife died after a long illness, then a nephew, then two of his daughters at an early age, then his sister. He lost his money in a failed publishing venture and had to sell his beautiful home. Among his later works were two short books *The Diary of Adam* and *The Diary of Eve*, gentle, maybe not so gentle parodies of the biblical story. His last work, *The Mysterious Stranger,* was not gentle. It was clever, entertaining, amusing and a harsh critique of the religious and ethical mores of his day. "Bitter" may not be too strong a term to describe a man who had seen through the pretensions of life and found little to admire. At the end of the book the mysterious stranger says bluntly to the amazed children who are telling the story, "There is no other life." His message was unambiguous; whatever we might expect from that long and widely held belief was delusion, in Mark Twain's case, painful delusion.

He reached that point as his life progressed. Epicurus reached that point at the beginning of his adult life. Mark Twain soured gradually as the result of his life's experiences. Epicurus found it a relief to be rid of the fears that religion generated. For Mark Twain it was, in Wilfred Owens's phrase, "A drawing down of blinds". For Epicurus, it was a pulling up of blinds. Not having to worry about what did not exist freed men and women to be truly themselves, to find within themselves, by themselves, their inner strength. Yet for Twain, and those like him, abandoning religious belief was hard. Existentialism, wrote Sartre, "is strongly opposed to a certain kind of secular ethics which would like to abolish God with the least possible expense." He explains that it is "very distressing that God does not exist... man is forlorn, because neither within him nor without does he find anything to cling to."[24] But for Epicurus it was something to celebrate. One might describe it as the difference in a life between the spare furnishing of a Japanese home and the clutter of a mid-Victorian parlor.

Is Epicurus's spare philosophy relevant today? Is it a workable option? Having asked the question of my students and myself for several years my conclusion is yes. It offers a courageous alternative to Christianity and all other kinds of supernaturalism.

But having said that, we should consider what it costs. Epicurus's

---

24 Jean-Paul Sartre, "Existentialism", in *Existentialism as a Humanism* (New York: Philosophical Library, 1947).

---

arguments are not proven; they are hypotheses. One of his claims is plain wrong. It does not follow that a knowledge of science eliminates religious belief. Geological data now provide compelling evidence for the age of this planet, a lot older than 4004 BC which was widely believed a hundred years ago and now is widely disbelieved.

But a considerable number of scientists are persons of faith. As I write, a news article describes a meeting of the Institute of Religion in the Age of Science, a gathering of scientists interested in various ways in religious issues.[25] If by philosophy we mean examining an issue, attempting to understand and evaluate its various sides, in this connection Epicurus did not do that. He was moved by emotion. The Iphigenia passage is a passionate objection to religion. It is not a strong argument. An argument is no stronger than the counter-examples that can successfully be brought against it. An emotional argument is especially vulnerable.

I doubt that any contemporary religion would approve the killing of a young woman to persuade the gods to grant a favorable wind for a fleet of ships. Religious thinking has changed since then. This is especially true of the period since the end of the Second World War which has seen penetrating, if not destructive criticism of traditional religious belief, and a much greater awareness of and allegiance to non-western religion.

Epicurus could not have imagined this. We, however, can imagine it and should take it into account if we are thinking about becoming Epicureans. As far as we know Epicurus was unacquainted with Buddhism, Hinduism, Confucianism, although aspects of his teaching may be found in them. But a philosophic teaching that is ignorant of them when they existed at the time may be less relevant to contemporary needs than at first appears.

From such writings of his that have survived, Epicurus did not pursue these kinds of critical reflections. They were not important to him. What was important was that people release themselves from the burdens of religious superstition, and the means to that was by accepting his teachings, a familiar approach to achieving peace of mind from the Athanasian Creed to the *Communist Manifesto*. It rests not on evidence, despite Epicurus's careful description of physical phenomena, but on faith.

Is Epicureanism simply another dogma, rather dated now, but interesting as part of the history of philosophy? If that were all, why has it persisted for twenty three hundred years?

We might consider two reasons. When human beings emerged as self-reflective creatures there must have been a time before the development of religious dogma. The terminology of good, bad, right, wrong as applied to

---

25 G. Jeffrey MacDonald, "Scientists Wrangle with Issues of Faith", *The Christian Science Monitor*, September 5, 2002, p. 16.

---

metaphysical speculation, imagination or revelation would not have developed quickly. In the early part of the 70,000 years, which we now know is the span of human existence (as compared with pre-hominids), people just dealt with their immediate physical existence. No doubt the somber reality of death impelled them to find explanations, but until then they were religiously unencumbered. It is to such a time that Epicurus's teaching returns us, even though we are enmeshed in a forest of intellectual and emotional religious ideologies. Epicurus's teaching offers us a clearing in the forest, perhaps a way out of the forest, perhaps, as if in a time machine, the clarity of life before the forest.

Another reason for the persistence of Epicureanism is that it is a continuously attractive ethic of self sufficiency, self discipline, courage, and the cultivation of friends. It looks inward and outward. Its goal, given these, is to live a pleasurable life as Epicurus defined pleasure.

He provided an example in his own life of how to live according to his teaching. In this he can be compared with Socrates, with Buddha and with Christ. They were humble men who would be shocked at the adulation they now receive, as would Epicurus.

The American theoretical physicist, Steven Weinberg, has written that the more he understands the universe, the more it seems to be pointless.[26] Weinberg is a non-supernaturalist, as was Epicurus, but Epicurus reached a different conclusion. He valued life and enjoyed it for its own sake. It was not pointless to him. When life ceases to be pleasurable, as, physically, it did for Epicurus at the end, there are friends. When friends cannot help there is courage, which draws upon what was for Epicurus the ultimate and self-validating strength of life, the self. That, I would say, is Epicurus's contemporary relevance.

---

26 Steven Weinberg, *The First Three Minutes* (New York: Basic Books, 1977), p. 143.

WORKS CITED

Apulius, *The Golden Ass.*

Beauvoir, Simone de, *The Ethics of Ambiguity*, trans. Bernard Prechtman (New York: Citadel Press, 1964).

Epicurus, *The Epicurus Reader*, trans. and ed. Brad Inwood and L. P. Gerson, introduction by D. S. Hutchinson (Indianapolis: Hackett Publishing Co. Inc., 1994).

Frankfort, Henri, *Ancient Egyptian Religion* (New York: Harper and Row Publishers, 1948, 1961).

Fuller, Robert C., *Spiritual But Not Religious: Understanding Unchurched America* (Oxford and New York: Oxford University Press, 2001).

Grant, Michael, *From Alexander to Cleopatra: The Hellenistic World* (New York: Collier Books, Macmillan Publishing Co., 1982).

Jacobsen, Thorkild, *The Treasures of Darkness* (New Haven: Yale University Press, 1976).

Lucretius, *On the Nature of Things*, trans. with Introduction and Notes by Martin Ferguson Smith (Indianapolis: Hackett Publishing Co. Inc., 2001).

MacDonald, G. Jeffrey, "Scientists Wrangle with Issues of Faith", *The Christian Science Monitor*, September 5, 2002.

Menander: Plays and Fragments, trans. with Introduction by Norma Miller (London: Penguin Books, 1987).

Sartre, Jean-Paul, "Existentialism", in *Existentialism as a Humanism* (New York: Philosophical Library, 1947).

Time, September 2, 2002.

Weinberg, Steven, *The First Three Minutes* (New York: Basic Books, 1977).

Zeller, E., *The Stoics, Epicureans and Skeptics*, trans. Rev Oswald J. Reichel, new and revised edition (London: Longmans, Green and Co., 1892).

PHILODEMUS, THE HERCULANEUM PAPYRI, AND THE THERAPY OF FEAR

David Armstrong

Since they were discovered in the mid-18th century, the papyri of the teaching library of Philodemus of Gadara (c. 110–30 BCE), taken from the Villa of the Pisones (more strictly: the Villa of the Papyri, though few doubt the Pisonian ownership of the Villa anymore),[1] at Herculaneum have been a stimulating and disturbing presence in Epicurean studies. Stimulating, because it has been known since their earliest unrollment and decipherment in the 1760s that they would give us a window into the development of the Epicurean school in the days of Cicero and Lucretius, not to mention Philodemus's younger contemporaries Horace and Vergil. (Besides the works of Philodemus and a few others of the later Epicureans, the most important fragments in the collection are those of Epicurus's own otherwise almost totally lost major work for initiates, *On Nature*, a priceless addition to our knowledge of the school's canonical origins.) Disturbing, because they are damaged, difficult to read, full of gaps, composed in a Greek prose very much of its specific period, for which the nearest parallels are that of Polybius two generations before and Dionysius of Halicarnassus and Diodorus Siculus a generation after. Until recently, in addition, many of the fragments were published out of order because of the way the papyri were sawn open originally—in a method which, if the best the 18th century could evolve, would cause nothing but dismay today. Fragments peeled off backwards from the stiffer, sawn-through outer layers, sometimes destroying them as the unrollers went, after they were drawn one by one, were capriciously numbered (sometimes, even, precisely backwards); and only the inner parts of rolls that came apart and unrolled easily and are still in trays at the great Officina dei Papiri in the Naples National Library were—more or less—securely arranged in order.[2] Since its initiation in 1993, it has been the arduous task of those of us in the Philodemus Translation Project of the National Endowment for the Humanities, especially (besides myself) Richard Janko, James Porter, David

1   For the English-speaking reader, the current state of knowledge about the Villa and its contents and ownership is well summarized in various chapters of Marcello Gigante's *Philodemus in Italy*, trans. Dirk Obbink (Ann Arbor: University of Michigan Press, 1995); much more will come from the current revived excavations.

2   For an account of the problems caused by the earlier methods of unrolling cf. Dirk Obbink, *Philodemus On Piety, Part I: Critical Text with Commentary* (Oxford: Oxford University Press, 1996), pp. 24–80.

Blank, Dirk Obbink and Jeffrey Fish, aided by parallel discoveries by continental scholars such as Daniel Delattre, to restore order to many of these, building on the wonderful work of Marcello Gigante (1923–2001) and his colleagues and students at the Centro per lo Studio dei Papiri Ercolanesi from 1969 onwards, especially as found in the journal *Cronache Ercolanesi* (1971–) and the series of texts *La Scuola di Epicuro*,[3] which together, journal and series, have made all but a few of the most important texts available in readable form with translations into one or other of the principal modern languages. We have also introduced and/or profited from new technologies for recovering lost and faint letters, such as new and more powerful microscopes and above all the new Multiple Spectrum Imaging (MSI) photography brought in in 2000 by Brigham Young University's ISPART, the Institute for the Study and Preservation of Ancient Religious Texts, under the leadership of Roger Macfarlane and Steven Booras, which has now made clearer and better contrasted images than ever of the entire library available to Herculaneum students.[4] (Figures 1–4.)

As the proliferation since the 1980s of books and collections of essays on Epicureanism like the present one amply demonstrate, Epicurus's philosophy, with its calm, joyful, religious and devoted attitude to a world strikingly like

---

3 *La Scuola di Epicuro* (Naples: Bibliopolis).

4 Steven W. Booras and David R. Seely, "Multispectral Imaging of the Herculaneum Papyri", *Cronache Ercolanesi* 29 (1999), pp. 95–100.

FIGURE 3, LEFT: *Original and enhanced images of a fragment from PHerc 1084. Photo by Steve Booras.*
FIGURE 4, RIGHT: *Rolled scroll. Photo by Mark Philbrick, Brigham Young University. Both images Courtesy of Biblioteca Nazionale, Naples, Italy.*

that of modern science, a world that operates entirely according to natural laws without the intervention of gods or spirits or providence, a world that offers no hope (and therefore no fear either) of life after death, has become central to modern research in ancient or at least in Hellenistic philosophy. Probably none of the essayists in this volume would dispute the special intensity of the school's contemporary appeal. In the eighteenth and early nineteenth centuries neither the religious nor the "enlightened" regarded Epicurus and his school with any similar enthusiasm. When our papyri were first dug up in the 1750s, and the nature of their contents ascertained by primitive and damaging techniques of unrollment, they excited far less interest. Charles III of Naples, the patron of the excavations of Herculaneum and Pompeii, was an enlightened Bourbon for his day. One of the first acts of his reign, for example, was to rescue Giambattista Vico, the author of *La Scienza Nuova*, whose works had gained him nothing but suspicion from the Neapolitan clergy, from poverty and pension him. The king was nonetheless immensely disappointed in the papyri: as was natural, he had assumed that a treasure trove of lost great poetry or prose, the lost plays of Aeschylus and Sophocles or the missing decads of Livy, had been discovered, one that would equal the amazing discoveries in architecture, painting, mosaic and sculpture which were giving at last his impoverished and hitherto little-visited kingdom an obligatory place on the Grand Tour of Europe.

Instead, after the amateur chemists and scientists of his court had destroyed a few dozen precious rolls trying to open them, and the (for the period) relatively superior opening and unrolling methods of Camillo Paderni and Padre Piaggio had been evolved, it was finally ascertained that the library was the teaching library of a minor Epicurean philosopher briefly mentioned by Cicero and Horace, of whom otherwise the major surviving work was a few dozen, mostly rather flippant, epigrams in the Greek Anthology.[5] Even a liberal Catholic monarch in that age might have been forgiven for feeling a certain exasperation at the discovery that his supposedly precious new texts were all or mostly the difficult and badly damaged writings of an Epicurean heretic who denied providence and the afterlife; not only that, the writings, not even of Epicurus himself or his immediate disciples like Metrodorus and Pythocles but of a later, minor, and little known member of the school. Philodemus had been the house philosopher of Julius Caesar's father-in-law, Calpurnius Piso Caesoninus, who ever since has been presumed to be the owner of the Villa; and his views on Epicureanism were well known in the Rome of the late Republic, forming the basis of Cicero's portrayal of that philosophy in his philosophical dialogues; there were indications that he had perhaps known Lucretius, Catullus and Vergil; but that was hardly a consolation. Charles III's disappointment is evident mainly from the practical results. Serious work now turned entirely to the archaeology of the two cities and the study of their physical remains, the Villa was not re-opened, after poison gas killed some of the king's workers there in the early 1760s, until the end of the 1980s (it is now at last being seriously re-excavated and many new discoveries have been made), and no serious work was done on the papyri until the late 1790s—they were apparently not even ticketed and numbered until then.

By this time, Charles III had inherited the throne of Spain and given the kingdom of Naples to a younger son, Ferdinand IV of Naples, later to style himself Ferdinand I of the Two Sicilies (his long and stormy reign lasted from 1759 to 1825). Ferdinand, who became king at eight and married at sixteen, was a dull and frivolous ruler entirely dominated by his masterful wife, Queen Maria Carolina, the sister of Marie Antoinette, and therefore by the late 1790s a princess badly traumatized and infuriated by the French Revolution. Many readers of this essay unfamiliar with the history of Naples will know this unpleasant woman as the offstage queen that Tosca in Puccini's opera thinks might show her radical lover Cavaradossi some mercy (wrongly, since Maria Carolina loathed revolutionaries and intellectuals even more than Baron Scarpia). By a kind of historical paradox Maria Carolina's obsessions and the damage she did the people of Naples resulted in the decipherment and publication between 1802

---

5 The edition of these by David Sider, ed., *The Epigrams of Philodemus* (Oxford: Oxford University Press, 1997) contains a far superior account of Philodemus in its introduction to that given by A. S. F. Gow and D. L. Page in their *The Garland of Philip*, 2 vols (Cambridge: Cambridge University Press, 1968).

and 1876 of (for all practical purposes) as much of the papyri as Europe was destined to know till the last quarter of the 20th century.

All Philodemus scholars are obliged to familiarize themselves with this history and what follows up to our time to some extent, because of its immense impact on the papyri and their publication; fortunately the immense labors of Marcello Gigante and his circle not only in the publication of the papyri but on the elucidation of their scholarly history since the first excavations are excellently summarized in Mario Capasso's *Manuale di Papirologia Ercolanese*[6] (see especially pp. 67–148 for both what precedes and what follows), and a quick summary may help.

A few of Naples's rather provincial classical scholars had begun work on the papyri in the 1780s and 1790s, to satisfy what at last was the growing curiosity of contemporary European scholars. It did not progress quickly and very little of importance had been achieved when a French-inspired Republic was proclaimed in Naples in 1798 and the royal family fled to Palermo, taking the papyri along at no one knows what cost in physical damage to them—but at least this shows that they were considered among the most valuable crown possessions after the renewed interest in them. This revolution and its aftermath, the terrible vengeance the queen was able to wreak on the rebels with the help of the British fleet under Horatio Nelson, the lover of the queen's favorite and confidante Emma Hamilton, in which the leading Neapolitan papyrus scholars perished along with almost everyone else in Naples who read foreign newspapers or was suspected of "liberal" opinions, is the subject of Susan Sontag's brilliant 1992 novel *The Volcano Lover*. For our purposes, it is enough to note that the violence and cruelty of the vengeance the British fleet helped the queen inflict on the rebels and their brief Parthenopean Republic outraged European public opinion even in those days. The suppression of the rebellion in Naples became a sort of late eighteenth century My Lai, and nearly ended in Nelson's court martial instead of his later ascent to glory after his victories over Napoleon in Egypt. The kingdom of Naples, necessary to British sea power in the Mediterranean, became a virtual British protectorate until the overthrow of Napoleon, but, because of its corrupt and reactionary government, a discreditable and compromising one, and the papyri were at last unrolled and deciphered on a large scale in a manner that for that age counted as scientific and responsible directly because of England's casting round for ways to lessen the odium of their alliance with Ferdinand and Maria Carolina.

One of the Prince of Wales's chaplains, the Rev. George Hayter, persuaded the future George IV to pay for an expedition to Naples in which he would at last hire Neapolitan workmen to unroll and record the papyri with the hitherto little used unrolling machines that Padre Piaggio had invented for

---

6   Mario Capasso, *Manuale di Papirologia Ercolanese* (Galatina: Congedo, 1991).

Charles III. Between 1802 and 1806, when Napoleon's troops rolled unstoppably down the Italian peninsula and installed his marshal Joachim Murat as King of Naples, and the court fled to Palermo, this time leaving the papyri behind, Hayter achieved a miracle that makes him immortal in Philodemus studies: he unrolled and deciphered for the first time over two hundred major papyri. The drawings he had made of them by Neapolitan artists and checked over with the aid of his own Greek and that of various Neapolitan academicians are indispensable in Philodemus studies, since they are by far the best early drawings, preserving in many places text that has decayed or is unreadable today. They were made, also, just after the papyri were opened and before they were pasted in trays, which caused the loss of a good deal of readable text. They are called in Philodemus studies the "O disegni" because Hayter kidnapped them all when the court fled and presented them to Oxford (they are still kept in the Bodleian Library), thus compelling the authorities in Naples to redraw all or most of them after he left from the slightly damaged papyri in their trays (the "N disegni"). Hayter is known from the correspondence that is preserved at Oxford with the "O disegni" to have been a drunken and immoral clergyman, a true Regency rake, who died penniless abroad after the Oxford and Cambridge dons mercilessly exposed his pretensions as an amateur classical scholar on his return to England. It seems amazing that he and his workmen achieved so much more important and crucial results with the papyri than nearly anyone else who had touched them since they were dug up and in fact than most of those who have worked with them since; but it is basically Hayter's work, and that of the Neapolitans who carried that on for a while after he left in his footsteps and following his techniques, that gave us the Philodemus we have today.

But Hayter's results took a long time to bear fruit. In the decade after his death, the Oxford University Press engraved and published some of his better disegni as *Herculanensium voluminum Pars prima/secunda* (1824–5) and these and the disegni themselves were studied to some profit by Walter Scott.[7] At Naples, decipherments of papyri continued and the government subsidized the collections *Herculanensium voluminum quae supersunt* (*Collectio Prior*, with Latin translation and commentary: 19 papyri, 1793–1855; as the commentaries by various Neapolitan academics were poorly received, the *Collectio Altera*, 1862–76, gives only engraved reproductions of the Naples disegni of 176 papyri; a more professional *Collectio Tertia* edited by Domenico Bassi in 1914[8] went only as far as the first volume, which made *de Morte* or *On Death*, PHerc 1050, available as a whole for the first time: all these are rather difficult to find in American libraries). Though for the most part the German scholars who began

---

7 Walter Scott, *Fragmenta Herculanensia* (Oxford: Clarendon Press, 1885).

8 Domenico Bassi, ed., *Herculanensium voluminum quae supersunt: Collectio tertia* (Milan: Hoepli, 1914).

professional Philodemus studies in the second half of the 19th century worked with these engravings only without seeing the papyri or with only brief visits to Naples, some of the texts—at a rather long last—became more or less known, or at least knowable. In the light of what we now know, Bassi's *On Death*, and some Teubner texts like Wilke's *On Anger*,[9] Olivieri's *On the Good King According to Homer*[10] and *On Frank Criticism*,[11] not to mention such major efforts as Siegfried Sudhaus's two-volume *On Rhetoric*,[12] and Christian Jensen's *On Poems V*,[13] made good readable texts available enough for the classical reading public to judge their contents at least generally—if they had provided translations into some modern language, which only Jensen did; and if his translation was into German sometimes more difficult even than the Greek, it was the only one that produced any really satisfactory amount of discussion. Taco Kuiper's rather good Dutch edition, translation and commentary of *On Death* (a dissertation) after Bassi, *Philodemus over den Dood*[14] fell utterly flat for being in an unfamiliar language and was barely even reviewed. (For the present study it is important to note both that the text given in Kuiper and improved for cols. 1–9 and 37–39 by Marcello Gigante in *Richerche Filodemee*,[15] can be still further improved at many points, but is basically reliable.) What boomlet there was in Philodemus studies between about 1915 and 1945 on the basis of these Teubner texts, almost unreviewable without a trip to Naples in person in days when foreign scholars were sometimes but not always welcome to inspect the papyri, depended on an expectation, not fulfilled, that further reliable studies would appear in quantity and provoke further and more reliable discussion. In spite of such exceptions as the editions of Francesco Sbordone and his pupils, mainly of the aesthetic works (*On Poems, On Rhetoric*) published as *Richerche sui Papiri Ercolanese*,[16] or Philip and Estelle DeLacy's edition of the logical work *Philodemus: On Methods of Inference*,[17] and above all Graziano Arrighetti's pioneering edition of Epicurus's own *On Nature* in his *Epicuro: Opere*,[18] these failed to materialize. The history of

9 Carl Wilke, ed., *Philodemide ira liber* (Leipzig: Tuebner, 1914).

10 Alexander Olivieri, ed., *On the Good King According to Homer* (Leipzig: Teubner, 1909).

11 Alexander Olivieri, ed., *On Frank Criticism* (Leipzig: Teubner, 1914).

12 Siegfried Sudhaus, ed., *On Rhetoric* (Leipzig: Teubner, 1892–1896).

13 Christian Jensen, *On Poems* (Berlin: Weidmann, 1923).

14 Taco Kuiper, *Philodemus over den Dood* (Amsterdam: H. J. Paris, 1925).

15 Marcello Gigante, *Richerche Filodemee*, 2nd ed. (Naples: Macchiaroli, 1983).

16 Francesco Sbordone, ed., *Richerche sui Papiri Ercolanese*, 4 vols. (Naples: Giannini, 1969–83).

17 Philip DeLacy and Estelle DeLacy, *Philodemus: On Methods of Inference* (Philadelphia: American Philological Association, 1941), revised for the series *La Scuola di Epicuro* (Naples: Bibliopolis, 1978).

18 Graziano Arrighetti, *Epicuro: Opere* (Turin: Einaudi, 1960; 2nd edn., 1973).

this frustrating period is given in Capasso[19] and need not be gone into further here; it suffices to say that the real beginning of modern Philodemus studies, including the long delayed introduction of microscopes into the Officina dei Papiri, the foundation the Centro Internazionale per lo Studio dei Papiri Ercolanesi, of *Cronache Ercolanesi* and the series *La Scuola di Epicuro*, and the enthusiastic welcoming of international scholars to do work at the Officina, was entirely the work of Marcello Gigante and his collaborators at Naples since 1969—Francesca Longo Auricchio, Giovanni Indelli, Gioia Maria Rispoli, and many others, without whose hospitality and help to myself and many others in the last two decades studies like the present essay would not exist.

A cardinal point in the restoration of Philodemus's library to its true importance in the modern world was the publication by Gigante and Capasso in 1989 of the news that in a recently opened papyrus, *PHerc Parisinus* 2, the names of Vergil himself and three friends, Varius Rufus, Quintilius Varus and Plotius Tucca (all four also close friends of Horace) had been discovered as addressees of a treatise on flattery (confirming a conjecture made by Alfred Koerte as early as 1890).[20] Since then much has been done to confirm the importance of Philodemus's influence on Vergil and the Augustans, already studied by Jane Tait in a pioneering dissertation of 1941,[21] and it is particularly sad to mention Marcello Gigante's death in late 2001 just as I had finished translating his essay in the forthcoming *Vergil, Philodemus and the Augustans: the Cumae Conference, 2000*,[22] a volume which will reveal much about the current state of thought on Philodemus's influence on the Augustan poets. Few scholars who die at 78 can truly be said to suffer a *mors immatura*, but as Vergil says, for the gods even old age is green and fresh. I personally have great hopes that the current excavations at the Villa will give us new classical texts that go beyond Philodemus and the Epicureans and reveal at least some of the great authors Charles III hoped for and was so impatiently disappointed of. I know that Marcello Gigante hoped for them and was also disappointed. Herculaneum studies over two and a half centuries have indeed been a Sargasso sea of hopeful progress and disappointed hopes—including the fact that even the best preserved and most interesting of

19 Capasso, *Manuale*, pp. 135–139.

20 Mario Capasso and Mario Gigante, "Il Ritorno di Virgilio a Ercolano", *Studi Italiani di Filologia Classica* 7 (1989), pp. 3–6—a momentous four pages!

21 Jane I. M. Tait, *Philodemus' Influence on the Latin Poets* (Ph.D. dissertation, Bryn Mawr, 1939). See now David Sider's *The Epigrams of Philodemus*, the introduction to which is by the way the best general account in English of Philodemus's life and work and the evidences for it.

22 *Vergil, Philodemus and the Augustans: the Cumae Conference, 2000*, ed. D. Armstrong, J. Fish, P. Johnston and M. Skinner (Austin: University of Texas Press, forthcoming).

Philodemus's texts have received disappointingly little attention so far. But this is at last changing.

One of these is *On Death*, which along with the recently translated *On Frank Criticism*[23] can be studied to some profit from the texts already known and mentioned above. They do not need to wait for "perfect" texts to be understood. Besides Kuiper's 1925 text there is the edition, translation and commentary by Marcello Gigante of the opening and closing columns in his *Ricerche Filodemee*. These, with Bassi's 1914 edition in the above-mentioned third series (one volume only) of the *Volumina Herculanensia*, give us a fairly reliable text, particularly for the sections I quote below; though in the case of both *On Death* and especially *On Frank Criticism*, we may expect many improvements in text and translation as the study of the new MSI photographs mentioned above progresses. I am preparing a translation and brief commentary of *On Anger* and *On Death* for the Society of Biblical Literature (SBL) series, *Texts and Translations: Graeco-Roman*, in which *On Frank Criticism* has already appeared;[24] here it is enough to say that I have selected passages I know to be fairly reliable in text. As with many Philodemus rolls, the text of this particular work, *PHerc* 1050, becomes clearer and fuller column by column towards the end, whereas much is missing, in this case at least the first two thirds, because the method of opening by Hayter and his assistants sacrificed that much before the papyrus could be unrolled. In *On Death* no outer fragments survived, only the inner consecutive columns. Thus (approximately) the higher the column number the better the text.

There has been much interest generated by *On Frank Criticism*, *PHerc* 1471, since its translation and publication in the SBL series and the book *Paul and Philodemus: Adaptability in Epicurean and Early Christian Psychagogy* by Clarence Glad.[25] Glad compares the personal and communal therapy of vices and inappropriate emotions, which is recommended for Philodemus's Epicurean community and school in this treatise, to Paul's rules and recommendations for his early Christian communities; and certainly in our time, along with the greater favor accorded to ideas like the basic ideas of Epicureanism, it has become a more attractive analogy to compare the techniques of the ancient ethical philosophers toward their students to those of modern psychotherapists, both in giving individual and group therapy, instead of comparing the philosophical

---

23 *Philodemus on Frank Criticism*, ed. and trans. David Konstan, Clarence E. Glad, Johan C. Thom, James Ware, and Diskin Clay (Atlanta: Scholars Press, 1998). Some corrections will be needed in the earlier parts of the translation—the separate fragments are less well done than the columnar part at the end—but the introduction, pp. 1–24, is particularly to be recommended.

24 Ibid.

25 Clarence Glad, *Paul and Philodemus: Adaptability in Epicurean and Early Christian Psychagogy* (Leiden: Brill Academic Publishers, 1995).

"diatribe" to the Christian sermon, or even the philosophers' personal counselling to the advice given by priests in confession. I think it will be clear in what follows that this is in fact a far superior analogy.

And indeed we might hope to answer several questions at once about the importance of Philodemus's library, even *before* any possible new discoveries of greater literature by greater writers in the current new excavations at Herculaneum: Charles III was in fact wrong to be disappointed. To put it in another way: as early as 1810, the Egyptologist and classical scholar Dr. Robert Young, in an anonymous article in the great Tory journal *Quarterly Review*,[26] both tore poor Hayter's borrowed scholarly feathers off in reviewing his incompetent first publication of *PHerc* 1428 *On Piety*, suggesting far better emendations of his own, and questioned the value of the whole collection. Did we not have more voluminous and boring compilations of the fragments of Hellenistic philosophy in Plutarch, Athenaeus, Stobaeus, Sextus and elsewhere than any even of the greatest classical specialists cared to read through twice? What was the use of trumpeting a fragmentary and torn up and confusing and apparently somewhat ill-written series of texts by a confessedly minor philosopher of the age of Cicero, on the same dreary series of topics, as a great new discovery? There are indeed students of Epicureanism who still value the texts of Epicurus himself preserved at Herculaneum far above anything Philodemus had to say, and for just exactly the reasons Young outlined so long ago, but I do not agree. Besides the unique information on Epicurean logic and aesthetics outlined in the various summaries of the library mentioned above (and the beautiful epigrams edited first by Gow and Page and then by Sider for the English reader!), Philodemus's ethical treatises are a mine of information not only on ancient ethical argument but on the personal side of ancient philosophy. They are indispensable in particular to our understanding of how such Roman writers as Lucretius, Vergil, Horace and Seneca saw the interaction of interpersonal therapy conceived as philosophical consolation with poetry and artistic prose's relation to its formal addressees and its readers.

On Frank Criticism (which was itself an epitome of the lectures of Philodemus's teacher in Athens, Zeno of Sidon, and is referred to as such both in its subscription and in *On Anger* col. 36, as being a source for that treatise also) describes the work of the Epicurean therapist as he treats students and beginners in the philosophy individually and together. For Epicureans tried to create communities of friendship in which like-minded people sharing the same philosophy could escape the ordinary prejudices of Greco-Roman society and live together as much as possible, and Philodemus, with the help of another Epicurean, Siro, was the leading figure of an Epicurean community and perhaps also school for the young which centered round Naples and Herculaneum. The

---

26 Robert Young, *Quarterly Review* (Feb., 1810), pp. 1–20.

---

treatise, like *On Anger*, and many other ethical treatises of Philodemus and many other Hellenistic philosophers, is filled with *medical* imagery: at every point the work of the philosophical therapist is compared to that of the ancient doctor, including the fact that the limited ancient pharmacopeia relied heavily on cathartics and purges, and the repetition of severe and sarcastic criticism till results are achieved is compared to repeated purges (fr. 63–5). So also harsh frankness is compared to the surgeon's knife (col. 17a). In *On Anger*, similarly, we are told in col. 44 that the Epicurean wise man accepts "natural" anger as he would a bitter medicine or the surgeon's knife. That is, there are pains that even for the pleasure-oriented Epicureans are worth suffering because they lead to good things, and accepting harsh criticism in order to improve oneself, like accepting the pain of feeling indignant and angry in order to be motivated to correct wrongs or relieve injustice, counts as a good thing in that scale.

On the other hand, there are many reasons for the Epicurean therapist to use gentler speech and gentler means of "treatment". A poignant passage (col. 22a) warns the therapist that women are easily upset by criticism by male intellectuals and "[think it right] that the weakness of their nature be pitied and that they meet with sympathy (*syngnome*) and not be directly ridiculed by those who are stronger than they, and they quickly come to tears thinking they are being reproved out of contempt." (At least, however, the Epicureans accepted women students—and I have identified in Caesar's wife Calpurnia, the daughter of Philodemus's patron, one more of the many known happy Epicurean great ladies of antiquity, like the empress Plotina, wife of the emperor Trajan[27]—so Philodemus's advice to himself and other Epicurean teachers must have worked!)

With the callower pupils in particular, and where no great offence has been given, the therapist will soften his criticisms with affectionate words (fr. 14) and (this is rather charming) will claim that in his own youth he was intemperate also (fr. 14), thus softening the "sting", however healthy and "natural", of his frankness. In fr. 26, Philodemus recommends both *kedemonike nouthetesis* ("caring admonishment") and "an irony which pleases while it gently bites at all men" like that of Socrates or the Roman satirists like Horace and Persius (cf. Gigante, *Ricerche Filodemee*, p. 81; here I agree with him against the SBL translators: my versions here are all slightly different from theirs, but the reader can compare their Greek text, which I follow).

With this much as a premise from Philodemus's theory of therapy, which deserves much longer quotation, we can look at *On Death*, which (as the following quotations may show) is one of the finest of the surviving treatises in

---

27 The proof about Calpurnia is to be found in my article "The addressees of the *Ars Poetica*", *Materiali e discussioni per l'analsi dei testi classici* 31 (1993), pp. 185–230, at p. 200 n. 29.

---

literary style as well as thought. Philodemus's often slipshod Greek has struck me in many other treatises as savoring of the shorthand transcript, minimally revised, but that is not true here. In my opinion this treatise was a showpiece delivered to an audience containing philosophers of many schools and Romans of many philosophies or none, showing to a larger audience than the normal one at his school "what Epicureanism can do for you" and taking the subject "fear of death" as the fulcrum of his demonstration. That accounts for its unusually elaborate and worked up rhetoric and style.

The opening nine columns that survive I will not treat here; they argue more or less effectively that not all deaths are painful and that those that are end in perfect insensibility and are thus "nothing to us" at least in the end and not to be feared. When sense returns after a distressing passage of torn columns among which words are legible only singly and in pairs, and we get more or less continuous intelligible passages (unfortunately whole columns only toward the end) from cols. 12–39, Philodemus is on the subject of various reasons for fearing death. Or, I would rather say, on the subject of *how the Epicurean therapist should treat* various reasons for fearing death advanced by a patient. The Epicurean contention that death is "nothing to us" and not a serious evil experienced by all mankind, one that proves a perfectly happy human life to be impossible, has been much discussed in recent secondary literature, almost always disapprovingly, as though the Epicureans were on this topic "facile eudaemonists", whistling in the dark about the tragedy of the human condition. Not much but a few fragments remain to show us how the Master treated this topic, and the lecture on the fear of death at the end of Lucretius III takes a contemptuous tone toward human fears that does not placate Epicurus's critics. I should think, however, that if *On Death* were better known, its alternation of sarcasm (harsh frank criticism) with the gentler medicine of genuine human sympathy for the worst aspects of the fear of death and its recommendation of deep, continuous and serious religious meditation on reality and the stark facts as the only escape from these difficult aspects would have rendered all or most of this scholarly dispute otiose.[28]

---

28 For a good overview of this debate, see the chapter on Lucretius's view of death in Martha Nussbaum, *The Therapy of Desire* (Princeton: Princeton University Press, 1994), pp. 192–239, itself based on her earlier "Mortal Immortals: Lucretius on Death and the Voice of Nature", *Philosophy and Phenomenological Research* 50 (1989), pp. 303–351. Some chief contributions: Bernard Williams, "The Makropulos Case: Reflections on the Tedium of Immortality", in *Problems of the Self* (Cambridge: Cambridge University Press, 1973); F. Miller, "Epicurus on the Art of Dying", *Southern Journal of Philosophy* 14 (1976), pp. 169–177; Thomas Nagel, "Death", in *Mortal Questions* (Cambridge: Cambridge University Press, 1979); Harry Silverstein, "The Evil of Death", *The Journal of Philosophy* 77 (1980), pp. 401–424; Joel Feinberg, "Harm and Self-Interest", in *Rights, Justice and the*

From column 12 to the first line of column 20, Philodemus's topic is "dying too young", and here we see a striking instance of "harsh" succeeded by "gentle" therapy. When a man has attained wisdom, the Epicureans held, he has attained all the joy that there is in the universe, even for the gods, and can depart rejoicing even if young; but a fool's life has nothing desirable in it, however long. This theme is expanded throughout the eight columns, and the peroration can serve as a summary of Philodemus's alternate "gentle" and "rough" speech:

> 19.1 … But as things are, once he has become wise, and has
> lived a certain additional time, the greatest of goods has
> been fully grasped by him. Once his journey has achieved

Bounds of Liberty (Princeton: Princeton University Press, 1980); Ernest Partridge, "Posthumous Interests and Posthumous Respect", *Ethics* 91 (1981), pp. 243–264; O. H. Green, "Fear of Death", *Philosophy and Phenomenological Research* 43 (1982), pp. 99–105; Amélie Rorty, "Fearing Death", *Philosophy* 58 (1983), pp. 175–188; George Pitcher, "The Misfortunes of the Dead", *American Philosophical Quarterly* 21 (1984), pp. 183–188; Anthony L. Brueckner and John Martin Fischer, "Why is Death Bad?", *Philosophical Studies* 50 (1986), pp. 213–227; David Furley, "Nothing to Us?" in *The Norms of Nature: Studies in Hellenistic Ethics*, ed. Malcolm Schofield and Gisela Striker (Cambridge: Cambridge University Press, 1986), pp. 75–91; Steven Luper-Foy, "Annihilation", *Philosophical Quarterly* 37 (1987), pp. 233–252 (an especially brilliant piece on whose arguments Philodemus's *On Death* could have shed much light); Palle Yourgrau, "The Dead", *Journal of Philosophy* 84 (1987), pp. 84–101; F. M. Kamm, "Why is Death Bad and Worse than Pre-Natal Non-Existence?" *Pacific Philosophical Quarterly* 69 (1988), pp. 161–164; Phillip Mitsis, "Epicurus on Death and Duration", in *Proceeedings of the Boston Area Colloquium for Ancient Philosophy*, Vol. 4, ed. John J. Cleary and Daniel C. Shartin (Lanham, MD: University Press of America, 1989), pp. 303–322; Fred Feldman, "On Dying as a Process", *Philosophy and Phenomenological Research* 50 (1989), pp. 375–389; Ishtiyaque Haji, "Pre-Vital and Post-Vital Times", *Pacific Philosophical Quarterly* 72 (1991), pp. 171–180; Anthony Brueckner and John Martin Fischer, "Death's Badness", *Pacific Philosophical Quarterly* 74 (1993), pp. 37–45; Walter Glannon, "Epicureanism and Death", *The Monist* 76 (1993), pp. 222–234. Except for Stephen Rosenbaum's brilliant defences of Epicurus's positions in detail, "How to Be Dead and Not Care: a Defense of Epicurus", *American Philosophical Quarterly* 23 (1986), pp. 217–225, "The Symmetry Argument: Lucretius Against the Fear of Death", *Philosophy and Phenomenological Research* 50 (1989), pp. 353–373, "Epicurus and Annihilation", *Philosophical Quarterly* 39 (1989), pp. 81–90, "Epicurus on Pleasure and the Complete Life", *The Monist* 73 (1990), pp. 21–41, most of these articles would need radical revision if the *On Death* of Philodemus had been part of modern scholarship's apparatus of Epicurean texts.

balance and consistency it would be perfectly in accord with his nature to continue it to eternity,[29] if that were possible; but if the deprival of his happiness comes to pass that is not a deprival of the happiness that has been, just a prevention of its further presence; but neither will there be any perception of its no longer being there.... and Metrodorus, and Epicurus, as many years as he was at the head of....

(17 lines missing)

—but he will not be hurt in any way by being taken from among the number of existing things, (it will be) as if he did not even perceive this cessation of activity. But the fool will have no happiness worthy of consideration to forget, not even if he lasts out the years of Tithonus, nor is it more alien to his nature to depart hence, once he is born, by the swiftest road and right now, than to leave life more slowly—
20. even if *we* would not advise him thus.[30]

Similarly (cols 20–22 init.) Philodemus treats a theme that perhaps would be more intelligible to a modern Mediterranean than the average Anglo-Saxon—that our enemies will rejoice over our extinction and laugh at us for our failure to survive and achieve our projects—with both satire and the feeling that the emotion is forgivable and "natural":

But this portion of one's pain is easily forgivable; what is unforgivable folly is the part about how one's enemies will rejoice. For no one will perceive them rejoicing, since he will have completely vanished. There is a natural trouble that an enemy mocking us gives us—when he does this to people who perceive and feel it, and when besides this evil effects result to those mocked; but to the man who is good in character no one once he has got to know him is an enemy, and it is those (who know us) whose hatred would be painful.... [20.1–14]

Thus, Philodemus not only sympathizes with those who are hurt by insults but makes the striking point that only our Epicurean "friends", who know what good people we are or are not, would have the right to judge, and they will judge us correctly whatever the rest of the world thinks.

---

29 as the Epicurean gods do.

30 The Epicureans were against suicide—even for fools.

In columns 22–25, Philodemus considers the pangs of an ancient person dying childless, with no one to perpetuate his name. Here he is full of wonderful sarcasms: the universe is infinite, and so must be people named (e.g.) Philodemus; Epicureans remember each other's virtues far more faithfully than most families, and there is no afterlife in which our ancestors can rejoice that we exist as their descendants:

> 24.31 ... but as far as concerns those who lament over just this, that those will command their testamentary property whom they do not wish to, it's just as possible to weep and wail even though they have children living, since Fortune the tyrant of all humanity is quite
> 25. capable of tearing (the inheritance) from their childrens' hands and tossing it down before whomsoever she will.
> Now, leaving behind parents or children or a spouse or others who are close to us, who will be in straits because of our death or even deprived of life's necessities, I admit brings with it a truly natural pang and can rouse a flow of tears especially and like nothing else from a man of understanding mind....

Philodemus's theme throughout this part of the lecture—that some kinds of fear of, and pain at the thought of, death are natural, and cause a "natural pang", *phusikon degma*, which even a philosopher will sympathize with, is expressed very beautifully and forcefully here. This is a crucial passage: here at last we see what is entailed by the Epicureans' belief in "natural emotion" and Epicurus's various admissions that the wise man will weep, love, be angry, at least to some extent, because that is a human being's "natural" good, however exempt the gods may be from fear and favor. As in *On Frank Criticism* the philosopher conciliates his patient by admitting his own vulnerability—indeed, since the ultimate Epicurean value is friendship, without which life is not worth living, the wisest feel the severing of ties to friends most deeply! This is not facile eudaemonism: before some of the most painful aspects of human mortality and especially the severing of affections, quite literally, the most reasonable reaction is "first you cry".

Immediately after in column 25 and 26 we learn that

> Now, when death occurs in a foreign land, it is natural even for learned men to feel a pang, and most of all if they leave parents or other family members at home, but only a pang, not such as to bring them in addition as they lie dying something that could truly be called a great grief, over and above the other difficulties that follow upon life in a foreign country. And in general, neither does this kind of

death matter to us, since we are going to be without any
sensation, including the sensation that our bones are lying in
a foreign land.... Yet even this belongs rather to people who
debase themselves far enough to believe in the myths, unless
indeed they are to believe that they will end up too far from
the place allotted to them in Hades; but they forget in their
stupidity that the way to Hades from wherever begun is of
equal length and equally direct. [25.37–26.11, 27.8–15]

Amusingly, by "learned men" (*philologoi*) Philodemus is indicating
"philosophers" (in common Epicurean terminology) like himself—for he was
born at Gadara in Jordan, and has family members there he has not seen for
decades of living first in Athens and then at Rome and Naples working for the
Roman aristocracy and teaching their children. We will see that this is not the
last passage in which he points humorously at himself. He also hints at what
is to be the ultimate consolation of the "pangs" one really does and must feel:
meditation on the lack of all sensation for good or for evil in death, as the
treatise makes clear at its eloquent end.

Philodemus deals after this with the fear that one's death will be
inglorious (cols. 28–9), that is, that one will not be remembered for heroism
but die uselessly in bed (a topic which reminds us that Roman grandees of
high military rank, perhaps even Piso's son-in-law Caesar himself, may well
have been in the audience); but this topic provokes only "harsh" sarcasm. "An
unimaginable quantity of those who died in battles, however 'gloriously', have
died no one knows how", Philodemus scornfully says, and (he argues) there is
far more glory, if that is important, in the life of philosophers and wise men,
noble as it undoubtedly is to defend one's country. Next, in cols. 30–33, distress
at the disfigurement of corpses in death and (that universal ancient terror) the
fear of being cheaply buried or not buried at all or dying at sea and receiving
only a cenotaph are treated with equal sarcasm: "Now those indeed, by Zeus, it
is natural actually to criticise and consider miserable, who for love of monetary
gain spend their whole life on the seas, and for its sake[31] are at last sunk into the
abyss, but really it's their life that's pitiable—not their death, when they are no
longer even there."

A very striking passage (cols. 33–35) appeals, I would argue, to Stoics in
the audience: the Stoics held that the Wise Man could always escape degradation
and flee to his God, the World-Soul, by suicide, and while the Epicureans
discouraged this (the Founder had set the example by enduring the pangs of
strangury of the bladder on his deathbed to the end, claiming that the memory
of his happy life and friendships counterbalanced the pain), Philodemus wants

---

31 A passage that impressed Horace; cf. *Odes* 1.1. 13–18, *Satires* 1.1. 4–8.

to show that the Wise Man will also defy tyrants or mobs and scorn death at their hands as reflecting on them, not himself:

> ... it is so certain that the standard-bearers of virtue among men can endure such things nobly, that one can see even ordinary men not just enduring with neck unbowed, but displaying the profoundest contempt for those who put them there, never mind Socrates and Zeno the Eleatic and Anaxarchus as historians tell us, and others of the philosophers. [35.25–34]

We should note that the Epicureans were not really great admirers of Socrates or of rival philosophers: this conciliatory note towards other schools and towards the wisdom of "the many" is frequent in the treatise, and is part of my argument that it is a showpiece for a general audience, not a technical treatise for the school.

Philodemus considers the objection "no one will remember me" with the same mixture of sympathy and brilliant sarcasm: once more, only the memory of friends is worth having, because only they knew who you really were, and even that is dispensable because (striking thought) the true use of friendship is for living anyway, not for dying, and the "naturalness" of this "pang" is less impressive to him:

> Now, to feel a pang that no one will ever even remember you seems natural, because in many cases this is the result of a friendless life, that is, one that has had nothing good about it. But if someone who has lived well and won himself affection comes to some misfortune that deprives him of those he knows, he will in the large picture lose nothing he needs, for we need these concomitant things not for their own sake, but that of the approved life which it is their nature to accompany. And so when that life is completed, what anxiety will come to us for that which is nothing to us nor even in our mind? But they seem to think that the not being remembered *after* life is painful, when they do not exist, turning their thoughts to what it is *during* life to be taken no notice of by human beings. And they rave on to no point about the blessedness of that remembrance, that follows on the sort of thing, forsooth, that attracts the wonder of mankind, and accompanies unhappy lives, not limiting themselves to that remembrance which follows on the good things a person has enjoyed.

But in fact if it's a misfortune not to be remembered, we must think *most* men wretched who have lived since whatever time it was when things came to be dignified with historical remembrance, and *all* men who lived before it, since nobody has preserved any historical facts about them at all. Or why should we hesitate to call simply everybody that's been born, and everybody that will be born, in the whole universe wretched? since when that falls apart nobody will remember them, for it will all be out of existence! [35.34–36.27]

By similar arguments, Philodemus concludes, such objections to death may be taken seriously or dismissed with contempt according as they happen to deserve; a man lamenting that some good project or purpose of his will be frustrated is to be treated with respect; a man merely complaining "why me, when so and so can still live, and I have so many material goods to lose" is to be treated as not even worth talking to.

The most impressive part, however, is reserved for the end. Philodemus, shrewd rhetorician that he was, knows very well that if he has made so many concessions to human grief, he could be asked whether he has given the show away: life *is* after all an existential tragedy, a banquet no guest wise or foolish ever leaves in perfect happiness. But that is not what he means at all. Philodemus's wise person thinks of life as a precious gift *precisely because of its transience*: he (or she) contemplates death as continually as the medieval monk did, as a fact of life, but not out of any kind of religious superstition; instead, from his contemplation he learns from the mere brute facts of life and death a special, thankful joy and a kind of invulnerability, Philodemus hopes, even to the terror of a death which he acknowledges might come at any instant unexpectedly:

But at any rate, to be caught unprepared when death comes upon us by chance, as though it were meeting us as a thing unexpected and paradoxical, does not happen to us,[32] but does happen to most men, ignorant as they are that every human being, were he stronger even than the Giants, is an ephemeral creature in his life and his death, and it isn't just tomorrow that is uncertain but the right-here-and-now. For we all inhabit "an unwalled city"[33] where death is concerned and all things are full of its causes, both according to our physical makeup, since we are so weak, and our soul has so many passages by which to breathe out and leave us,

---

32 Epicureans and philosophical people in general.

33 A quotation from Epicurus (or Metrodorus)—*Sententiae Vaticanae* 31.

and because the world around us generates innumerable causes of dissolution that attack us as swift as chance and frequently as swift as thought,[34] and there is the wickedness of mankind that brings on us in addition both these roads to death and others impossible for themselves to guess at and innumerable; so that unless a person is the greatest of fools, he might well think the absurd and paradoxical thing to be not that one should die, but that he should stay here some little while, and his lasting it out to old age a wonder and a miracle. But some have dwelt in human life as such aliens in it, not just ordinary men but some at any rate *called* philosophers, that they draw up plans to spend so many years at Athens in the pursuit of learning, so many years seeing Greece and what is accessible of barbarian lands,[35] so many years back at home in philosophical dialogue and the rest with their circle of friends—"and suddenly, unnoticed", Necessity "comes forward, cutting off our long hopes."[36] But

---

34 *hama noemati*, the usual Epicurean phrase for instantaneous events like the "atomic swerve".

35 A pleasant joke aimed at his Roman audience; Philodemus is describing his own life-story, which took him from Athens to the "barbarians" of Italy. For this use of the word "barbarian" to refer to Roman audiences listening to Greek works of literature, cf. Plautus, e.g. *Asinaria* 11, *Trinummus* 19, *Miles Gloriosus* 211 (Gonzales Lodge, *Lexicon Plautinum* [New York: Georg Olms Publishers, 1971]).

36 From some verses from an unknown tragedy, recited by the actor Neoptolemus before Philip II of Macedon not long before his murder (quoted in Diodorus Siculus 16.92.3):

>Think now things higher than highest heaven,
>and than the boundless plains of earth,
>think, rising in pride above
>the gods' own houses, in folly
>assigning a long term to your life:
>yet He comes on you swiftly,
>walking His shadowy path,
>and suddenly, unnoticed, comes forward,
>cutting off our long hopes,
>the Woe of mortals, Hades.
>
>[August Nauck, *Tragicorum Graecorum Fragmenta* (Leibzig: B. G. Teubner, 1889), 127]

Philodemus as an Epicurean substitutes "Necessity" (*to chreon*) for "Hades" in his quotation.

---

the man of sense, when he has come to understand that he can attain that which is self-sufficient to a happy life, from that point on walks about as one already laid out for burial in his shroud (*entetaphiasmenos*) and enjoys every single day as if it were an age, and when that is taken from him, goes forth (to die) not mourning, that thus, having somehow missed something that belongs to the best possible life, he joins the company of those who have died before. And all supplement to his time, he receives as in reason, he ought, as one who has lighted upon an unexpected piece of good fortune, and gives thanks accordingly to—the nature of things (*tois pragmasin eucharistei*). But every useless drone of a man, even when he grows old, is still mindless of the mortality and perishability of his makeup; he thinks the man unconvincing who said "what a paradox to see an old ship-captain—or an old tyrant", nor does he believe in the universality of the human condition, but even as pestilences are grasping him, fails to expect this. Or rather in the confusion of his thoughts he does not even despair of immortality, as appears from his planting cypresses still, and choking with rage over the loss of two brass pennies, and laying the foundations of dwelling-places that will not be able to be finished even a thousand years hence. And yet one could hardly say that such feelings differ in any way from thinking that glass and pottery vessels colliding over and over with adamantine steel will remain unbroken. But it seems that from a clinging to life produced by their terror of death—not from any pleasure in their life—they push away even the thinking about death, and then when the vision of it is near and vivid,[37] it comes as a surprising thing to them. Though from this cause they did not even abide to write their wills they are suddenly caught and surrounded, and are as Democritus says "borne about in different direction". But with persons of stable mind, even if through some unavoidable cause they were unsuspecting in advance of the fact that already the paragraph and limit[38] of their life was approaching, when it comes into actual view,

---

37 In Greek *enarges*, as a clear Epicurean perception should be, and in our grasp.

38 The literary metaphor in the Greek words *paragraphe* and *periodeuein* makes for an elegant, self-referential rhetorical "closure" in the Hellenistic tradition. As Philodemus says this, the "paragraph and limit", couched in one "period" (periodic sentence) of his own speech, appears at the end of his page. Cf. for a similar effect

they summing up in one period systematically, and with keenest vision (in a way that is a mystery unexplainable to the ignorant),[39] their own complete enjoyment of life and the utter unconsciousness that is to come over them, breathe their last as calmly, as if they had never put aside their act of attention[40] for an instant of time.

And just at this point comes—the blank page at the end, with the coronis or "finis" mark, and the subscription "Philodemus on Death, book Four". Besides the marvelous self-referential literary gesture—the "period" and "paragraph" of life disturb the philosopher as little as the blank space at the end of his roll, which Philodemus probably held up and showed the audience smilingly when he gave this lecture in public[41]—there are many interesting things to comment on in this splendid peroration. Let me single out two only.

First, Philodemus once more satirizes himself, as *On Frank Criticism* suggested the sympathetic therapist might do: *he personally* is the "man of sense" and yet he personally could conceivably be so foolish as to believe his life secure from mortality, laying plans to be first educated in Athens, then work for "the barbarians" as he calls the Romans, as long as he wants to, and then return to Syria (which probably he never did) to bask in the affection of his family—if better thoughts, at least better grounded in reality, had not been given him by the Garden. The "gentle" therapist always points to his own weaknesses as well as his patients'.

---

the last words of Seneca, *Ep. ad Lucil. 77* (on suicide): *nihil ad rem pertinet quo loco desinas; quocumque voles desine; tantum bonam clausulam impone* (itself a "good clausula": cretic +iambic). (I must thank Jeffrey Fish for this reference.)

39 Notice the characteristic Epicurean metaphor, so common in Lucretius of *clear mental presentation* throughout this sentence, contrasted with the dim and confused grasp of the common man of the images that he chooses to focus on in his dishonesty and fear; also the imagery of initiation.

40 to the concept "death": the word for "act of attention" is *epibole*; see below.

41 Philodemus writes in Greek, not only because it was the principal language of the Greek East where he was born, and the preferred language of professional philosophy in the Roman Empire, but because every upper class Roman responsible for government and business in the Empire as a whole was bilingual in Greek and Latin—which meant everyone in the circle and family of his patron Calpurnius Piso Caesoninus. He probably knew Latin well enough to speak it fluently, but not well enough to feel sure of himself in writing it as literature or philosophy, and besides in South Italy (especially Naples and Herculaneum) where he lived by preference most of the time, probably more people spoke Greek in the streets than Latin.

Secondly, Philodemus has an answer for the objection that if some things about death cause not just bites but pangs, and pangs that bite deepest for the wisest as we saw, life cannot be happy. Life is not happy, rather, because fools pay no real attention to it and are afraid to see it steadily and for what it really is: a dance on the edge of mortality, in which we always turn our eyes away from the facts. We should remember that in Epicureanism, there are three criteria of truth: sense-perception (which is always really there), *aisthesis*; general notions correctly formed on its basis by the mind, *prolepseis*; and "focussing" on things, *epibole*.[42] In some contexts, *epibole* is a relatively trivial word, just "attention", but not so where "unremitting attention", as in our present passage, is in question. It seems, from a parallel passage in Philodemus's *De Dis*, to have been when directed to spiritual truths an important spiritual act, for "the most continual focussing", *sunechestate epibole*, "on goods past present and to come" is there apparently said to be a support to the wise man's piety (*De Dis* 3. col. 2.23–27). This "most continual focussing" is what Philodemus describes again here—a focussing on the truth of death that even when left aside for a time is so effective that when death itself appears it is as if its contemplation had never been suspended. The apparently casual flock of detailed examples, the many roads to death, the ship

---

42 Diogenes Laertius 10.31 says that later Epicureans added this to the criteria
of truth, and sure enough Philodemus (De Lacey, *On Signs and Inferences*, fr.
1) lists it among them. A classic acount of *epibole* is Cyril Bailey, *Epicurus: the
Extant Remains* (Oxford: Clarendon Press, 1926), pp. 259–274, and there are good
discussions also in Elizabeth Asmis, *Epicurus' Scientific Method* (Ithaca: Cornell
University Press, 1984). It is relevant to our passage that one of the chief contexts
for the use of this criterion is religious, the contemplation of the gods as they
actually are and must be, and that Lucretius uses the Latin translation *animi
iactus* to describe the bold adventure of contemplating the infinity of the universe
outside our cosmos: *DRN* 2.1044–47. Cf. on the same subject Cicero *De Natura
Deorum* 1.54: *se iniciens animus et intendens* (derived from Philodemus). Modern
literature tends to deal with the logic of *aisthesis* and *prolepsis* by preference and
leave the question of "focussing" a little to the side. Cf. A. A. Long and D. N. Sedley,
The Hellenistic Philosophers (New York: Cambridge University Press, 1987), where
"focussing" is glossed rather unexcitingly "that we can test a theory about external
objects *merely* by closing our eyes and examining them" (p. 90; authors' italics).
Bailey seems to have shown conclusively that a more intense act of intellection
and understanding than that is intended, and I would add that when the passage
specifies "intense" or "continuous" attention we can be sure that an important
"act of attention" is meant. Sedley's theory that it includes only "the visualization
of perceptible objects" (expounded in his "Epicurus, On Nature, Book XXVIII",
Cronache Ercolanesi 3 [1973], pp. 5–84, at pp. 23–25) unfortunately did not take this
passage of *On Death* into account.

---

captain and the tyrant, the folly of planting trees one will not live to see, are all examples of those "facts", *pragmata*, that lead the wise person to place himself correctly in life and understand his own mortal nature, as he contemplates them, fearlessly, till they become continually part of him. He becomes grateful to them at last for being as they are. The fool's *epibolai* or "focussings" on death were only such as all or any of us might have, momentary, trivial and such as he could push away (*apothein*); the wise man willingly takes the contemplation of death into himself seriously and permanently, and is fortified and made happy. When death comes, it is as if his clear contemplation had never been suspended at all; for "never suspended for the least instant of time" and "most continual" in *De Dis* 3 mean the same thing. Those who knew the Epicurean system would have seen exactly what Philodemus meant. But for those of his audience who did not know the technical term, the description of continual, unbroken, intense "attention" (for that is what the word means in ordinary Greek also) as opposed to uneasy apprehensions we push away would have been quite enough. The brilliant conclusion was meant to be equally intelligible to philosopher and layman.

It takes long and weary study, and many a visit to Naples, to be certain of what Philodemus said and did not say, at least in the current condition of scholarship, which we in the Philodemus Translation Project are attempting year by year to remedy. One can see that from the lack of attention given in the history of scholarship to even this brilliant treatise: how could scholars judge whether its text is even reliable or not, when in fact in the current state of things it takes a Philodemus expert simply to guarantee it is more or less there to read? I can in fact make that guarantee for this bright and striking piece of ancient consolatory rhetoric—unique in so many of its attitudes, and so very relevant to how we think about death today. The summary and quotations I give are all reliable, at least according to my personal inspection of the original papyrus, and I am confident that none of the passages I quote in detail can any longer be altered very significantly by new readings, though the MSI photographs I described will inevitably produce some. It is truly thrilling to be involved with the National Endowment for the Humanities Philodemus Translation Project, and with bringing Philodemus's theories back to a modern audience, and I hope this sample helps show why.

WORKS CITED

Armstrong, David, "The addressees of the *Ars Poetica*", *Materiali e discussioni per l'analsi dei testi classici* 31 (1993), pp. 185–230.

Arrighetti, Graziano, *Epicuro: Opere* (Turin: Einaudi, 1960; 2nd edn., 1973).

Asmis, Elizabeth, *Epicurus' Scientific Method* (Ithaca: Cornell University Press, 1984).

Bailey, Cyril, *Epicurus: the Extant Remains* (Oxford: Clarendon Press, 1926).

Bassi, Domenico, ed., *Herculanensium voluminum quae supersunt: Collectio tertia* (Milan: Hoepli, 1914).

Booras, Steven W. and David R. Seely, "Multispectral Imaging of the Herculaneum Papyri", *Cronache Ercolanesi* 29 (1999), pp. 95–100.

Brueckner, Anthony L. and John Martin Fischer, "Why is Death Bad?", *Philosophical Studies* 50 (1986), pp. 213–227.

———, "Death's Badness", *Pacific Philosophical Quarterly* 74 (1993), pp. 37–45.

Capasso, Mario, *Manuale di Papirologia Ercolanese* (Galatina: Congedo, 1991).

Capasso, Mario and Mario Gigante, "Il Ritorno di Virgilio a Ercolano", *Studi Italiani di Filologia Classica* 7 (1989), pp. 3–6.

DeLacy, Philip and Estelle DeLacy, *Philodemus: On Methods of Inference* (Philadelphia: American Philological Association, 1941), revised for the series *La Scuola di Epicuro* (Naples: Bibliopolis, 1978).

Feinberg, Joel, "Harm and Self-Interest", in *Rights, Justice and the Bounds of Liberty* (Princeton: Princeton University Press, 1980).

Feldman, Fred, "On Dying as a Process", *Philosophy and Phenomenological Research* 50 (1989), pp. 375–389.

Furley, David, "Nothing to Us?" in *The Norms of Nature: Studies in Hellenistic Ethics*, ed. Malcolm Schofield and Gisela Striker (Cambridge: Cambridge University Press, 1986), pp. 75–91.

Gigante, Marcello, *Philodemus in Italy*, trans. Dirk Obbink (Ann Arbor: University of Michigan Press, 1995).

———, *Ricerche Filodemee*, 2nd edn. (Naples: Macchiaroli, 1983).

Glad, Clarence, *Paul and Philodemus: Adaptability in Epicurean and Early Christian Psychagogy* (Leiden: Brill Academic Publishers, 1995).

Glannon, Walter, "Epicureanism and Death", *The Monist* 76 (1993), pp. 222–234.

Gow, A. S. F. and D. L. Page, *The Garland of Philip*, 2 vols (Cambridge: Cambridge University Press, 1968).

Green, O. H., "Fear of Death", *Philosophy and Phenomenological Research* 43 (1982), pp. 99–105.

Haji, Ishtiyaque, "Pre-Vital and Post-Vital Times", *Pacific Philosophical Quarterly* 72 (1991), pp. 171–180.

Jensen, Christian, *On Poems* (Berlin: Weidmann, 1923).

Kamm, F. M., "Why is Death Bad and Worse than Pre-Natal Non-Existence?" *Pacific Philosophical Quarterly* 69 (1988), pp. 161–164.

Kuiper, Taco, *Philodemus over den Dood* (Amsterdam: H. J. Paris, 1925).

Lodge, Gonzales, *Lexicon Plautinum* (New York: Georg Olms Publishers, 1971).

Long, A. A. and D. N. Sedley, *The Hellenistic Philosophers* (New York: Cambridge University Press, 1987).

Luper-Foy, Steven, "Annihilation", *Philosophical Quarterly* 37 (1987), pp. 233–252.

Miller, F., "Epicurus on the Art of Dying", *Southern Journal of Philosophy* 14 (1976), pp. 169–177.

Mitsis, Phillip, "Epicurus on Death and Duration", in *Proceeedings of the Boston Area Colloquium for Ancient Philosophy*, Vol. 4, ed. John J. Cleary and Daniel C. Shartin (Lanham, MD: University Press of America, 1989), pp. 303–322.

Nagel, Thomas, "Death", in *Mortal Questions* (Cambridge: Cambridge University Press, 1979).

Nauck, August, *Tragicorum Graecorum Fragmenta* (Leibzig: B. G. Teubner, 1889).

Nussbaum, Martha, "Mortal Immortals: Lucretius on Death and the Voice of Nature", *Philosophy and Phenomenological Research* 50 (1989), pp. 303–351.

———, *The Therapy of Desire* (Princeton: Princeton University Press, 1994).

Obbink, Dirk, *Philodemus On Piety, Part I: Critical Text with Commentary* (Oxford: Oxford University Press, 1996).

Olivieri, Alexander, ed., *On the Good King According to Homer* (Leipzig: Teubner, 1909).

———, ed., *On Frank Criticism* (Leipzig: Teubner, 1914).

Partridge, Ernest, "Posthumous Interests and Posthumous Respect", *Ethics* 91 (1981), pp. 243–264.

Philodemus on Frank Criticism, eds. and trans. David Konstan, Clarence E. Glad, Johan C. Thom, James Ware, and Diskin Clay (Atlanta: Scholars Press, 1998).

Pitcher, George, "The Misfortunes of the Dead", *American Philosophical Quarterly* 21 (1984), pp. 183–188.

Rorty, Amélie, "Fearing Death", *Philosophy* 58 (1983), pp. 175–188.

Rosenbaum, Sephen, "How to Be Dead and Not Care: a Defense of Epicurus", *American Philosophical Quarterly* 23 (1986), pp. 217–225.

———, "The Symmetry Argument: Lucretius Against the Fear of Death", *Philosophy and Phenomenological Research* 50 (1989), pp. 353–373.

———, "Epicurus and Annihilation", *Philosophical Quarterly* 39 (1989), pp. 81–90.

————, "Epicurus on Pleasure and the Complete Life", *The Monist* 73 (1990), pp. 21–41.

Sbordone, Francesco, ed., *Richerche sui Papiri Ercolanese*, 4 vols. (Naples: Giannini, 1969–83).

Scott, Walter, *Fragmenta Herculanensia* (Oxford: Clarendon Press, 1885).

Sedley, David, "Epicurus, On Nature, Book XXVIII", *Cronache Ercolanesi* 3 (1973), pp. 5–84.

Sider, David, ed., *The Epigrams of Philodemus* (Oxford: Oxford University Press, 1997).

Silverstein, Harry, "The Evil of Death", *The Journal of Philosophy* 77 (1980), pp. 401–424.

Sudhaus, Siegfried, ed., *On Rhetoric* (Leipzig: Teubner, 1892–1896).

Tait, Jane I. M., *Philodemus' Influence on the Latin Poets* (Ph.D. dissertation, Bryn Mawr, 1939).

Vergil, Philodemus and the Augustans: the Cumae Conference, 2000, ed. D. Armstrong, J. Fish, P. Johnston and M. Skinner (Austin: University of Texas Press, forthcoming).

Wilke, Carl, ed., *Philodemide ira liber* (Leipzig: Tuebner, 1914).

Williams, Bernard, "The Makropulos Case: Reflections on the Tedium of Immortality", in *Problems of the Self* (Cambridge: Cambridge University Press, 1973).

Young, Robert, *Quarterly Review* (Feb., 1810), pp. 1–20.

Yourgrau, Palle, "The Dead", *Journal of Philosophy* 84 (1987), pp. 84–101.

THE ANGRY GOD:
EPICUREANS, LACTANTIUS, AND WARFARE

James I. Campbell

In his letter to Menoeceus, Epicurus wrote "Do and practise what I constantly told you to do, believing these to be the elements of living well. First, believe that god is an indestructible and blessed animal, in accordance with the general conception of god commonly held, and do not ascribe to god anything foreign to his indestructibility or repugnant to his blessedness";[1] and the first of the forty items of the "Principal Doctrines" which is attributed to him, stated that "What is blessed and indestructible has no troubles itself, nor does it give trouble to anyone else...."[2] While thus unequivocally affirming the existence of god (or gods), Epicurus nevertheless rejected the popular conception which held the gods to be involved in the operations of the universe and the affairs of individual lives. Instead, the immortal gods enjoyed a state of perpetual and undisturbed blessedness. Having nothing to do with the motions of the universe or with natural processes here on earth, blissful in themselves, and without unfulfilled desires, they experienced neither anger nor gratitude because of what human beings do or fail to do.[3]

With nothing to fear from the gods, the Epicurean did not fear death either. The aggregate of atoms out of which the soul is constituted is scattered at death, marking the end of sense perception: "all good and bad consists in sense-experience, and death is the privation of sense-experience." Freed, then, from fear of both the gods and of death, an Epicurean could live a virtuous and pleasant life "as a god among men", enjoying a state of untroubled peace of mind, or *ataraxia*.[4]

---

1   Epicurus, "Menoeceus", in Diogenes, *Lives*, X.123, in Brad Inwood and L. P. Gerson, *The Epicurus Reader* (Indianapolis, IN: Hackett Publishing Co., Inc., 1994), p. 28. All references to Epicurus's works will be to this volume.

2   The "Principal Doctrines" are also known as the "Authorized Doctrines" (Norman Wentworth DeWitt, *Epicurus and His Philosophy* [Cleveland, OH: The World Publishing Co., 1967], p. 276), and the "Sovran Maxims" (*Diogenes Laertius, Lives of Eminent Philosophers*, trans. Robert D. Hicks, 2 vols. [Cambridge, MA: Harvard University Press, 1965], vol. 2, p. 663). Hicks notes that while it is uncertain whether they were composed by Epicurus himself, they may be regarded as an accurate summary of his teachings (pp. 662–663, note *b*).

3   "Principal I"; "Menoeceus".

4   "Menoeceus", 124, 132; "Principal II", and "Letter to Herodotus". Cf. also Andre-

These teachings concerning the gods became standard Epicurean orthodoxy. Approximately two hundred years after Epicurus, Lucretius wrote

> the nature of gods must ever in itself of necessity enjoy immortality together with supreme of repose, far removed and withdrawn from our concerns; since exempt from every pain, exempt from all dangers, strong in its own resources, not wanting aught of us, it is neither gained by favours nor moved by anger.[5]

In his *On the Nature of God* (*De Natura Deorum*), Cicero had Velleius, his Epicurean spokesman, say

> [the gods] spend their time in such a manner that nothing can be conceived which is more blessed or better supplied with all kinds of good things. For a god is idle, is entangled with no serious preoccupations, undertakes no toilsome labour, but simply rejoices in his own wisdom and virtue, being certain that he will always be in the midst of pleasures which are both supreme and eternal.[6]

Those who teach that the gods are actively involved in the world, Velleius continued, have put obstacles in the way of *ataraxia* since they

> have burdened us with the yoke of an eternal master whom

Jean Festugière, *Epicurus and His Gods*, trans. C. W. Chilton (New York: Russell and Russell, 1955), pp. 51–72, esp. 56–57: "So fear of the gods, fear of their anger towards the living and of their vengeance on the dead, played a great part in Greek religion.... [Epicurus] was convinced ... that *deisidaimonia* ['a feeling of constant terror ... in regard to the divine power', p. 52] ... prevailed all about him, and ... felt it to be his first care to banish this fear which utterly prevents peace of mind (*ataraxia*)." For further discussion of Epicurus's attitude towards religion, see De Witt, *Epicurus*, pp. 249–288, and Howard Jones, *The Epicurean Tradition* (London: Routledge, 1989), pp. 52–55.

5 Lucretius, *On the Nature of Things* (*De Rerum Natura*) in *The Stoic and Epicurean Philosophers*, ed. Whitney J. Oates (New York: The Modern Library, 1940), II.646. Lactantius quotes it in *On Anger*, 8, arguing that Epicurus thereby "destroys religion."

6 Cicero, *De Natura Deorum*, I.xix, 51 in Inwood and Gerson, *Epicurus*, p. 53. A standard translation of this work is by H. Rackham (Cambridge, MA: Harvard University Press, 1967).

---

we are to fear by day and by night; for who would not fear an inquisitive and busy god who foresees everything, thinks about and notices everything, and supposes that everything is his own business?[7]

The "true maxim" taught by Epicurus, namely, that "what is blessed and eternal … is subject to neither anger nor gratitude" thus liberates us from all fear of the gods.[8]

St. Paul, on his missionary journey to Athens prior to 50 A.D., had argued with Epicurean philosophers;[9] later on writers of the first few Christian centuries discussed one or another element of the Epicurean canon. Their comments were not always negative: indeed Tertullian, Clement of Alexandria, and Athenagoras found so much to admire in Epicureanism that Richard Jungkuntz has warned that "any generalizations about patristic antipathy to Epicureanism really need careful qualification to be valid."[10] The Epicurean practice of the social virtues, emphasis on forgiveness and mutual helpfulness, and suspicion of worldly values so closely paralleled similar Christian attitudes that Norman Wentworth DeWitt has observed that it "would have been singularly easy for an Epicurean to become a Christian"[11]—and, one might suppose, a Christian to become an Epicurean.

Concerning the nature of God (or the gods), and God's relationship

---

7   Ibid., I.xx, 54. Cf. Lucretius, *De Rerum*, V.1198–1203. Yet Epicurus taught his followers to participate in solemn religious festivals. Since "the gods are indescribably happy, to praise them in prayer, to draw near to them on those solemn occasions when the city offers them a sacrifice, and to rejoice with them at the annual festivals is to take part in their happiness" (Festugière, *Epicurus*, p. 62).

8   Cicero, *De Natura Deorum*, I.xvii, 45.

9   "The Acts of the Apostles", 17: 18 ff., *The Anchor Bible*, ed. William Foxwell Albright and David Noel Freedman, 51 vols. (Garden City, NY: Doubleday & Co), vol. 31 (1967), trans. Johannes Munck. Apparently, the excessive religiosity of the Athenians had not abated in the centuries after Epicurus. Paul famously remarked on the altar to an unknown god (the God he himself was proclaiming), erected for fear that some god might be ignored. See "Acts" 17: 22 ff.

10 Richard P. Jungkuntz, "Christian Approval of Epicureanism", *Church History* 31 (1962), pp. 279–293, at p. 291. For Epicurean influence on Christianity, see Adelaide D. Simpson, "Epicureans, Christians, Atheists in the Second Century", *Transactions and Proceedings of the American Philological Association* 72 (1941), pp. 372–381; Richard P. Jungkuntz, "Fathers, Heretics and Epicureans", *The Journal of Ecclesiastical History* 17 (1966), pp. 3–10; Norman Wentworth DeWitt, *St. Paul and Epicurus* (Minneapolis, MN: University of Minnesota Press, 1954).

11 DeWitt, *Epicurus*, pp. 31–32.

---

to the world and human affairs, however, there could be no agreement between the two movements. An unfeeling God who does not care for the human race and takes no notice of what human beings may or may not do was not the God revealed in the Old and New Testaments, namely, a God to whom various emotions including anger, jealousy, and vengeance no less than love, pity, tenderness, and kindness are ascribed.[12] This was not the God whose son had died to save sinful humanity, who had given human beings commands, who would raise the dead, and who rewards the good and punishes the wicked. The fundamental teachings of Epicurus's theology thus struck at the heart of the Christian's faith, his belief in divine providence.

Towards the beginning of the fourth century Lactantius, a native of northern Africa and the last of the Latin apologists, wrote a number of treatises in defense of the Christian faith. A convert from paganism to Christianity, he was born between 240 and 250.[13] After the Diocletian persecution, and with Christianity growing in imperial favor, he was appointed tutor to Constantine's son, Crispus. The historian Philip Schaff identifies him as one of three important Christians to serve as the Emperor Constantine's "chief advisers and helpers in that great change which gave to the religion of the cross the moral control over the vast empire of Rome."[14] Not only an educator, Lactantius thus seems to have been an important participant in what turned out to be one of the most

---

12 There are many scriptural references to *anger*, including "Exodus" 4:14; "Deuteronomy" 4:25; 1 "Kings" 14:15; "Jeremiah" 4:8; to *wrath*: "Exodus" 22:23–24; "Psalms" 79:5–6; 2 "Chronicles" 28:11; "John" 3:36; "Romans" 1:18; "Ephesians" 5:6; to *hatred*: "Psalms" 139:22; "Revelation" 2:6; to *jealousy, vengeance, fury*: "Deuteronomy" 4:24; "Nahum" 1:2–3; to *mercy*: "Deuteronomy" 4:31; to *love, pity, tenderness*, etc.: "Exodus" 22:27; "Psalms" 86:13, 15; "Psalms" 36:5–7; to *kindness*: "Genesis" 24:12; "Deuteronomy" 7:13.

13 There are different estimates of the dates of Lactantius's birth and death. Louis J. Swift, *The Early Fathers on War and Military Service*, vol. 19, in *Message of the Fathers of the Church*, ed. Thomas Halton, 23 vols. (Wilmington DE: Michael Glazier, Inc., 1983), gives those dates as c. 240 to c. 320; Michael P. McHugh, "Lactantius", in *Encyclopedia of Early Christianity*, ed. Everett Ferguson (New York: Garland Publishing Co., 1990), pp. 524–525, gives c. 250 to c. 325; Etienne Gilson, *History of Christian Philosophy in the Middle Ages* (New York: Random House, 1955), p. 577, states that the dates of his birth and death are unknown.

14 Philip Schaff, *History of the Christian Church*, 8 vols. (Grand Rapids, MI: William B. Eerdmans Publishing Co., 1910, reprinted 1967), vol. 2, p. 866. See *Lactantius Divine Institutes*, trans. Sister Mary Francis McDonald, vol. 49 of *The Fathers of the Church* (Washington, D.C.: The Catholic University of America Press, 1964), p. xviii: Lactantius "became the emperor's spokesman for the change in policy which would so affect the welfare of the times."

---

significant changes in human history.

At his death in the early 320s, he left a number of writings, including the *Divine Institutes* (*Divinae institutiones*), composed prior to the accession of the Emperor Constantine, and completed about 308 or 309; *A Treatise on the Anger of God* (*De ira Dei*), written in 313–314; and a shortened and edited version of the *Institutes*, *The Epitome of the Divine Institutes* (*Epitome divinarum institutionum*) completed in about 317.[15] These works included a defense of the Christian doctrine of divine providence, including the notion that anger in God was not only compatible with His perfection but was necessary for His caring for the human race.

In the course of his argument, and arising out of his response to Epicurean theology, Lactantius found it necessary to propose a new way of interpreting Jesus's instruction to his followers concerning anger. Later on, this new hermeneutic allowed him to imply that a similar reinterpretation of what Jesus had taught concerning violence was also possible. He was the first Christian writer to have done so, the harbinger of what in other hands would become a full-blown Christian theology of permissible violence. Whether directly or through reaction to one another, hostile ideologies can, of course, influence each other's development and direction. Because of Lactantius, Epicureanism became a catalyst in the emergence of a new and important way of interpreting some of Jesus's teachings. That is the topic of this paper.

The *Institutes* criticized pagan beliefs and practices, argued in favor of monotheism, and explained and defended some of Christianity's foundational beliefs and moral principles. In the course of his discussions, Lactantius examined the role of emotions (*affectus*: passions, affections) in moral life, presenting his own views in relation to and in contrast with the views of the Stoics and Peripatetics (Aristotelians). About the Epicureans he said little; about their denial of anger in God, he said nothing. That would be the subject of Lactantius's later work, *On Anger*.

The Stoic teaching that the emotions are "diseases" and must be entirely removed, Lactantius wrote, was contrary to human nature and was "almost mad" since they "wish by some means or other to deprive man of powers implanted in him by nature." Besides, if it is virtuous to restrain and check oneself "in the midst of the impetuosity of anger", then to remove anger is to remove virtue. And so for the other virtues which control lust and greed.[16] The Peripatetics, on the

---

15 The dates of Lactantius's writings are given in Michael P. McHugh, "Lactantius", p. 524. Variant dates are given *Institutes*, pp. xi–xv. McDonald provides a useful general introduction to Lactantius's life, writings, and theological teachings (pp. ix–xxv). In this paper, translations of the writings of Lactantius are from *The Ante-Nicene Fathers*, ed. Alexander Roberts and James Donaldson, 10 vols. (Grand Rapids, MI: Wm. B. Eerdmans Publishing Company, 1979), vol. 7.

16 *Institutes*, VI, 14 and 15.

---

other hand, while correct in realizing that emotions are natural in human beings, were to be faulted for thinking that anger has value in being the "whetstone of virtue", thus making bravery in battle possible, and for holding that although the emotions are "vices" they can be permitted in moderation. If the value of anger is that it allows us to kill, then what, Lactantius asks, "is to be thought more savage than man, what more resembling the wild beasts"? Furthermore, emotional moderation is not always virtuous (one can rightly experience an excess of joy in what is good); and if the emotions are vices, then they should not be allowed, even in moderation.[17]

Lactantius's own position was that emotions are morally neutral. Badly used, they become vices; well used, they are virtues. Guided by Biblical teaching, Christians know that anger-driven behavior is not vicious when confined within the "fixed limits" established by God.[18] In fact, anger is both just and necessary when used to restrain "the faults of those who are in our power", namely children, "lest by useless love and excessive indulgence they should be trained to evil and nourished to vices." But should angry behavior exceed the divinely appointed limits and be directed against our "equals in age", evils arise, including disagreements and wars.[19] In response to those who harm him, the Christian reacts with patience, blessing those who abuse him, bearing injury with calmness and moderation rather than responding with vengeance. The Christian "should not himself inflict injury … [and] should not avenge it even when inflicted on himself."[20] Anger itself is thus morally neutral. Anger-driven behavior is not always evil but becomes so when it goes beyond the limits set by God.

Lactantius returned to the topic in the *On Anger*, a treatise designed primarily to refute the Epicurean denial of anger in God (a teaching with which Stoicism agreed)—and which Lactantius considered to be the premise that led ultimately to Epicurus's denial of divine providence.[21] In its opening lines Lactantius summarized the positions held by "some philosophers" who taught either

---

17 Ibid., 15, 16, 19.

18 These guidelines appear to be dependent on "Proverbs" 13:24; 15:1; 16:32; 22:6; 22:15; 23:13; "Psalms" 7:6 ff.; 38:8; Paul, "Letter to the Ephesians", 6:4.

19 *Institutes*, VI, 15, 16, 19. Despite strong elements of Aristotelean philosophy present in Lactantius's teaching, he seems to have been unaware of the more complete discussion of anger in the *Nichomachean Ethics*, IV, 5 (1125b26–1126b10).

20 *Institutes*, VI, 18.

21 *On Anger*, 4. The Epicureans were the principal target of this treatise. See *Lactantius The Minor Works*, trans. Sister Mary Francis McDonald, vol. 54 of *The Fathers of the Church*, ed. Roy J. Deferrari (Washington, D.C.: The Catholic University of America Press, 1965), p. 59.

that God is not subject to anger; since the divine nature is either altogether beneficent, and that it is inconsistent with His surpassing and excellent power to do injury to any one;

or that

at any rate, He takes no notice of us at all, so that no advantage comes from His goodness, and no evil from His ill-will.[22]

In a few brief paragraphs, he disposed of the Stoic doctrine that anger is incompatible with divine benevolence, arguing that it is inconsistent since, if God is "mild, calm, [and] propitious", loving the pious and the righteous, He would have to be angry with the impious and unrighteous since "in opposite matters it is necessary to be moved to both sides or to neither."[23] The Epicureans may have committed the "greatest error" due to having "assumed premises which are altogether false", but their denial of God's anger was consistent with the broader view of the divine power as existing in "supreme repose, far removed and withdrawn from our concerns", utterly self-sufficient, "not wanting aught of us" and "neither gained by favours nor moved by anger."[24] This doctrine, however, is not only incorrect (as he had pointed out earlier in the *Institutes*) but has two important consequences.

The first is, in effect, atheism. God, to be God, must be a being of "surpassing excellence, distinction, and blessedness" and this would be impossible if there were no plan, art, or workmanship governing the universe, and if God did not know past, present, and future. For "what greater, what more worthy administration can be attributed to God, than the government of the world, and especially of the human race? ... [what] so worthy of God, and so befitting to Him, as providence?" A God who is inactive, always at rest and immovable, caring for nothing and foreseeing nothing, unaware of those who worship Him; who "has no will at all, no action, ... no administration", and who is "neither moved, which is peculiar to a living being, nor does anything impossible for man" is a God who is deprived of "all power and all substance". But then, what is left to say other than "there is no God at all"? Epicurus's denial of providence is tantamount to a denial of God's existence, and though "he leaves the gods in words" he has taken away their reality "since he gives them no motion, no office".[25]

---

22 *On Anger*, 1.

23 Ibid., 5.

24 Ibid., 5 and 8. Lactantius appears to have been quoting Lucretius's account of Epicurus's teaching. See above, note 5.

25 *On anger*, 9 and 4.

Second, if Epicurus is correct, of what use is religion? Why serve a God by sacrifice and offerings if one could receive no favor in return? Is any honor due to a God "who pays no regard to us, and is ungrateful"? If God does not know our words and secret thoughts no less than our actions, and does not reward the good and punish the wicked, human life becomes "full of folly, of wickedness, and enormity". For with nothing but civil law to restrain us, why not resort to criminal behavior if we could escape detection? Epicurus has effectively destroyed religion and "confusion and perturbation of life will follow."[26] For it is

> the fear of God alone which guards the mutual society of men, by which life itself is sustained, protected, and governed. But that fear is taken away if man is persuaded that God is without anger; for that He is moved and indignant when unjust actions are done, not only the common advantage, but even reason itself, and truth, persuade us.[27]

Epicureanism (and, to a lesser extent, Stoicism) is thus the unwitting enemy of religion and of good social order. For "religion, and majesty, and honour exist together with fear; but there is no fear where no one is angry."[28] Neither Epicureanism nor Stoicism but Christianity alone, teaching a God of both generous rewards and angry punishments, can safeguard religion and society.

The false teachings concerning God's anger arise, Lactantius suggests, from philosophical misunderstanding of the nature of anger itself. Seneca, for example, described anger as "the desire of avenging an injury"; Cicero defined it as "the desire of taking vengeance", others as "the desire of punishing him by whom you think that you have been unfairly injured" or as "the desire of requiting pain". But these definitions refer to *unjust* anger. *Anger* itself "is an emotion of the mind arousing itself for the restraining of faults"; and anger is *justified* when "we arise to take vengeance, not because we have been injured, but that discipline may be preserved, morals may be corrected, and licentiousness be suppressed."[29] This is anger that "ought not to be taken away from man" since it is both "serviceable" and "necessary" and is "plainly in accord

---

26 Ibid., 8.

27 Ibid., 12. Cf. Ibid., 6: "God is angry, since He is moved by kindness.... [T]his is the sum and turning-point on which the whole of piety and religion depend: and no honour can be due to God, if He affords nothing to His worshippers; and no fear, if He is not angry with him who does not worship Him."

28 Ibid., 8.

29 Ibid., 17. Lactantius reports these as definitions given by various philosophers "which Seneca enumerated in the books which he composed on the subject of anger."

with justice and wisdom."[30] In this description, another element going beyond what had been said in the *Institutes* has now been introduced: justified anger requires *righteous motivation*, namely, the correction of morals and suppression of licentiousness. Once more those who are properly the targets of just anger are identified: children again, but—another advance—now also including slaves, pupils, and wives, that is, all those under our power and for whose behavior and moral development men bear responsibility.[31] Censure is not always wrong, Lactantius reminds his reader, as is apparent from the fact that we praise judges who condemn criminals:[32] and if the anger which drives us to punish the wicked is thus recognized as a source of virtuous action, how can it be denied to God? His wisdom and justice require that He would be angry with wrongdoers and would seek, through punishment, to correct them and to bring their evildoing to an end.[33] It would be clearly unjust if both those who break His commands and those who keep them were to be treated equally by Him, from which it follows that it is only right that He should be moved by just anger to punish evildoers.

All of this, however, seemed to fly in the face of Jesus's teachings in the "Sermon on the Mount" where he had apparently condemned both anger and violence, the one linked to the other. These are his words, as reported in the Gospel of Matthew:

> You have heard that it was said to the ancients, "You shall
> not murder, and whoever murders will be liable to judgment."
> But I tell you that everyone who is angry with his brother
> shall be in danger of (divine) judgment. Whoever insults his
> brother will answer to the Sanhedrin, while whoever says
> "Rebel! (against God)" merits a fiery death.[34]

Until this time Christian writers had taken a literal and absolutist view of Jesus's instructions. While it is natural for people to experience anger, Jesus's followers were not to harbor it or to react in anger towards others, regardless of the offense given, lest their anger lead to killing. The seeming conflict between Jesus's words and Lactantius's argument thus needed to be resolved,

---

30 Ibid., and 18: "[God] has … given anger for the sake of restraining faults."

31 Ibid., 17. Lactantius appears to be dependent again on the Old and New Testaments, including "Proverbs" 13:24; 22:6; 15:1; 16:32; 22:15; 23:13; "Psalms" 7:6 ff; 37:8; Paul's "Letter to the Ephesians" 6:4.

32 *On Anger*, 17.

33 Ibid., 16, 17, 18.

34 "Matthew" 5:21–23, *Anchor Bible*, vol. 26 (1971) trans. William F. Albright and Christopher S. Mann.

---

and towards the end of the *On Anger* Lactantius noted that "some ... will perhaps say, that in His precepts [God] ... forbids man to be angry."[35] But those unnamed persons (including, perhaps, his teacher, Arnobius)[36] are incorrect. For if anger were entirely forbidden, God Himself "would have been in some measure the censurer of His own workmanship" since he had placed anger in the human being He had created. God does not forbid us to be angry but rather to "persevere in anger" since (and here Lactantius alludes to one of the Psalms, repeated by Paul in his "Letter to the Ephesians") "He enjoined us to be angry, and yet not to sin." It is plain, Lactantius concludes, that "He did not tear up anger by the roots, but restrained it, that in every correction we might preserve moderation and justice."[37] The polemic against the Epicureans' denial of divine providence and of anger in God has thus led Lactantius to argue for an "anger-restrained" position, to move from the "no anger" of earlier Church teaching to a "no unjust anger" way of interpreting Jesus's command.[38]

---

35 *On Anger*, 21.

36 Arnobius believed that a display of anger was inconsistent with the divine nature. His view placed him "particularly with Epicureanism but also to some extent with Stoicism" (George E. McCracken, "Introduction" to Arnobius of Sicca, *The Case Against the Pagans* [*Adversus nationes*], trans. George E. McCracken, 2 vols. [1949] of *Ancient Christian Writers*, ed. Johannes Quasted and Joseph Plumpe, 40 vols. [New York: Newman Press], vol. 1, pp. 28f).

37 *On Anger*, 21. The scriptural quotations he uses are from "Psalms" 4, 4 and Paul's "Letter to the Ephesians", 4, 26 (in which Paul repeats the psalm). Translations of these texts are varied: The King James Version, the Jerusalem Bible, the Revised Standard Version, the Knox translation, and the New English Bible differ, sometimes significantly, in the rendering of one or other of these passages. Mitchell Dahood, the translator of the Psalms (*Anchor Bible*, "Psalms" 1 [1–50], vol. 16, [1965]), renders it "Be disquieted, but do not sin" and a note explains that the disquiet is due to lack of rainfall since the entire psalm is a prayer for rain. Markus Barth, translator of "Ephesians", renders the verse as "If you are angry yet do not sin." In an extensive note which begins by noting that "be angry and sin not" is the literal translation, he describes this as a "concessive imperative" which does not command that one be angry (*Anchor Bible*, "Ephesians" [4–6], vol. 34A, p. 513, n. 26). Citing other scriptural verses, he suggests that righteous anger aroused by injustice is not forbidden. Lactantius's statement that God has "enjoined us to be angry" would thus seem overdrawn.

38 See, for example, Origen, *On First Principles*, IV, 1 (*The Ante-Nicene Fathers*, vol. 4); cf. *Pastor of Hermas III*, 15 (*The Ante-Nicene Fathers*, vol. 2) and Tertullian, *On the Resurrection of the Flesh*, 47 (*The Ante-Nicene Fathers*, vol. 3). Tertullian, however, implies a distinction between just and unjust anger in *On Modesty* [*On Purity*], 19: "there are some sins of daily committal, to which are all liable: for who will

---

But, in the same sermon in which he had seemingly condemned anger, Jesus had also said that

> You have heard that it was said "An eye for an eye and a tooth for a tooth." But I tell you not to resist the one who is evil. But if anyone strikes you on the right cheek, turn the other to him as well.... You have heard that it was said: "You shall love your neighbor and hate your enemy," but I tell you to love your enemies and pray for those who misuse you.[39]

If divinely ordained limits and proper motivation are the twin factors that make anger righteous and, so understood, allow a new way of interpreting what Jesus had commanded, could those factors not also allow a parallel new interpretation of his teachings in response to evildoers? Lactantius did not raise the possibility in the *On Anger*: it was hardly necessary since anger, properly motivated and kept within the divinely appointed limits, would presumably not give rise to violence. But that possibility would be suggested by him—suggested, not stated—a few years later when the Church began to find it necessary to reconsider its stance against violence not only as it related to private life but also with respect to public policy and statecraft.

For the first 300 years of Christianity's existence, non-violence was an integral, and even distinctive, part of its moral teaching. No matter the

be free from the accident of either being angry unjustly, and retaining his anger beyond sunset ..." (*The Ante-Nicene Fathers*, vol. 4). But his other observations on anger reflect the view of anger-driven behavior as inimical to Christian life, and he does not suggest that Jesus's teaching allows just but not unjust anger. Cf. *On Prayer*, 19 (*The Ante-Nicene Fathers*, vol. 3): "How will he appease his Father who is angry with his brother, when from the beginning 'all anger' is forbidden us?.... After that, the Lord ... openly adds the prohibition of anger against a brother to that of murder. Not even by an evil word does He permit it to be vented. Even if we must be angry, our anger must not be maintained beyond sunset, as the apostle admonishes. (Ephesians, 4:26)"; *Of Patience*, 6 (*The Ante-Nicene Fathers*, vol. 3): "Anger has been prohibited, our spirits restrained, the petulance of the hand checked, the poison of the tongue extracted"; *On the Resurrection of the Flesh*, 47 (*The Ante-Nicene Fathers*, vol. 3) and again quoting Paul's admonition to "be angry and sin not" (see the previous note): "Never have grudges against others, or lose your temper, or raise your voice to anybody, or call each other names, or allow any sort of spitefulness." I have been unable to find any pre-Lactantian writer who used the just/unjust anger distinction to interpret Jesus's words in the "Sermon on the Mount".

39 "Matthew" 5:39–40, 43–44 (*Anchor Bible*).

cause or reason, whether in self-defense, or in defense of an innocent third party, as a soldier in battle or a state official exercising judicial functions, severe ecclesiastical penalties were imposed on the Christian who performed any act of bloodshed. War was especially evil. In the words of one historian of this period, the early Church considered it "organized iniquity", an "institution of the realm of darkness", with which Christians could not be associated.[40]

In the early decades of the fourth century, however, social and political developments occurred which exerted pressure on this aspect of Church teaching and policy. The growing number of Christians within the empire,[41] the Edicts of Toleration in 311 and of Milan in 313, and the accession of Constantine

---

40 William P. Paterson, "War", in *Encyclopedia of Religion and Ethics*, ed. James Hastings (New York: Charles Scribner's Sons, n.d.), vol. 12, p. 678a. There are a number of general and specialized studies on the subject of pre-Constantinian Christian teachings, attitude, and practice with respect to war and military service. See, for example, Roland H. Bainton, *Christian Attitudes Toward War and Peace: A Historical Survey and Critical Re-evaluation* (New York: Abingdon Press, 1960), and his "The Early Church and War", *Harvard Theological Review* 36 (1946), pp. 189–212; Peter Brock, *The Military Question in the Early Church: A Selected Bibliography of a Century's Scholarship* (Toronto, Ont.: Peter Brock, 1988); C. John Cadoux, *The Early Christian Attitude to War* (London: George Allen & Unwin Ltd., 1940); Hans von Campenhausen, "Christians and Military Service in the Early Church", in *Tradition and Life in the Church*, trans. A. V. Littledale (Philadelphia, PA: Fortress Press, 1968), pp. 160–170; John Driver, *How Christians Made Peace With War* [Peace and Justice Series, #2] (Scottdale, PA: Herald Press, 1988); Adolf von Harnack, *Militia Christi: The Christian Religion and the Military in the First Three Centuries*, trans. David M. Gracie (Philadelphia, PA: Fortress Press, 1981); John Hegeland, "Christians and the Roman Army: AD 173–337", *Church History* 43 (1974), pp. 149–163; Jean-Michel Hornus, *It is Not Lawful For Me To Fight: Early Christian Attitudes Toward War, Violence, and the State*, revised edition, trans. Alan Kreider and Oliver Coburn (Scottdale, PA: Herald Press, 1980); James Moffatt, "War", in *Dictionary of the Apostolic Church*, II, ed. James Hastings (New York, 1919), pp. 646–673; E. A. Ryan, "The Rejection of Military Service by the Early Christians", *Theological Studies* 13 (1952), pp. 1–32; H. F. Secretan, "Le Christianisme des Premiers Siecles et le Service Militaire", *Revue de theologie et de philosophie* 2 (1914), pp. 345–365; and Swift, *The Early Fathers*.

41 Rodney Stark, *The Rise of Christianity* (Princeton, NJ: Princeton University Press, 1996), pp. 4 ff., estimates that the Christian population of the Roman empire grew at the rate of 40% per decade. Starting with approximately 1,000 Christians in 40 AD (0.0017% of the population), by the year 300 there were more than six million Christians (10.5% of the population) and by 350 there were nearly 34 million (56.5% of the population).

---

to the throne in 312, put Christianity's political quietism and historic pacifism under severe stress. No longer a marginalized and persecuted cult whose members played no prominent role in affairs of state, the Church now began to grow in political power and influence. Since the Emperor required his armies and his magistrates to preserve the safety and well-being of his dominions, a Christian policy of non-involvement in state-sanctioned violence was now difficult, if not impossible, to maintain.

It was during this period, some three years after the *On Anger* and five years after Constantine's accession, that the *Epitome* was written. Although described as but a summary of the main arguments of the *Institutes*,[42] the *Epitome* is, in fact, no mere abridgement: small but significant changes in Lactantius's thinking have now occurred, both in what he has to say there about anger, and in what he says and fails to say about violence.

As we have seen, the *Institutes* had criticized the Peripatetics on two grounds: first, that they approved of anger because it made bravery in battle possible and, second, that in approving anger, they were approving of what they considered to be vice. In the *Epitome*, however, only the second criticism (that vice should not be allowed, even in moderation) appeared. Not only did Lactantius not repeat his disapproval of the Peripatetic association of anger with the battlefield, but in the same chapter (LXI) and in a surprising turnabout, the following passage—absent from the *Institutes*—was added:

> And as bravery, if you fight in defence of your country, is a good, if against your country, is an evil, so the passions, if you employ them to good purposes, will be virtues, if to evil uses, they will be called vices. Anger therefore has been given by God for the restraining of offences, that is, for controlling the discipline of subjects, that fear may suppress licentiousness and restrain audacity. But they who are ignorant of its limits are angry with their equals, or even with their superiors. Hence they rush to deeds of cruelty, hence they rise to slaughters, hence to wars.[43]

---

42 *Epitome*, "Preface". Cf. Pierre de Labriolle, *History and Literature of Christianity from Tertullian to Boethius*, trans. Herbert Wilson (New York: Barnes and Noble, Inc., 1968), p. 206: "The Epitome ... is like an amended second edition of the *Institutiones* after the elimination of useless developments, repetitions and quotations from profane authors." The *Institutes* is made up of seven books (179 chapters) and the preface, and covers 215 pages in *The Ante-Nicene Fathers* edition; the *Epitome*, originally 73 chapters long (68 of which survive), covers 32 pages in the same edition.

43 *Epitome*, LXI; italics mine.

Our writer who, a few years earlier, had criticized killing in war as bringing human beings to the level of beasts now presented bravery in warfare as virtuous and praiseworthy. A divinely ordained limit and a righteous motive, identified earlier as making anger justified and so permitted to Christians, now also allowed violence-driven actions provided they are battle-related (the limit) and performed in order to defend one's country (the motive). It seems that Lactantius had by this time moved so far in the direction of seeing some forms of violence as justified that bravery in warfare now was identified as the "given" which helped explain how anger-driven action could sometimes be virtuous. Finally, although the chapter reproduces much of Lactantius's earlier thinking about the acceptable motive and limits of righteous anger, it now adds a new member to the earlier group of those with whom one can be justly angry—namely, "subjects". Especially since this is introduced within the context of bravery in battle, it seems that the Emperor and those serving him were now being included among those who can be righteously driven by anger, provided that they are motivated by the desire to discipline and restrain the "audacity" and "licentiousness" of their subjects.

The modification of Lactantius's thinking on violence is again present in his treatment of the Biblical commandment against killing. In the *Institutes* he had reproduced the traditional teaching of the Church on this topic. Not only must Christians avoid all killing and violence, he wrote, but they must also refuse even to take pleasure in witnessing any form of violence, especially the gladiatorial arenas so popular in ancient Rome. For

> when God forbids us to kill, He not only prohibits us from open violence, which is not even allowed by the public laws, but He warns us against the commission of those things which are esteemed lawful among men. Thus *it will be neither lawful for a just man to engage in warfare … nor to accuse any one of a capital charge, because it makes no difference whether you put a man to death by word, or rather by the sword, since it is the act of putting to death itself which is prohibited. Therefore, with regard to this precept of God ["Thou shalt not kill"], there ought to be no exception at all; but that it is always unlawful to put to death a man, whom God willed to be a sacred animal.*[44]

---

44 *Institutes*, VI, 20; italics mine. De Labriolle in *History and Literature* includes his opposition to all bloodshed as among his "traits of absolutism [that] are so much the more surprising because, taken as a whole, his work is of a moderate and tranquil tone" (p. 210).

To quote the patristic scholar Louis Swift, this is "pacifism pure and simple."[45] The section of the *Epitome* which parallels this fails, however, to include most of the content of this passage.[46] While Lactantius repeated his condemnation of attendance at blood sports, about war he said only that it is "detestable";[47] and in the following chapter he remarked that

> It is an old precept not to kill, which ought not to be taken in this light, as though we are commanded to abstain only from homicide, which is punished even by public laws. *But by the intervention of this command, it will not be permitted us to apply peril of death by word, nor to put to death or expose an infant, nor to condemn one's self by a voluntary death.*[48]

Homicide, death threats, infanticide, and suicide are still forbidden to Christians; but killing in battle is not now included in the list of those forms of forbidden killing. Nor was anything said here or elsewhere in the *Epitome* about its not being lawful for a just man to engage in warfare; nothing about its being always unlawful to put a man to death; nothing about there being no exception at all to the "old precept" that condemns killing; nothing about the act of killing itself that is forbidden; nothing about its being unlawful to put to death a human being, God's sacred animal—all of them elements of his earlier teaching on the topic. The "pacifism pure and simple" of the *Institutes* is neither as pure nor as simple any longer.

Orthodoxy does not change overnight. In the handful of years that separated the composition of the *Institutes* and the *Epitome*, the alliance

---

45 Swift, *The Early Fathers*, p. 63.

46 *Epitome*, LXIII, LXIV. Note as well the *Institutes* in which he sharply criticizes the Romans' admiration and even deification of warlike heroes and leaders. To think that these men ascend to the region of the gods because they have "slaughtered countless thousands of men" is a "miserable wave of errors". Further, if only through mass bloodshed can immortality be obtained, the warlike will not tolerate public tranquillity if all people were to live harmoniously together. Instead they "will plunder and rage; and by the infliction of outrageous injuries will disturb the compact of human society, that they may have an enemy whom they may destroy with greater wickedness than that which they attacked" (I, 18). Although this material is not to be found in the extant chapters of the *Epitome* (see above, note 43), the five missing chapters of that work would in all likelihood have coincided with this section of Book I.

47 Ibid., LXIII: "What is so dreadful, what so foul, as the slaughter of man? Therefore our life is protected by the most severe laws; therefore wars are detestable."

48 *Epitome* LXIV.

---

which the Church was beginning to forge with the Empire[49] would have been impossible were the emperor to be deprived of the services of his Christian citizens in protecting the state and its inhabitants from the violence of its enemies.[50] In those few years, a small but significant development in official Church thinking on the subject of war had occurred. In 314, a scant two years after Constantine's accession and three years before the *Epitome* was written, the Western bishops meeting in council at Arles decreed that anyone who deserted the armies "in time of peace" would suffer excommunication; nothing was said about desertion in time of war.[51] The meaning of the Arles decree has been widely debated,[52] but this much is clear: Church leaders were beginning to rethink their policy of involvement by Christians in the life of the state. The religious/political situation was fluid when Lactantius wrote the *Epitome*, and so he moved carefully, pointing by cautious word and significant omission a direction in which some of those moral challenges could be resolved.

By the end of that century the tide of orthodoxy had changed. Prior to 356, Athanasius (c. 296–373) wrote to the monk Amun that "one is not supposed to kill, but killing the enemy in battle is both lawful and praiseworthy."[53] He did not seem to think it necessary to justify his view. Ambrose of Milan (340?–397), in his *On The Duties Of The Clergy (De Officiis ministrorum)* written prior to the spring of 386, contained an early formulation of principles that would evolve, in Augustine's hands, into an articulated moral defense for Christian participation in war and other forms of state-sponsored violence.[54] Those principles, a

---

49 Basil Studer, "The Situation of the Church", in *History of Theology*, ed. Angelo Di Berardino and Basil Studer, 4 vols. (Collegeville, MN: The Liturgical Press, 1996), vol. 1 (*The Patristic Period*), p. 256.

50 René Pichon, *Lactance Étude sur le Mouvement Philosophique et Religieux sous la Règne de Constantin* (Paris: Librairie Hachette et Cie, 1901), p. 454, and de Labriolle, *History and Literature*, p. 211.

51 Canon 3 of the Council of Arles stated: *De his qui arma projeciunt in pace, placuit abstineri eos a communione* (Concerning those who throw away their arms in time of peace, it is fitting that they should not be admitted to communion), as cited in Hornus, *It is Not Lawful*, p. 172.

52 For discussions of Canon III and its significance, see Bainton, *Christian Attitudes*, pp. 80–81; Cadoux, *The Early Christian Attitude*, pp. 256–257; Hornus, *It is Not Lawful*, pp. 171 ff.; and von Harnack, *Militia Christi*, p. 100.

53 As cited in Swift, *The Early Fathers*, p. 95. Swift observes that, at this time, "the issue is no longer whether Christians may take human life but what conditions are necessary to justify such action. That kind of shift marks a significant departure from the concerns of the ante-Nicene period...."

54 For the dating of the *De Officiis*, see F. Holmes Dudden, *The Life and Times of St. Ambrose*, 2 vols. (Oxford: Clarendon Press, 1935), vol. 2, p. 695. For Ambrose on

foundation of "just-war" or "limited-war" theory, remain today an important part of much mainstream Christian thinking concerning the morality of war.[55]

Mainstream: for in the immediate post-Constantinian period, even as today, there were both individual Christians and Christian communities that refused to endorse the new orthodoxy of the later fourth and early fifth century. They continued, and continue, to hold that violence itself is inherently evil, rejecting the notion of "just war" as a betrayal of Jesus's authentic teaching, as an unacceptable compromise of Christian teaching with the world and its values, and as an alliance with the "realm of darkness".

---

warfare, see *De Officiis ministrorum libri tres* (*On The Duties Of The Clergy*), I, 27, 129; 29, 139–140; 35, 175–176; 36, 179; III, 3, 23; 4, 27; 13, 84. See also Letter LXXXVI, 1; Letter XC (Letter XXV in Benedictine edition), 1–3; 8–9; *De Tobia* (*On Tobius*), 15.51; *Expositio Evangeli secundum Lucam* (*Discourse on Luke's Gospel*), 5, 58; *Expositio in Ps. CXVIII* (*Discourse on Psalm 118*), 15, 22; *De Incarnationis dominicae sacramento l. unus* (*The Sacrament of the Incarnation of Our Lord*), 1, 3. Ambrose's writings can be found in various translations and in Jacques-Paul Migne, *Patrologia Latina* (Paris: Apud Garnier Fratres, 1844–1864), vols. 14–17. Augustine's theology of war evolved from its earliest appearance in the *On Free Will* (*De libero arbitrio*) and his anti-Manichaean writings, most of which were completed by the end of the fourth century, to the later *On the City of God* (*De civitate Dei*) which was completed in 427. Some of his more important ideas can be found in his letters and Scriptural commentaries. Cf. *On Free Will*, 4, 9 and 5, 11–13; *On the Sermon on the Mount* (*In sermone Domini in monte*), I, 20, 63–64; I, 21, 69, 71–72; I, 22, 76–77; *Against Faustus the Manichaean* (*Contra Faustum Manichaeum*), XXII, 70, 73–77, 79; *On the City of God*, I, vii, 21, 26; III, x; IV, xv; XV, iv; XVII, xiii; XIX, vi, vii, xii, xv; XXII, vi; *Exposition on the Book of Psalms* (*Ennarationes in Psalmos*), XXXVIII, 13; LXXII, 4; LXXIX, 14; CXI, 24; CXIX, 24; CXXV, 7; CXXXIX, 18; *Letters* (*Epistulae*), XLVII, 5; LXXXVII, 7–8; CXXXVIII, 9, 12–15; CLIII, 3, 5, 16–17, 19; CLXXIII, 2; CLXXXV, 7–8; CLXXXIX, 4–6; CCXXIX, 2. Augustine's writings can be found in various translations and in Migne, *Patrologia Latina*, vol. 32–47.

55   For example, in "The Challenge of Peace: God's Promise And Our Response", the pastoral letter of the Roman Catholic Bishops issued in 1983, "just war" criteria are explicitly stated in items 80–110, and introduced (in 79) as "moral principles within the Catholic tradition which provide guidance for public policy and individual choice" that reflects "Catholic teaching on the nature of peace, avoidance of war, and the state's rights of legitimate defense...." The pastoral letter may be found in Jim Castelli, *The Bishops and the Bomb* (Garden City, NY: Doubleday and Company, 1983), pp. 185ff. See also the U.S. Conference of Bishops' statement "Living With Faith and Hope After September 11", www.nccbuscc.org/sdwp/sept11.htm.

But to return to Lactantius. He seems to have had no significant theological or philosophical influence on writers of the later fourth century. Ambrose does not mention him. Augustine, who seems to have read both the *Institutes* and the *Epitome*, refers briefly to him but not with respect to either anger or violence.[56] In the centuries after his death, with Epicureanism no longer a challenge to Christianity, he was no longer known for his arguments against it, but rather for his distinguished literary talents.[57]

He is hardly remembered today. In standard histories of philosophy and theology, if he is mentioned at all, it is usually brief and patronizing. He "was not an intelligence of the first order", one scholar has written; "the refreshing candor of his heart sometimes affected his intellect", said yet another.[58] Others have been kinder. Thomas B. Kilpatrick credits the *On Anger* with formulating the "classical theological statement" of the view that anger is harmonious with

---

56 Augustine's discussion of anger appears to be independent of any Lactantian influence. See, for example, *On the City of God*, XV, 25 in *Basic Writings of Saint Augustine*, ed. Whitney J. Oates, 2 vols. (New York: Random House, 1948), vol. 2, p. 311: "The anger of God is not a disturbing emotion of His mind, but a judgment by which punishment is inflicted upon sin." Augustine continues that Scripture uses expressions such as "anger" to "familiarly insinuate itself into the minds of all classes of men … that it may alarm the proud, arouse the careless, exercise the inquisitive, and satisfy the intelligent…."

In *On Nature and Grace* (*De natura et gratia*), 71, Augustine quotes from the *Institutions*. In *On the City of God*, XVIII, 23, he wrote that "Lactantius … inserted in his work the prophecies about Christ of a certain sibyl, he does not say which." While in both the *Institutes*, IV, 13, and the *Epitome*, 42, Lactantius mentions pagan prophesy of Christ, Augustine's reference seems to be to the *Epitome* since the *Institutes* links pagan prophesy of Christ specifically to the oracle of Apollo (the "Milesian Apollo") while the *Epitome* refers simply to "the Sibyl". In *Institutes*, I, 6, Lactantius observes that the name "Sibyl" could refer to one of at least 10 oracles because "[all prophetesses] were called by the ancients Sibyls." Hence Augustine's "certain sibyl, he does not say which".

57 His elegant prose was praised by St. Jerome and was widely admired by the Renaissance humanists, some of whom called him the "Christian Cicero". Cf. *The Nicene and Post-Nicene Fathers*, Second Series, ed. Philip Schaff and Henry Wace, 14 vols. (Grand Rapids, MI: Wm. B. Eerdmans Publishing Company, 1979), vols. 3 and 4, and Michael P. McHugh, "Lactantius", p. 525.

58 de Labriolle, *History and Literature*, pp. 199 and 207; Gilson, *History*, p. 50. De Labriolle writes that "Even when we exert ourselves to say something good of him it would be puerile to cover up the weaknesses in the train of thought of this conscientious professor, whose traditionalism was more pronounced that his critical sense was acute" (p. 200). James Stevenson, "Lactantius", in *New Catholic*

the divine nature, and Thomas C. O'Brien identifies him as being "the first to formulate a general concept of Christian virtue".[59]

There is, however, more to be said. In his efforts to refute Epicurean theology, Lactantius became the first Christian writer to use the distinction between just and unjust anger as a way of understanding Jesus's instructions in the "Sermon on the Mount" and, as he moved away from the literal and absolutist interpretation of them that had been the common practice of earlier writers, he was later able to imply that a just/unjust distinction could also be used to understand Jesus's teaching about violence and bloodshed. He was, again, the first Christian writer to have done so, and in this he showed one way in which Christianity's historic pacifism could be reconciled with the political necessities of the age.

Because of Lactantius's polemic, Epicureanism deserves another modest footnote in the history of Christian development—not for direct influence but rather for being a catalyst for a new and original way of Christians thinking about anger and violence.[60]

Encyclopedia, ed. William J. McDonald (New York: McGraw Hill, 1967), vol. 8, writes that he is "of little value as a theologian" (p. 308). Approximately a half-page is devoted to him in McHugh, "Lactantius", where he is described as a "rhetorician and not a theologian" (p. 524). Frederick Copleston, *A History of Philosophy* (Garden City, NY: Image Books, 1962), vol. 2, Part 1 (Mediaeval Philosophy), p. 39, devotes all of three lines discussing him, referring solely to his teaching on the origin of the human soul. There is no article on him in the *Encyclopedia of Philosophy*, ed. Paul Edwards (New York: Macmillan Publishing Company, 1967) or in *Encyclopedia of Religion and Ethics*, ed. James Hastings (New York: Charles Scribner's Sons, n.d.). There is no mention of him in Paul Tillich's *A History of Christian Thought*, ed. Carl E. Braaten (New York: Simon and Schuster, 1968).

59 Thomas B. Kirkpatrick, "Anger (Wrath) of God", *Encyclopedia of Religion and Ethics*, vol. 1, pp. 477b–482a, at p. 480a; Thomas O'Brien, "Virtue", in *New Catholic Encyclopedia*, ed. William J. McDonald (New York: McGraw Hill, 1967), vol. 14, pp. 704b–708a, at p. 704b.

60 I am grateful to the librarians at the Rochester Institute of Technology Wallace Library, especially Linda Coppola, for invaluable help in preparing this paper.

WORKS CITED

The Anchor Bible, ed. William Foxwell Albright and David Noel Freedman, 51 vols. (Garden City, NY: Doubleday & Co., Inc.).

"Ephesians" (4–6), trans. Markus Barth, vol. 34A (1974).

"Matthew", trans. William F. Albright and Christopher S. Mann, vol. 26 (1967).

"Psalms" 1 (1–50), trans. Mitchell Dahood, vol. 16 (1965).

"The Acts of the Apostles", trans. Johannes Munck, vol. 31 (1967).

The Ante-Nicene Fathers, ed. Alexander Roberts and James Donaldson, 10 vols. (Grand Rapids, MI: Wm. B. Eerdman Publishing Company, 1979).

Augustine, *Basic Writings of Saint Augustine,* ed. Whitney J. Oates, 2 vols. (New York: Random House, 1948).

Bainton, Roland H., *Christian Attitudes Toward War and Peace: A Historical Survey and Critical Re-evaluation* (New York: Abingdon Press, 1960).

——, "The Early Church and War", *Harvard Theological Review* 36 (1946), pp. 189–212.

Brock, Peter, *The Military Question in the Early Church: A Selected Bibliography of a Century's Scholarship* (Toronto, Ont.: Peter Brock, 1988).

Cadoux, C. John, *The Early Christian Attitude To War* (London: George Allen & Unwin Ltd., 1940).

Castelli, Jim, *The Bishops and the Bomb* (Garden City, NY: Doubleday and Company, 1983).

Cicero, *De Natura Deorum* and *Academica,* trans. H. Rackham (Cambridge, MA: Harvard University Press, 1967).

Copleston, Frederick, *A History of Philosophy,* 9 vols. (Garden City, NY: Image Books, 1962).

de Labriolle, Pierre, *History and Literature of Christianity from Tertullian to Boethius*, trans. Herbert Wilson (New York: Barnes and Noble, Inc., 1968).

DeWitt, Norman Wentworth, *Epicurus and His Philosophy* (Cleveland, OH: The World Publishing Co., 1967).

———, *St. Paul and Epicurus* (Minneapolis, MN: University of Minnesota Press, 1954).

Diogenes Laertius, *Lives of Eminent Philosophers*, trans. Robert D. Hicks, 2 vols. (Cambridge, MA: Harvard University Press, 1965).

Driver, John, *How Christians Made Peace With War* [Peace and Justice Series, #2] (Scottdale, PA: Herald Press, 1988).

Dudden, F. Holmes, *The Life and Times of St. Ambrose*, 2 vols. (Oxford: Clarendon Press, 1935).

Encyclopedia of Philosophy, ed. Paul Edwards (New York: Macmillan Publishing Company, 1967).

Encyclopedia of Religion and Ethics, ed. James Hastings (New York: Charles Scribner's Sons, n.d.).

Festugière, Andre-Jean, *Epicurus and His Gods*, trans. C. W. Chilton (New York: Russell and Russell, 1955).

Gilson, Etienne, *History of Christian Philosophy in the Middle Ages* (New York: Random House, 1955).

Hegeland, John, "Christians and the Roman Army: AD 173–337", *Church History* 43 (1974), pp. 149–163.

Hornus, Jean-Michel, *It Is Not Lawful For Me To Fight: Early Christian Attitudes Toward War, Violence, and the State*, revised edition, trans. Alan Kreider and Oliver Coburn (Scottdale, PA: Herald Press, 1980).

Inwood, Brad and L. P. Gerson, *The Epicurus Reader* (Indianapolis, IN: Hackett Publishing Co., 1994).

Jones, Howard, *The Epicurean Tradition* (London: Routledge, 1989).

Jungkuntz, Richard P., "Christian Approval of Epicureanism", *Church History* 31 (1962), pp. 279–293.

——, "Fathers, Heretics and Epicureans", *The Journal of Ecclesiastical History* 17 (1966), pp. 3–10.

Kirkpatrick, Thomas B., "Anger (Wrath) of God", in *Encyclopedia of Religion and Ethics*, vol. 1, pp. 477b–482a.

Lactantius, *Lactantius Divine Institutes*, trans. Sister Mary Francis McDonald, vol. 49 (1964) of *The Fathers of the Church*, ed. Roy J. Deferrari, 63 vols. (Washington, D.C.: The Catholic University of America Press).

——, *Lactantius The Minor Works*, trans. Sister Mary Francis McDonald, vol. 54 (1965) of *The Fathers of the Church*, ed. Roy J. Deferrari, 63 vols. (Washington, D.C.: The Catholic University of America Press).

Lucretius, *On the Nature of Things* (*De Rerum Natura*) in *The Stoic and Epicurean Philosophers*, ed. Whitney J. Oates (New York: The Modern Library, 1940).

McCracken, George E., "Introduction", to Arnobius of Sicca, *The Case Against the Pagans* [*Adversus nationes*], trans. George E. McCracken, in *Ancient Christian Writers* (New York: Newman Press, 1949), vols. 7 and 8 (1949) of *Ancient Christian Writers*, ed. Johannes Quasted and Joseph Plumpe, 40 vols. (New York: Newman Press).

McHugh, Michael P., "Lactantius", in *Encyclopedia of Early Christianity*, ed. Everett Ferguson (New York: Garland Publishing, Inc., 1990), pp. 524–525.

Migne, Jacques-Paul, *Patrologia Latina* (Paris: Apud Garnier Fratres, 1844–1864).

Moffatt, James, "War", in *Dictionary of the Apostolic Church*, ed. James Hastings, 2 vols. (New York, 1919), vol. 2, pp. 646–673.

The Nicene and Post-Nicene Fathers, Second Series, ed. Philip Schaff and Henry Wace, 14 vols. (Grand Rapids, MI: Wm. B. Eerdmans Publishing Company, 1979).

O'Brien, Thomas, "Virtue", in *New Catholic Encyclopedia*, ed. William J. McDonald (New York: McGraw Hill, 1967), vol. 14, pp. 704b–708a.

Paterson, William P., "War", in *Encyclopedia of Religion and Ethics*, vol. 12.

Pichon, René, *Lactance Étude sur le Mouvement Philosophique et Religieus sous la Règne de Constantin* (Paris: Librairie Hachette et Cie, 1901).

Ryan, E. A., "The Rejection of Military Service by the Early Christians", *Theological Studies* 13 (1952), pp. 1–32.

Schaff, Philip, *History of the Christian Church*, 8 vols. (Grand Rapids, MI: William B. Eerdmans Publishing Co., 1910, reprinted 1967).

Secretan, H. F., "Le Christianisme des Premiers Siecles et le Service Militaire", *Revue de theologie et de philosophie* 2 (1914), pp. 345–65.

Simpson, Adelaide D., "Epicureans, Christians, Atheists in the Second Century", *Transactions and Proceedings of the American Philological Association* 72 (1941), pp. 372–381.

Stark, Rodney, *The Rise of Christianity* (Princeton, NJ: Princeton University Press, 1996).

Stevenson, James, "Lactantius", in *New Catholic Encyclopedia*, ed. William J. McDonald (New York: McGraw Hill, 1967), vol. 8.

Studer, Basil, "The Situation of the Church", in *History of Theology*, ed. Angelo Di Berardino and Basil Studer, 4 vols. (Collegeville, MN: The Liturgical Press, 1996), vol. 1 (*The Patristic Period*).

Swift, Louis J., *The Early Fathers on War and Military Service*, in *Message of the Fathers of the Church*, ed. Thomas Halton, 23 vols. (Wilmington DE: Michael Glazier, Inc.), vol. 19 (1983).

Tillich, Paul, *A History of Christian Thought*, ed. Carl E. Braaten (New York: Simon and Schuster, 1968).

United States Conference of Bishops, "Living With Faith and Hope After September 11", www.nccbuscc.org/sdwp/sept11.htm.

von Campenhausen, Hans, "Christians and Military Service in the Early Church", in *Tradition and Life in the Church*, trans. A. V. Littledale (Philadelphia, PA: Fortress Press 1968), pp. 160–170.

von Harnack, Adolf, *Militia Christi: The Christian Religion and the Military in the First Three Centuries*, trans. David M. Gracie (Philadelphia, PA: Fortress Press, 1981).

PLOTINUS AND EPICUREAN EPISTEMOLOGY

Lloyd P. Gerson

The *index fontium* of Henry and Schwyzer's great edition of Plotinus's *Enneads* lists about fifteen references to doctrines of Epicurus. This is a modest amount in comparison with the hundreds and hundreds of references Plotinus makes to Stoics and Peripatetics and, of course, to Plato. The relatively few references, however, are sufficient to show that Plotinus was acquainted with the basic lines of Epicureanism. In fact, these references themselves do not tell the full story.[1] For Plotinus was deeply engaged with all those he perceived to be opponents of Platonism. This engagement, especially in Plotinus's oral teaching, is documented for us in Porphyry's remarkable biography of him. But his level of engagement was often at a fairly abstract level. Let me explain.

As paradoxical as it might sound at first, Plotinus was firmly committed to Platonism, not Plato, though I hasten to add that he believed Plato to be the outstanding exponent of Platonism. His expositions of Plato were strictly subordinate to his constructive Platonism. That is why Plotinus felt he should— always with appropriate caution—draw out the implications of what Plato was claiming in the dialogues or even what witnesses like Aristotle reported that Plato held in oral discussion. This paper is not about Neoplatonic hermeneutics, but I suggest that much of the astonishment that some contemporary scholars feel when they read accounts by the Neoplatonists about what Plato taught stems from an assumption that they did not share. The assumption is that one aims to discover what Plato thought on the basis of whatever evidence is held to be legitimate and that is the end of the matter. That was not the assumption of Neoplatonism generally. Rather, they assumed that what they were after was truth and that Plato was their best, though certainly not their only guide to this.

Plotinus's engagement with Epicureanism should be understood in the light of his defense of Platonism. For Plotinus, Platonism was practically synonymous with what we might call a top down approach to the full array of problems faced by philosophy. In a top down approach, the sensible world is to be explained ultimately by the intelligible world. In a bottom up approach, the order is reversed. Both a top down approach and a bottom up approach agree that the relatively complex is to be explained by the relatively simple. But in a top

---

1 Plotinus's interest in Epicurus was, principally, as a proponent of atomism. So to the fifteen or so direct references to works of Epicurus should be added another fifteen or so references to general atomistic doctrines.

down approach, the relatively simple is identified with the intelligible, whereas in a bottom up approach the relatively simple is identified with the sensible. The top down approach identifies the relatively simple with the intelligible principles, soul, intellect and the intelligible Forms, and ultimately, the One; the bottom up approach identifies the relatively simple with elements of some sort and the intelligible as in some way epiphenomenal or supervenient on the sensible.[2] This is, very briefly, why Plotinus takes Atomism generally, and Epicureanism in particular, as the polar opposite of Platonism, and the epitome of misguided philosophy.

A naturalistic or naturalized account of cognition such as we find in Epicurus is an expression of "bottom uppism". Such an account sees the study of epistemological questions as belonging to natural science. In particular, it inquires into the generation of beliefs from the sense-experience of human organisms. In a naturalistic epistemology, this is the *only* way in which beliefs ultimately can be explained. Thus, there is, I believe, a direct line from Epicurus to Quine, something that is especially useful to recall in confronting some of the odder things Epicurus is inclined to say.

Plotinus's critique of Epicurean epistemology should be seen as "top downism" in confrontation with "bottom uppism" expressed in particular as a naturalized account of cognition. That critique is focused on the Epicurean idea of ἐνάργεια or evidence. Sextus Empiricus informs us of the importance of this idea in Epicurean epistemology.[3] The branch of philosophy called "canonic" deals with the evident and the non-evident and also the relationship between the two. According to Epicurus's *Letter to Herodotus*, we learn that the evident is to provide a sign (σημειωσόμεθα) of the non-evident.[4] In the central epistemological section of the *Letter*, we learn further that in sense-perception "outlines" (τύποι) or "images" (ἔιδωλα), consisting of atoms and streaming off of sensibles, enter the eyes or mind and produce a "presentation" (φαντασία).[5] As Sextus helpfully notes, Epicurus uses the term "presentation" as synonymous with the term "evidence".[6] This presentation or evidence is always true and provides the "base

---

2 See the entire treatise V 9 (5) which is an extended description of the difference between the top down and bottom up approaches and the individuals oriented to each. Here, Plotinus lumps the Stoics and Epicureans together. One might question the interpretation of the Stoics as "bottom uppists". But Plotinus simply views their top down claims—such as the priority of the active principle to the passive principle—as inconsistent with their essentially bottom up (read: materialist) position.

3 See Sextus Empiricus, *Adversus Mathematicos*, VII.22.

4 See *Letter to Herodotus*, 37–38.

5 Ibid., 49.

6 See Sextus Empiricus, *Adversus Mathematicos*, VII.203.

and foundation of all [true judgments]".[7] "That which is false and in error" (τὸ δὲ ψεῦδος καὶ τὸ διημαρτημένον) always (ἀεί) lies in an "additional belief" (ἐν τῷ προσδοξαζομένῳ).[8] In this additional belief, whether it be about the evident or the non-evident, resides the possibility of knowledge. Thus, true belief which has been confirmed by additional or sufficient evidence is knowledge.[9]

Before turning to Plotinus's critique, we should briefly look at the contrasting, that is, Skeptical critique of Sextus. He argues in effect that there is no such thing as sufficient evidence. That is, the confirming or "witnessing" evidence adduced by Epicurus is unable to turn belief into true belief that is not merely accidentally true because there is nothing added to the original presentation that entails the truth of the belief.[10] There is no belief that o, which, added to the belief that p, entails q. So, it is not enough that presentations of sensibles should all be true and even that they should all be "real" or "existent" (ὑπάρχον).[11] That is, it is not enough for knowledge that one have a belief expressing the presentation, a belief that is, by definition, true. It is the skeptic's position generally that, once it is admitted that there is *some* logical gap between belief and knowledge, one must immediately recognize that the gap is unbridgeable. This is the case even if it is stipulated, according to Epicurean principles, that the belief is true. Adding more true beliefs about more evidence nigh unto eternity will not do the trick.

Plotinus's critique of Epicurean epistemology is especially interesting because it is not a skeptical critique. It is well known that one of the motivations of a naturalized epistemology is to circumvent skeptical attacks. Various proponents of this approach argue that skepticism is rendered irrelevant by the scientific milieu within which they operate. Since cognition is a natural process, skepticism can only arise within the scientific framework of the description of that process. Thus, one cannot argue in general whether knowledge is possible when it is knowledge that is being investigated. One can only argue whether knowledge has occurred in this case, and one may answer this question only by applying the relevant scientific criteria.

Plotinus's criticism is somewhat different. In *Ennead* V 5 (32) titled "That the Intelligibles are not Outside the Intellect", Plotinus asserts that "that which is cognized (γινωσκόμενον) by sense-perception is an image (εἴδωλόν) of the thing (τοῦ πράγματος), that is, sense-perception does not grasp the thing itself. For that thing remains outside."[12] This is, of course, literally what

---

7 Ibid., VII.216.

8 *Letter to Herodotus*, 50.

9 Sextus Empiricus, *Adversus Mathematicos*, VII.210–217.

10 Ibid., VIII.362–366.

11 Ibid., VIII.9.

12 *Ennead*, V 5.1, 17–19. Cf. V 3.3, 15–18.

Epicurus says himself in the *Letter to Herodotus*, though he is clearly using the term "image" in a way intended not to drive a wedge between that image and reality.

This argument alluded to by Plotinus should put one in mind of a similar argument made by Plato himself in *Theaetetus*.[13] Here it is shown that sense-perception cannot be knowledge because it is not possible to "attain" (τυχεῖν) truth if one does not attain "being" (οὐσίας) and it is not possible to attain knowledge if one does not attain truth.[14] Therefore, if one does not attain being, one does not attain knowledge. But attaining being is precisely *not* equivalent to having a sense-perception. Therefore, sense-perception is not knowledge. If, however, we take this argument as germane to Plotinus's critique of Epicurus, we might want to say that it is patently question-begging. For Epicurus surely insists that sense-perception *does* attain being. Is that not exactly what even Sextus says when he concedes that all sensibles are "real" or "existent"?

In order to answer this question, we need to probe a little further into Plato's argument. In order to attain being, one must cognize "common terms" (τὰ κοινά) that "apply to everything".[15] Among these common terms are "being" and "not-being", "likeness and unlikeness", "sameness and difference", "one" and "number", "odd and even" and so on.[16] These are not perceived by us; rather, the soul operating through itself investigates and reaches out to them.[17] The issue then becomes why cognition of the "common terms" is thought to be necessary for attaining being. The answer, I believe, is that these common terms should not be understood as "universals" as opposed to particulars, as they often are in the literature, but as objective properties of things, as opposed to what is available to sense-perception, namely, "unique or personal or subjective properties" (τὰ ἴδια).[18] What is wrong with the claim that sense-perception is knowledge, and by extension, with the theory of Epicurus, is that it substitutes "being for me" for "being" and "true for me" for "true". In order to attain the latter, one must, as Plato claims, employ the mind.

If this is basically correct as an interpretation of Plato's argument, then the belief wherein Epicurus thinks resides knowledge is to be contrasted with the deliverances of mind in relation to the common terms. That is, since belief is capable of attaining only more evidence, in effect, more of what is "true for me" as opposed to what is "true", it is not capable of attaining being and so is

---

13 See *Theaetetus*, 184B–186E.

14 Ibid., 186C7–10.

15 Ibid., 185B–E.

16 Ibid., 185C9–D4.

17 Ibid., 185E1–2, 186A4.

18 Cf. ibid., 158A7, 160B8–C2, 162D1, 166D4–E4, 167C5.

---

not a candidate for knowledge. Further, Epicurus seems open to the charge of doing exactly what Plotinus implies he is doing—substituting "true for me" for "true"—when he insists that all sense-perceptions are true.[19]

Returning to Plotinus's argument, the words "sense-perception does not grasp (λαμβάνει) the thing itself" should, therefore, not be understood as holding up sense-perception to an impossible Kantian criterion. What sense-perception does not do but must do if it is to be the "base and foundation" of knowledge is to attain being, that which is objectively the same for everyone. But it cannot in principle attain being. It attains only an image of being. The image is always the "image-for-someone" and thus "true" is conflated with "true for me".

The larger story about the metaphysics of imagery in the Platonic tradition is, fortunately, not in need of telling here. I limit myself here to the discussion of imagery as applied to cognition. For Plotinus, all cognition other than the highest form, knowledge, is representational. When Plotinus says that sense-perception grasps only an image of "the thing itself" he means that what is "in" the perceiver is a representation of something else. When a subject represents something "outside" itself, it does not have knowledge. It is important to see what sort of argument Plotinus employs to arrive at this startling claim. In V 3 (49), "On the Knowing Hypostases and That Which is Beyond", Plotinus argues that if the hypothetical object of knowledge is not "inside" the subject, then the putative knower will only possess an "impression" (τύπον) and not the truth.[20] And the reason given is, "the truth should not be the truth about something different, but rather it should be what it says it is." In other words, what is supposed to make a representation true, namely, that it represents something different, guarantees that the representation itself is not the truth.[21]

We are perhaps inclined to reply in Epicurus's defense that it is hardly fair to require of a representation anything other than that it be a good or accurate or, indeed, true, representation. This is a fair point, one to which Plotinus would assent. Where he would demur is with the assumption that *all* cognition, including knowledge, must be representational. One who holds such an assumption, for example, an Epicurean, must face the obvious objection that a representation can be judged to be a true one if and only if one can compare it with that which is represented. But, of course, if one *could* compare the representation with that which it is supposed to represent, then one would not need the representation in the first place in order to attain being and hence truth.

The way Epicurus responds to this objection is, in the passage from the *Letter to Herodotus* to which I briefly referred, to insist that if enough

---

19 See on this doctrine especially Elizabeth Asmis, *Epicurus' Scientific Method* (Ithaca: Cornell University Press, 1984), pp. 141–159.

20 *Enneads*, V 3.5, 23–25.

21 Cf. V 5.1, 56–58.

---

representations of the favored kind are added to the original representations, then knowledge is achieved. Three things should be said about this. First, this position quite clearly wants to reappropriate or take back the honorific term "knowledge" which has been kidnapped by the Platonic/Aristotelian tradition. This is, generally, a typical Epicurean strategy. Why, after all, should a materialist like Epicurus concede that knowledge needs to be anything other than representational? Second, the stipulation that all sense-perceptions are true shifts the focus away from the potential embarrassment that we can never know that our representations actually represent. A true belief is just basically one pursuant upon a necessarily true sense-perception that is not defeated (I do not say *defeasible*) by any other sense-perception. And, again, this seems reasonable on materialist principles. According to these, the acquisition of knowledge must, after all, be some sort of physical process. In this regard, I am reminded of the insistence of the eliminative materialist that our cognition of numbers must just be neurological events or states since that is all there is. Third, the Epicurean reappropriation of the concept of knowledge has more force against a skeptical claim that knowledge is impossible than it does against a Platonic (or if you like Neoplatonic) claim that knowledge is indeed possible for us, but no representational state is it. Clearly, the latter is more genuinely a threat to Epicurus than the former, which denies that knowledge, as traditionally conceived, does exist. Against the skeptic, Epicurus can maintain that materialists recognize that representational states based on sense-perception are the only game in town. As for the Platonists, Epicurus must explain why his account of knowledge is superior to theirs.

From the perspective of the Platonists, the issue is actually somewhat more complicated. They want to insist not only that knowledge is possible for us, but that if we were not the sort of thing capable of knowing, then embodied forms of cognition would not be available to us either. In short, if we were not immaterial entities, then we would not be capable of having the very beliefs that the Epicurean claims are knowledge. To put it slightly differently, unless our embodied cognitive states were authentic representations of a disembodied supreme cognitive state, namely, knowledge, we could not represent cognitively to ourselves what is "outside" us, or things in the sensible world. For the remainder of this paper, I am going to try to flesh out these presuppositions of the Plotinian critique of Epicurus.

The first presupposition is the definition of knowledge as an infallible mental state in which the knower is cognitively identical with what is known. This is actually a presupposition of both Plato and Aristotle and perhaps of Academic skeptics as well. That knowledge must be infallible is equivalent to holding that "I know but I may be mistaken" is incoherent. The infallibility of knowledge is actually the basis for the distinction between knowledge and belief in Book V of Plato's *Republic*.[22] Thus, "s knows p" must entail p, whereas "s believes p", of course, does *not* entail p. It is plain enough, I think, that no representational state entails anything about what it represents. If, therefore, you put this traditional definition together with the claim that all cognitive states are representational, you arrive at the skeptical conclusion that knowledge is impossible. By contrast, if knowledge is possible and it is infallible, then it is not a representational state.

The second presupposition is that knowledge is essentially or primarily occurrent and self-reflexive. That is, "s knows p" if and only if "s knows that s knows p". In the latter formulation, "s" must, of course, stand for the identical subject in both places if there is to be genuine self-reflexivity.[23] The origin of this insight is in Plato's *Theaetetus* where we find the distinction between "possessing" (κεκτῆσθαι) and "having" (ἕξειν) knowledge.[24] The former is the dispositional state; the latter is the occurrent state. In the occurrent state, one is in a mental state, namely, identity with the object of knowledge, and simultaneously aware that one is in that state. The distinction and the presupposition are also adopted by Aristotle in his *De Anima* and expressed as the distinction between potentially and actually knowing and the identity of knower and object of knowledge.[25]

On the Platonic account of the matter, only of immaterial entities could the above two presuppositions be true. For one thing, no material entity could aspire to infallibility. If it is not sufficient merely to appeal to the laws of systems theory and ultimately to the laws of physics to support this claim, consider that no material entity could be aware of its own states except in an equivocal sense of "its own". All one could conceivably have is one putative state of knowing, call it "A" and another putative state of being aware that the entity is in state "A". Call that second state "B". But "A" and "B" cannot be states of the identical subject. The easiest case is to make "A" a switch in the "on" position. Then "B" must be another switch in, say, the "on" position. But the subjects of each switch obviously cannot be identical. The first switch cannot both be in the "on" and "off" positions nor can it be "twice" in the "on" position. So, in addition to the problem about how there could be self-reflexivity in the material entity, there could be no infallibility either because there is no way to guarantee that "B" will always correctly monitor the state "A". Thus, to put it simply, the fact that B "reports" that "A" is in the "on" position does not entail that "A" is truly in that position.

---

22 Cf. *Republic*, 477E6–7, where infallibility is given as the reason (and the only reason) for distinguishing knowledge and belief.

23 Cf. *Enneads*, V 3.13, 13–15; III 8.8, 26–29.

24 Cf. *Theaetetus*, 197B8–10.

25 Cf. *De Anima*, Γ6, 430a25–26; Γ7, 431b17, etc. Sextus Empiricus, *Adversus Mathematicos*, VII.310–314, argues that such self-reflexivity is impossible. See also *Enneads*, V 3.5 for Plotinus's reply.

The Epicurean will likely be unphased by the accusation that he cannot show how material entities compounded of atoms and void can have infallible self-reflexive cognition. This would be very much like accusing an atheist of being unable to explain how an omniscient being can know the future. But a potentially far more damaging accusation is that belief—which is what the Epicurean supposes knowledge is—would not be possible unless knowledge, defined as above, were possible. So, if knowledge is possible, belief is possible. But knowledge is possible only if persons are other than as the Epicurean science would have it. In addition, if knowledge is possible, then it is *not* what Epicurus says it is either. Consequently, true beliefs are available to the Epicurean only if Epicurus is wrong about what the ideal cognitive state is and about what a cognizer must be. For example, Epicurus's belief that we are made of atoms and so subject to disassembly at death could only be a true belief if it is a belief. But it must be a false belief or no belief at all if it is a belief held by Epicurus on Epicurean principles.

So, the question from the Epicurean to the Platonist becomes: why do you think that belief is possible only if persons are immaterial entities capable of knowledge? Plotinus's answer to this question is contained in a passage in which he is discussing the faculty of discursive reasoning and belief in relation to the faculty of knowing or intellect and in relation to sense-perception. It is worth quoting in full. He says,

> Is it then the case that the discursive part does not know that it is the discursive part and that it acquires understanding of externals, and that it discerns what it discerns, and that it does so by the rules that are in itself which it has from Intellect, and that there is something better than it that seeks nothing, but rather no doubt has everything? But after all does it not know what it [Intellect] is just when it understands the sort of thing it is and what its works are? If, then, it should say that it comes from Intellect and is second after Intellect and an image of Intellect, having in itself all its sort of writings, since the one who writes and has written is there, then will one who knows himself in this way halt at these? Shall we, employing another power, observe again Intellect knowing itself, or, sharing in that, since that is also ours and we are also its, in this way know Intellect and ourselves? Is it not that it is necessary that [we know it] in this way, if we are going to know what this self-knowledge in Intellect is. Someone has indeed himself become Intellect when letting go of the other things that are his, he looks at this [Intellect] with this

[Intellect]; he then looks at himself with himself. Then, it is as Intellect that he sees himself.[26]

The point in this unfortunately obscure passage is that in ordinary embodied cognition there is a measure of self-reflexivity. There is no perfect self-reflexivity because the objects cognized are external and there is here no entailment from "s cognizes p" to "p". Ordinary embodied cognition, according to Plotinus, is entirely different from the zombie like night of the living dead scenario that would obtain if Epicurus were correct. That is, unless we were aware that we were believing and judging and so on, we would not occurrently be doing so at all. But this *self-awareness* is available only for immaterial entities.

As I have constructed the argument, there may seem to be a devious slide from the self-reflexivity of knowledge, which may be acknowledged, even if only hypothetically, to the self-reflexivity of belief. Though one might allow that infallibility is available only to immaterial entities, if there be such, since, however, belief is not infallible, there is no reason to suppose that only immaterial entities can have beliefs. But note that Plotinus in the above passage adds that believing and judging are done according to "the rules" (τοῖς κανόσιν) had from intellect. I do not suppose that the use of the term "rules", one of Epicurus's most important epistemological concepts, is adventitious. In any case, what does Plotinus mean?

I suggest that Plotinus is here alluding to the argument from recollection, especially as that appears in Plato's *Phaedo*.[27] Briefly, the point of that argument is that unless we had knowledge of Forms, we could not make the judgment that sensibles, though they participate in Forms, are nevertheless deficient. We could not judge correctly that equal sticks or stones are equal, though they are nevertheless lacking something with respect to Equality itself. There is a considerable amount of misunderstanding of this argument, especially in regard to the difference between that in virtue of which we judge equal sticks or stones to be equal and that in virtue of which we judge them to be deficient. In the former case, it is sufficient that we observe what equals have in common and make a universal judgment about this particular case. But a universal judgment cannot be, in principle, a judgment of deficiency because a universal is precisely what all the particulars falling under it have in common. Forms are not needed to make a judgment that equals are equal nor is cognition of Forms needed to learn how to make such judgments. The recollection argument is typically dismissed because of a confusion over the judgment that two sticks are equal (a judgment that does not involve recollection itself) and the judgment that they are deficiently so (a judgment that *does* involve knowledge of Forms).

---

26 *Enneads*, V 3.4, 15–31. Cf. V 3.2, 24–26.

27 See *Phaedo*, 72E3–78B3.

So, I interpret these "rules" as the contents of the mental state of one who has had knowledge of Forms. But Plotinus does not say in this passage that the supposedly self-reflexive judgments made are exclusively or even primarily judgments of deficiency.[28] These rules, in an earlier passage called "laws", and in a later passage simply called "the power of intellect" may be variously construed.[29] There is an interesting passage in which Plotinus asks on what basis one makes a judgment like "Socrates is good" having already made the judgment "this is Socrates" based on sense-perception.[30] He answers that the one who judges has "the rule of good in himself". And in reply to the further question, "how does he have this rule?" Plotinus answers that he has it by being "goodlike"—in other words, because he is himself an image of the intelligible good. The central point is that unless we are the sort of entities that can and do have knowledge of Forms, albeit not occurrently, we could not make any judgments whatsoever about sensibles. That is, unless were are immaterial entities, we cannot have beliefs.

This is especially clear in the case of the inferences supposedly made from the evident to the non-evident. As Epicurus puts it, "so that we can have some sign (σημειωσόμεθα) by which we may make inferences both about what awaits confirmation (τὸ προδμένον) and about the non-evident (τὸ ἄδηλον)".[31] There are a number of problems here. First of all, if all sense-perceptions are true, this is because sense-perception is "a-rational" or "without an account" (ἄλογος), as Diogenes Laertius aptly notes.[32] But then the use of signs, whether as a basis for inference about that which awaits confirmation or about the non-evident is extremely puzzling, to say the least. What are the presumed grounds for inference? The "witnessing" or "testimony" and "non-witnessing" or "non-testimony" that is supposed to make beliefs true or false consists in itself

---

28 But cf. V 8.8, 2; V 8.9, 39; VI 2.7, 11–14.

29 See *Enneads*, V 3.4, 3; V 3.6, 22.

30 Ibid., V 3.3, 6–11.

31 See *Letter to Herodotus*, 38. On Epicurean signs generally see Asmis, *Epicurus' Scientific Method*, pp. 175ff and most recently, James Allen, *Inference From Signs* (Oxford: Oxford University Press, 2001), Study IV, "Epicurean sign-inference in Philodemus".

32 See Diogenes Laertius, *Lives of Eminent Philosophers*, X.31. On the Epicurean claim see especially Gisela Striker, "Epicurus on the Truth of Sense-Impressions", in her collection *Essays on Hellenistic Epistemology and Ethics* (Cambridge: Cambridge University Press, 1996), pp. 77–91; C. C. W. Taylor, "All Perceptions are True", in *Doubt and Dogmatism*, ed. M. Schofield, M. Burnyeat, and J. Barnes (Oxford: Oxford University Press, 1980), pp. 105–124; and Stephen Everson, "Epicurus on the Truth of the Senses", in *Companions to Ancient Thought 1. Epistemology*, ed. Stephen Everson (Cambridge: Cambridge University Press, 1990), pp. 161–183.

entirely in sense-perceptions.[33] Reason cannot be a genuine *corrective* to sense-perception at all.[34] Epicurus cannot have it both ways. Either sense-perceptions are contentful, that is, they have a λόγος or they do not. In the former case, they are not all true; in the latter case, they do not provide the grounds for inferences that conclude in knowledge.[35]

Nor is the way out by means of the Epicurean "preconceptions" or "basic grasps" (προλήψεις).[36] As Diogenes Laertius tells us, "a basic grasp is like an act of grasping or a correct opinion or a conception or a universal idea stored up [in the mind], i.e., a memory of what has often appeared in the external world".[37] These basic grasps or empirical concepts could never, *ex hypothesi*, be the basis for correcting sense-perceptions since they are themselves borne of sense-perceptions.

I suggest that the basis for the Platonic critique of Epicurus's epistemology is that, as a thoroughgoing materialist, he cannot account for knowledge even in his own terms, or for embodied cognition generally.[38] Returning to the top down versus bottom up approaches to philosophical explanation, we can frame the dispute quite nicely. Epicurus wants to give a naturalistic account of belief which he holds, under certain circumstances, to be knowledge. Plotinus thinks that such naturalistic accounts are necessarily inadequate. In order to account for any type of cognition, one must start with the paradigm of cognition, knowledge, and understand the other types as images of that. In antiquity, there were some who supposed that the *tertium quid* between top down Platonic immaterialism and bottom up Epicurean materialism was the top down materialism of the Stoics. Unfortunately, there is no time here to bring the Stoics into this debate. Suffice to say, Plotinus did not regard Stoicism as an acceptable alternative. He believed that top down materialism was not just false, but incoherent as well.

According to Plotinus, a naturalized epistemology such as that offered by Epicurus is doomed to failure because it is committed to a naturalized account of the paradigmatic cognitive state, namely, knowledge. Such an account necessarily misconstrues what knowledge is because such an account

---

33 Cf. *Letter to Herodotus*, 50–51; Sextus Empiricus, *Adversus Mathematicos*, VII.211.

34 See Diogenes Laertius, X.32. This despite the "slight assistance from reasoning" (συμβαλλομένου τι καὶ τοῦ λογισμοοῦ).

35 Thus, the point of the "grasp by the mind" (ἐπιβολή τῆς διάνοιας) is, as many scholars have noticed, quite obscure.

36 See D. K. Glidden, "Epicurean Prolepsis", *Oxford Studies in Ancient Philosophy* 3 (1985), pp. 175–218.

37 See Diogenes Laertius, X.33; Epicurus, *Letter to Herodotus*, 72.

38 As Taylor, "All Perceptions are True", pp. 122–123, points out, the claim that all perceptions are true follows from the physical theory, not the other way around.

---

cannot explain the infallibility of knowledge. If it is objected that this failure is no more troubling than, say, the failure to explain the rectilinearity of a circle, the Platonist will insist and insist again that if we were not apt for infallible mental states, then Epicurus could not have even one of the allegedly comforting beliefs that he wants to serve up to his followers.

WORKS CITED

Allen, James, *Inference From Signs* (Oxford: Oxford University Press, 2001).

Asmis, Elizabeth, *Epicurus' Scientific Method* (Ithaca: Cornell University Press, 1984).

Everson, Stephen, "Epicurus on the Truth of the Senses", in *Epistemology*, ed. S. Everson, in *Companions to Ancient Thought 1* (Cambridge: Cambridge University Press, 1990), pp. 161–183.

Glidden, D. K., "Epicurean Prolepsis", *Oxford Studies in Ancient Philosophy* 3 (1985), pp. 175–218.

Striker, Gisela, "Epicurus on the Truth of Sense-Impressions", in *Essays on Hellenistic Epistemology and Ethics* (Cambridge: Cambridge University Press, 1996), pp. 77–91.

Taylor, C. C. W., "All Perceptions are True", in *Doubt and Dogmatism*, ed. M. Schofield, M. Burnyeat, and J. Barnes (Oxford: Oxford University Press, 1980), pp. 105–124.

ATOMISM AND GASSENDI'S CONCEPTION
OF THE HUMAN SOUL[1]

Veronica Gventsadze

Pierre Gassendi is one of the most significant figures of the seventeenth century Scientific Revolution: an ardent reviver of the philosophy of Epicurus, a Catholic priest, a person of vast erudition and solid knowledge in the history of philosophy as well as the science of his day. The eclecticism of Gassendi's sources, much like the Renaissance humanism of Pico, is a testimony to his freedom to entertain all and any probable opinions on a given issue, and while the resulting plethora of ideas may not be self-consistent, it is vibrant and alive with antinomies in a way that a more systematic philosophy could not be. Despite the modesty of Gassendi's philosophical claims, his influence in his own time was immense, and one of his principal contributions is a theory of human psychology founded on Epicurean atomism with a simultaneous defense of freedom—a theory that provided a foundation for Locke's corresponding ideas.[2]

Gassendi's conception of the human soul proposes a two-tier arrangement whereby the sentient and appetitive soul, or *anima*, is corporeal and acts as a link between the body and the mind, or rational soul (*mens*, or *animus*, or *intellectus*). What about the nature of the rational soul? In his polemic with Descartes, published as the *Disquisitio metaphysica* (1644), Gassendi challenges his opponent to prove that a thinking substance cannot be extended at the same time. His earliest position is therefore a *prima facie* defense of the rational soul's corporeality. Gassendi's later views, expressed in the *Syntagma philosophicum* (posthumously published in 1658), are far more complex and include a positive defense of the mind's incorporeality and immortality on the one hand, and a

---

1   Earlier versions of this paper as well as parts of it have been read by David Suits, Dane Gordon, Daniel Garber, Elizabeth Asmis, Glenn Most, and Margaret Osler, to all of whom I am deeply grateful for their comments and suggestions.

2   The marked continuity between Gassendi's and Locke's philosophies, particularly in the areas of atomism, epistemology, and psychology in general, has been explicated in detail by Thomas Lennon, *The Battle of the Gods and Giants: The Legacies of Descartes and Gassendi* (Princeton, NJ: Princeton University Press, 1993). This continuity is notable in both Gassendi's and Locke's understanding of freedom as indifference of the intellect, and not least of all in Locke's none too clear conception of spiritual and corporeal substance, which I believe can be explained at least in part by the complicated and inconsistent treatment of this subject by Gassendi himself.

consistently empiricist epistemology on the other. The ambivalence of Gassendi's views is largely explained by a conflict of priorities resulting from Gassendi's position: natural philosopher and scientist on the one hand, and representative of the Christian faith on the other. As is invariably the case with ambivalent philosophical positions, sound arguments have been presented on behalf of two disparate interpretations of Gassendi's views of the rational soul. Margaret Osler, for example, maintains that Gassendi's priority of upholding the human soul's immortality puts an effective limit on his mechanical philosophy, meaning that the rational soul cannot be corporeal if its immortality is to be observed.[3] On the other hand, Olivier Bloch considers Gassendi to have been a closet materialist in his views of the human soul as well as matter's inherent mobility.[4]

At stake are the integrity and consistency of the newly-revived Epicurean atomism in the face of the demands of Christian doctrine, as well as the future of Epicureanism as a foundation for natural philosophy seen from a seventeenth century vantage point. Of immediate interest is the atoms' inherent capability to generate patterns of motion from within themselves rather than relying on an external cause (that is, God) to continually supply both their ends and their mobility. Based on evidence from Gassendi's works, both early and mature, I maintain that his accounts of the rational soul (*animus*) are elaborated in the spirit of Epicurean atomism: they proceed on the principle that atoms possess inherent mobility, that only a body can move another body, and that the nature of the rational soul emerges from this mobility as well as from the atoms' properties. I agree with Osler in that a purely mechanistic and reductionist interpretation of atomism fails to explain the functions of the rational soul. Yet I do not believe that the limitations of mechanical philosophy apply to Gassendi in the first place, although he is traditionally (and, I believe, inaccurately) classified as one of its representatives. As Osler points out, one characteristic of "mechanical philosophers" is that they "interpreted all causal action as external to the material particles".[5] This cannot be applied to Gassendi's atomism which reflects the Epicurean thesis of matter's inherent mobility in contrast to a Cartesian atomism which sees matter as fundamentally inert.

1. REVIVAL OF ATOMISM AND POLEMIC WITH DESCARTES

Gassendi's project of reviving Epicureanism was conceived around

---

3 Margaret J. Osler, *Divine Will and the Mechanical Philosophy* (New York: Cambridge University Press, 1994), pp. 59ff.

4 Olivier Bloch, *La Philosophie de Gassendi: Nominalisme, Matérialisme et Métaphysique* (The Hague: Martinus Nijhoff, 1971).

5 Margaret J. Osler, "Renaissance Humanism, Lingering Aristotelianism and the New Natural Philosophy: Gassendi on Final Causes", *Humanism and Early Modern Philosophy*, ed. Jill Kray et al. (London: Routledge, 2000), pp. 193–208.

1625 and finally begun in 1629, following a hostile reception of his passionate critique of scholasticism in the *Exercitationes paradoxicae contra Aristoteleos* (1624). As Olser suggests, the fact that Gassendi chose atomism as his alternative to the scholastic tradition of physics could be due largely to his admiration for Galileo, himself an atomist. Notwithstanding his emphasis on atomism as the foundation for the new science, Gassendi continues to operate with principles of Aristotelian physics and even metaphysics, as well as the Christian doctrine of creationism and incorporeal substance; as a result, his physics is both eclectic in origin and immensely complex in content. The *Physica* section of the *Syntagma Philosophicum* (*SP*) incorporates much of the material published in earlier works such as *De Vita et Doctrina Epicuri* (1629–1633), as well as later additions and emendations.

The gist of Gassendi's revision of Epicurean atomism is as follows. Gassendi amends the Epicurean doctrine of the atoms' eternity, and maintains that they have been created by God out of nothing (*SP* I.281b).[6] At their creation, they were endowed with motive power (*vis motrix*—*SP* I.285a), and with the ability to form bodies, which is their means of carrying out divine purpose: "[God] both instructed and permitted it [primary Matter] to henceforth carry out his will" (*SP* I.280a). Having created atoms and taught them to move and form compounds, God continues to afford them his concurrence, without which they could neither move nor even continue in existence: "I am not one to deny the constant influence of the primary cause on us", writes Gassendi (*Disquisitio* III.346a). The significance of this is that the primary source of motion in the universe, including human psychological processes, is no longer traced back to the atoms as its first cause, but to God. Strictly speaking, mobility cannot be seen as inherent in the atoms, but rather as "borrowed" from God: all atomic motions are now established as second causes in relation to God as their first cause. This would impart sanctity to all natural processes, and should be considered a firm guarantee against viewing matter as "profane" and *prima facie* unworthy of hosting the higher operations of reason. At the same time, Gassendi does not present the atoms as immediately dependent on God for every move they make: "Is it not so that if you imagined all soldiers so well trained and so familiar with all the functions applying to themselves that each one kept himself in his rank and place and performed the requisite movements by himself as if he were commanded…?"[7] It can be inferred that while the atoms and all their capacities

---

6   This and all subsequent references to Gassendi are from *Opera omnia*, 6 vols (Lyon: Anisson et Posuel, 1658 [reprinted Stuttgart-Bad Constatt: Friedrich Frommann Verlag, 1964]), with indication of title, volume, page and column. Unless specified otherwise, translations from Latin are my own.

7   *The Selected Works of Pierre Gassendi* [*SP*], ed. and trans. Craig Brush (New York: Johnson Reprint, 1972), I.336.

---

were indeed created by God, the execution of these capacities proceeds of itself and nature runs on autopilot precisely because God had provided all that is necessary for the unfolding of natural processes.

Gassendi's next step is to amend the particulars of the Epicurean theory of atomic motion. Following Epicurus's reasoning, he considers the atomic swerve as an alleged solution to the problems of the first collision(s) and of human freedom, but rejects the swerve for three distinct reasons. First, it would be a violation of God's monopoly on contingency in the universe (*SP* I.326a); secondly, it is an insult to the dignity of human beings to put their freedom at the mercy of "dumb chance"; and thirdly, even if the swerve did occur, it would not provide a physical foundation for freedom. In this, Gassendi follows Cicero and asserts that the motion of an atom that has swerved is not remarkable in any way, and to the extent that it is natural motion, it does not make any more contribution to autonomy than do collisions or the atoms' gravitation through the void:

> this swerving motion is just as natural, or congenial to the atoms, as rectilinear [motion] (which they certainly possess not from outside, but from themselves); for that reason everything takes place through Fate, in the same way as if the swerving motion was never assumed [to exist]. For the things that should happen, would always happen through the same necessity due to variety of motions, collisions, rebounds, swerves etc. in an endless series, and through a sort of chain of their own effects....[8]

The meaning of "Fate" in this passage is the same as "necessity". The import of this passage is that while the swerve does not fall under the category of absolute necessity (by definition, it may or may not take place), it is regarded by Gassendi as an event of natural necessity in terms of its results: the motion, and therefore causal impact, of an atom that has just swerved, are no different from the motion and causal impact of an atom moving by virtue of gravity, or following a collision.[9] In designing a hypothetical apology for the Epicureans on

---

8 "Cum hic declinationis motus tam sit naturalis, atomisve congeneus, quam qui ad perpendiculum est (quippe quem non extrinsecus, sed a seipsis habeant) ideo tam fient omnia Fato, tametsi ille concedatur, quam si admissus non fuerit; cum pari semper necessitate ea, quae evenient, sint eventura pro varietate motuum, ictuum, repulsuum, clinaminum, &c. aeterna quadam serie, & quasi catena sese consequentium ..." (*SP* II.838a).

9 A similar view of the atom's motion following the swerve is held by Elizabeth Asmis. She persuasively argues that the nature of the swerve is "a sideways move

behalf of Carneades, Gassendi writes:

> The Epicureans could have defended their cause [freedom]
> even without the fictitious atomic swerve. For since they
> taught that there can be some voluntary movement of the
> mind, they could have easily stood up to Chrysippus (as
> to Democritus), to whom they had granted that there is
> no motion without cause, but did not need to grant that
> everything takes place through antecedent causes, or that
> there are external and antecedent causes to our will.[10]

While Gassendi's rejection of the swerve is not the first critique of
its kind, it may not be a major deviation from Epicureanism itself. None of
Epicurus's surviving works mentions the swerve, and even Lucretius's account is
rather vague and does not present an actual mechanism of volition involving the
swerve. The closest he comes to connecting the swerve with volition is to posit
the swerve as that "from which this power [free will] is born in us",[11] without
mentioning what exactly a particular swerve could do to the mind's atoms and
how this could result in a volitional act. Lucretius's account suggests that the
swerve provides necessary fuel for volition to work on, but does not explicitly
indicate that a particular swerve triggers a volitional act. Neither is the swerve
mentioned in Book iv, in the passage explaining the algorithm of a free action
(*DRN* iv.877–906), and it is entirely absent from the discussion of the mind and

---

by a single minimal unit of space at a single minimal unit of time, followed
immediately by a renewed, straight downward motion of the atom" (*Epicurus'*
Scientific Method [Ithaca, NY: Cornell University Press, 1984], p. 280). This
spontaneous shift satisfies the requirement of breaking the chains of necessity,
but in physical terms it can be understood to be so negligible that it could hardly
change the trajectory of the atom, and therefore can afford no tangible options
for the will to work with, the conclusion being that the will simply does not rely
on it. Moreover, such a tiny shift of the atom bears no analogy to the ethical
magnitude of resisting an inherited disposition or a natural urge, or to
performing a visible action requiring volition.

10 "Carneades … docuit potuisse Epicureos suam causam, etiam sine commentitia
atomorum declinatione defendere. Nam, cum docerent esse posse quemdam animi
motum voluntarium, potuisse Chysippo (adde & Democrito) facile resistere, cui
cum concessissent nullum motum esse sine causa, poterant non concedere omnia,
quae fierent, fieri causis antecedentibus; voluntatis enim nostrae non esse causas
externas, & antecedenteis" (*SP* II.840a; Gassendi is referring to Cicero's *De fato* 23).

11 *De rerum natura* (*DRN*), trans. W. H. D. Rouse, revised with notes by Martin F.
Smith (Cambridge, MA: Harvard University Press, 1982), ii.286.

---

spirit in Book iii. One way in which Lucretius does use the swerve is to posit it as a metaphor for free actions, stating that we also "[swerve] our motions not at fixed times or fixed places, but just where our mind has taken us" (*DRN* ii.259–260). This use of the swerve in a metaphorical sense indicates that Lucretius was more comfortable using it as a symbol of free will than explaining how it can be a physical cause thereof.

Gassendi employs the swerve figuratively, as a metaphor for the indeterminacy of which a human being is capable. For him, Lucretius's description of the swerve symbolizes the mind's capacity to deflect its attention from one object to another, and thereby to maintain indifference to either.[12] This metaphorical interpretation of the swerve as the mind's focused and deliberate effort at maintaining indifference has little to do with the randomness of the swerve's occurrence, which is partly why Gassendi jettisons the swerve as physically irrelevant to freedom.

It remains to consider the role of the swerve in causing collisions between atoms, which would otherwise have moved along parallel lines and never met. For Gassendi this problem is solved through the very notion of creationism. Lisa Sarasohn writes regarding atomic motions as second causes in relation to God as the first cause: "This infused motion [of atoms] changes both the physics and the philosophy of atomism. It obviates the necessity for the *clinamen* in the Epicurean system, since world building becomes part of God's providential plan and operates according to the second causes he instituted."[13] Indeed, the need for a swerve in "world building" is obviated whether the atoms are seen to be moved by God, or whether their motion can be considered inherent, if no longer innate.[14]

Gassendi likewise modifies the Epicurean notion of parallel "fall" of the atoms through the void. He rejects the notions of "up" and "down" as irrelevant to the Epicurean conception of the cosmos, and says that the atoms simply move

---

12 "Quo loco, *declinare,* est flectere, ac dirigere motus: illudque, *nec tempore certo,* &c. notat cum ipsam animi indifferentiam, seu libertatem; quatenus animus ex se, non ad ista potius quam ad illa fertur..."(*SP* II.839a).

13 Lisa Sarasohn, *Gassendi's Ethics: Freedom in a Mechanistic Universe* (Ithaca, NY: Cornell University Press, 1996), p. 59.

14 The problem of "world building" remains outstanding in Epicurus's atomism, especially if the swerve is no longer relied on. I would suggest, however, that the problem itself is largely contrived. As Walter Englert points out, the notion of atoms falling through the void along parallel lines is the result of Epicurus's close attention to Aristotle's requirement to show the first cause of motion (*Epicurus on the Swerve and Voluntary Action* [Atlanta, GA: Scholars Press, 1987], p. 6). By positing weight as the atoms' inherent property, Epicurus has identified this first cause; however, the very notion of weight as well as the concept of falling

---

through, or across, the universe in one direction (*SP* I.279b). Gassendi identifies this faculty as weight (*pondus,* or *gravitas*), a faculty that is natural and internal to the atoms and due to which they stir and move themselves, and which he also calls their innate and inalienable propensity (*SP* I.273b). Thus not only has Gassendi reiterated the Epicurean notion of matter's inherent mobility due to weight, but in doing so he has gone beyond describing atoms as mere second causes in constant need of divine concurrence. In this context it is worth taking a brief look at Gassendi's formulation of the principle of inertia. The principle, published in 1642 in the work *De motu impresso a motore translato* yet formulated even earlier, states that a material body could ideally move forever in a straight line without change in speed, but that the initial impetus could come only from an external force. This statement, however, is supplemented and obscured by statements about matter's inherent mobility, with the emerging picture being rather inconsistent.[15] As with many other aspects of Gassendi's philosophy, I believe that the issue of inertia bears simultaneous influences of Aristotelianism and Epicureanism with the ensuing contradictions. The notion that no body can be its own efficient cause is distinctly Aristotelian (although it also lends excellent support to the notions of creationism and divine concurrence); equally Aristotelian is the view of a material body as a piece of homogeneous and undifferentiated substance, without inquiry into its internal structure. At the same time, Gassendi puts limitations on the stated principle of inertia when he regards matter from the Epicurean perspective. On this view, not only are individual atoms endowed with inherent mobility, but the composites formed from them must be regarded as conglomerates of inherently mobile units, with the ensuing conclusion that no body is ever at rest properly speaking, but is always in motion on an imperceptible level.

Besides uniform motion through the void as well as collisions and rebounds, Gassendi introduces what appears to be a new type of motion: a

---

downward are suited to Aristotle's geocentric cosmology rather than to Epicurus's undifferentiated cosmos.

15 The inconsistency of Gassendi's notion of inertia has been noted by Peter Anton Pav and Olivier Bloch. Pav states that Gassendi "faltered especially in the realms of the very large and the very small. First, he saw the immense celestial revolutions as a paradigm of force-free inertial motion; second, his atoms, matter par excellence, were unashamedly animistic." Pav concludes that "it is significant for a study of Gassendi and his influence that the inertial concept was conjoined with other clear notions—notions which were incompatible with it" (Peter Anton Pav, "Gassendi's Statement of the Principle of Inertia", *Isis* 57 [1966], pp. 24–34, at p. 25). Similarly, Bloch draws attention to the discrepancy between Gassendi's accounts of the properties and mechanics of larger bodies, and those of atoms (*La Philosophie de Gassendi*, pp. 220–27).

---

rolling motion due to which atoms disentangle themselves from compounds. Here is how Gassendi describes this motion:

> Indeed, it can be posited that [the atoms] possess some internal motion which, although it is not apparent to the senses, can nonetheless be deduced from the following. There is no body which, to the extent that it is compact, and even when an external cause is absent, does not have an internal reason to be unbound and annihilated; since this cannot be due to anything other than the fact that the body is compounded of beginnings which are never still but are in a perpetual effort to extricate themselves (*sint in pertetuo quasi emergendi conatu*) (helped along by the presence of minute intervals of void which, as has been mentioned previously, are found even in the most compact aggregates). Consequently, to the extent that they never cease to make a great effort, or to roll forth and seek freedom, they finally manage to unbind and annihilate the entire body. [*SP* I.277a][16]

Gassendi points out that a body's disintegration need not be caused by external blows (which would be the Epicurean position), but is primarily due to an inherent capacity of the atoms to break free of their bonds. Neither can such restlessness be explained by the property of weight due to which atoms move through the void in the same direction, since such motion does not account for the atoms' tendency to roll away from each other. This curious propensity for rolling forth (*vis evolvendi*) can be seen as a will to freedom on the part of the atoms, and is a good illustration of the animism which often emerges in Gassendi's discourse without thereby dominating his atomism as a whole. The rolling motion cannot be seen as analogous to the atomic swerve due to its continuous presence in the atoms, yet it does bear a resemblance to the "swerve", or volitional effort, of the mind as a whole. While this rolling motion appears

---

16 "corpus contextum est ex iis principiis, quae quiete nunquam se habeant, sed sint in perpetuo quasi emergendi conatu (ac faventibus quidem inanibus spatiolis, quae dictum est ante in densissimis etiam concretionibus intercipi) adeo proinde, ut conniti, evolvique, & libertatem quasi quaerere nunquam desinentes, evincant tandem, ac ipsum corpus exsolutum, ac nullum faciant" (*SP* I.277a). Gassendi reiterates this notion in his discussion of creationism: "Supponi etiam potest Atomos singulas accepisse a Deo creante ut quantulamcumque suam corpulentiam, magnitudinemve & figuram varietate ineffabili; sic & vim congruam sese movendi, ciendi, evolvendi; & consequenter sese extricandi, emergendi, prosiliendi, impingendi, retundendi, regrediendi..." (*SP* I.280b).

to be a questionable contrivance from the physical point of view, it retains its symbolic significance, in the same way as the swerve is used figuratively by Lucretius to refer to acts of will.

How is Gassendi's atomism applied to this conception of the human mind? As Osler points out, both Gassendi and Descartes were representatives of what came to be known as "mechanical philosophy" (a term introduced in retrospect by Robert Boyle).[17] This view combines creationism and divine concurrence and providence with the concept of motion and change as produced by interaction of parts of matter according to uniform mechanical laws. Yet while for Descartes the mechanical philosophy is limited to extended substance and does not apply to thinking substance, Gassendi attempts to apply his version of atomism as universally and consistently as possible.

In one of his objections to Descartes's second Meditation, Gassendi challenges his opponent to give positive proof that a thinking being cannot be corporeal at the same time; however, with characteristic caution he avoids committing himself to the view that the rational soul is indeed corporeal (*Disquisitio* III.297a–b).[18] Therefore, while this argument makes only a negative case for the mind's corporeality, it does contain the assumption that the mind's corporeality is a default position—an assumption that must stand until it has been proven wrong. At the same time, this argument touches only on the principle of corporeality, not on the specific nature and substance of the human mind: Gassendi operates with the term *corpus crassum* (*Disquisitio* III.297b) as if to signify that at this point, any and all kinds of matter should be taken into consideration.

Gassendi returns to this subject in his objections to Meditation Six, and here his argument is much more specific and focused. First, he argues that our imperfect knowledge, or even ignorance, of the nature of physical extension is no reason to exclude it from the qualities that describe a thinking being: such an exclusion would take away from the completeness and perfection of the object in question (*Disquisitio* III.397a). Next, Gassendi draws attention to the fact that the issue at hand is not just any thinking being, but the human mind, and the reasoning and extension that are specific to it. Toward the middle of the

---

17 Margaret J. Osler, "How Mechanical was the Mechanical Philosophy? Non-Epicurean Aspects of Gassendi's Philosophy of Nature", in *Late Medieval and Early Modern Corpuscular Matter Theories*, ed. Christopher Lüthy, John Murdoch, and William Newman (Leiden, Boston, Köln: Brill, 2001), pp. 423–439.

18 That Gassendi brought up the issue of mind as tenuous matter, but did not positively assert this scenario, is pointed out by Daniel Garber, "Soul and Mind: Life and Thought in the Seventeenth Century", in *The Cambridge History of Seventeenth Century Philosophy*, ed. Daniel Garber and Michael Ayers (Cambridge: Cambridge University Press, 1998), pp. 771–774.

---

argument, Gassendi substitutes the more general term "extension" for the more specific "body", and asks Descartes: "How would you then admit that no extended substance can be a thinking substance? By declaring it contradictory that a body, that is an extended thing, can produce thought?"[19] To Gassendi, the separation between matter and thought appears entirely arbitrary and unjustified. Further on, he hypothesizes on the nature of matter that constitutes the human mind: it is no longer an unspecified *corpus crassum*, but "a subtle body, or the mind itself [*agetur de corpore tenui, ac mentis proprio*]" (*Disquisitio* III.398a).

It is not difficult to discern the influence of Epicurean atomism in Gassendi's polemic with Descartes. Besides the most obvious common feature, namely the corporeal nature of the human mind, there are other Epicurean postulates that find their reflection in Gassendi's discourse. These include Gassendi's distaste for abstraction, and his insistence that any idea, at least at its inception, is a concrete idea, taking its origin in sensory data. Throughout the above polemic, Gassendi takes every opportunity to show how self-defeating Descartes's abstract reasoning is, and how unfruitful it is to consider qualities and attributes divorced from the objects they pertain to. Simultaneously, the *Disquisitio* presents a vigorous defense of the absolute veracity of sense perception, which in turn makes the faculty of judgment responsible for the correctness of inferences. Next, Gassendi treats the scholastic/Cartesian notion of extension in terms of the Epicurean dichotomy of "atoms–void": extension is either entirely empty space (in which case it is nothing at all), or body, however dense or rarefied. Thus wherever Descartes operates with the term "extension", Gassendi converts it into "body", and steers the discussion from abstract and undefined extension to corporeality. For instance, in an objection to the second Meditation, he indicates that if matter is allowed only extension, and not solidity, or weight, as its inherent property, there would be no action or active capacity in bodies (*Disquisitio* III.305b). Finally, with regard to the specific type of matter that constitutes the human mind, Gassendi suggests that it is tenuous and subtle—not at all like the crude and sluggish matter that constitutes the body itself.

No less important is Gassendi's epistemology, which is founded on empiricism and nominalism and thereby supports the hypothesis of a corporeal mind. Gassendi rejects the notion of innate ideas, and indicates that the source of all ideas is the imagination, which in turn draws exclusively on empirical evidence: "The Imagination is initially blind, as it were, and entirely devoid of images …"(*SP* II.456b). In *De simplici rerum imaginatione*, he states that all ideas, even the most general and abstract ones, have their origin in sense perception and are stored in the imagination.[20] Meanwhile, Gassendi's

---

19 "Quomodo ergo fidem facies nullam rem extensam cogitantem esse? An dicendo repugnare ut corpus, sive res extensa cogitationem eliciat?" (*Disquisitio* III.397b)

20 See Bloch, *La Philosophie de Gassendi*, pp. 141–142. He goes even further and

---

conception of sensation is based on the Epicurean notion of *simulacra*, or the thin films that escape the surface of objects and impact our sense organs (*SP* II.833ff). Admittedly, Gassendi's own conception of vision is more elaborate and comprises an early version of the corpuscular theory of light; yet the fact remains that light is corporeal (the concept of corpuscles itself being a development on atomism), and its impact on the eye is a variety of touch. Once perceptions are received and stored in the imagination, they form the basis of our entire gamut of ideas. Thus the origin of ideas in sense perception suggests that the mind, or the faculty that operates with ideas, must be of a kind with sensation, or the faculty which supplies data for ideas. At the very least, the mind must be able to communicate with the imagination which in turn proceeds from sensation, but such communication can only be direct and physical to the extent that sensation itself is physical. Neither does Gassendi consider it problematic for complex and abstract ideas to be generated by a corporeal mind, since in his polemic with Descartes he defends such a possibility: "From the proposed abstract formation of concepts, it is just as possible to infer the corporeal nature of the mind, or rather its inseparability [from body], as its separability" (*Disquisitio* III.398b).[21] The kind of abstract ideas to which Gassendi refers are not Platonic Forms or other mental realities whose existence is independent of human minds; the only legitimate abstractions according to Gassendi are generalizations based on particular instances of experience (*Exercitationes* III.159). Thus far Gassendi's conception of the mind and its operations is entirely consistent with atomism, and the next step would be a detailed inquiry into thinking substance which is at once corporeal. However, before such an inquiry can be undertaken, it is necessary to consider a major obstacle with which Gassendi as well as any other atomist of his time would have been faced: the issue of incorporeal substance.

---

suggests that the intellect and the imagination are altogether indistinguishable in the context of knowledge: "such a distinction does not proceed from the requirements of the theory of knowledge: the same act of the mind, with regard to the image of the thing in question, that receives without difference the name of imagination, conception, apprehension, intellection or notion, while the image can without difference be called idea, aspect, notion, prenotion, anticipation, concept, or figment ..." ("une telle distinction ne procede pas des exigences propres de la théorie de la connaissance: c'est le même acte de l'ésprit, visant l'image de la chose pensée, qui reçoit indifféremment le nom d'imagination, de conception, d'apprehension, d'intellection ou de notion, l'image pouvant de son cote être appelée indifferemment idée, espèce, notion, prénotion, anticipation, concept ou fantasme ...") (p. 142).

21 "Ex praecisione conceptuum proposita tam inferri mentem esse corpoream, imo confici potius inseparabilem, quam separabilem esse" (title of Article 11 of objections to Meditation 6 in *Disquisitio* III.398b).

---

2. THE NATURE OF THE RATIONAL SOUL

Not long after his polemic with Descartes, Gassendi elaborates a series of arguments for the rational soul's immortality which are included in the *Syntagma philosophicum* (*SP* II.620ff). There is little doubt that these arguments were a response to the exhortation of the Fifth Lateran Council in 1513 for philosophers to "use all their powers to demonstrate that the immortality of the soul can be known by natural reason, not by faith alone."[22]

Following an exposition of the history of the question of immortality, Gassendi proceeds to a defense of immortality, the first part of which is the argument from faith, or an exposition of the official Christian doctrine on the matter. The main points of this doctrine are as follows: each person possesses a discrete individual soul;[23] such a soul is rational and incorporeal, created by God and infused into the body as its form rather than a mere presence; upon the demise of the body, the soul survives; while it maintains itself in the body, the soul earns for itself either Paradise or Hell; together with these rewards or punishments, the soul is also provided with a body upon resurrection (*SP* II.627a).

Following this argument from faith is the argument from physics. Gassendi starts by making a necessary connection between immortality and incorporeality: the latter makes the former possible. Arguments for the rational soul's incorporeality are presented by Gassendi in a separate section of the *Syntagma* in conjunction with the customary operations of the intellect (*De habitibus intellectus—SP* II.440ff), and they are briefly summarized in the context of immortality. The particular functions that Gassendi presents as a testimony of the intellect's incorporeality are its ability to contemplate universals which do not and cannot proceed from the imagination (which latter is a corporeal faculty dealing with corporeal species or images), its self-reflection, and its ability to appreciate the very concept of universality. With regard to

---

22 Emily Michael and Fred S. Michael, "Early Modern Concepts of Mind", *Journal of the History of Philosophy* 27 (1989), pp. 29–48, at p. 31. Daniel Garber notes that "[t]here is much debate over whether Gassendi really changed his view, whether his later view is to be taken as sincere, and why his later writings are so different from his earlier" ("Soul and Mind", p. 771).

23 The postulate of a discrete, individual soul was reinforced by Bonaventura in the 13th century in opposition to the teachings of Siger de Brabant, who in turn reflected the views of Averroës and other Aristotelian scholars such as Avicenna and Maimonides. A similar view was held by the Stoics, who did not propound personal and individual immortality, but rather a collective of souls indistinguishable from one another and which partake in the Logos or divine Breath, and are immortal only to this extent and in this sense. Thus by 1513, the year of the Fifth Lateran Council's congregation, the view of a discrete, individual soul was a relatively new development even in Christianity.

self-reflection and the inability of matter to fulfill this function, it is worth noting that in his discussion of matter's hypothetical animism in the *Syntagma* Gassendi suggests the possibility of "[corporeal] substance not unaware of its workings" (*operis sui non ignara substantia—SP* I.114b) even with regard to matter in general, without specific reference to the human soul. Admittedly, this hypothetical self-awareness of matter does not yet amount to self-reflection, and Gassendi explicitly rejects the possibility that self-reflection can be achieved by one part of a body acting on another part (as when the hand touches the leg, both pertaining to the same body—*SP* II.441a). However, what is remarkable here is not the inability of matter to engage in self-reflection, but Gassendi's own admission of the human soul's inability to know itself with any degree of certainty or clarity (*SP* II.237a–b). How, then, can we claim to be in possession of an incorporeal soul which reflects upon itself when even the most fundamental truths about it are denied to our understanding? If the soul is in fact capable of self-reflection, how can it fail to shed light upon itself? Gassendi concludes that the only certainty regarding the human soul comes from doctrines of faith. Thus while the proof of incorporeality from self-reflection is consistent in and of itself, there is no positive evidence that we are in possession of such a self-reflecting soul, much less an indication of what such self-reflection might yield. As Emily and Fred S. Michael reasonably suggest, such self-reflection would be akin to the Cartesian act of *cogito*, a feature that is alien to Gassendi's epistemology.[24]

The first and third reasons for the intellect's incorporeality—its alleged contemplation of universals which cannot be derived on the basis of imagination, and its recognition of the nature of universality—are two reasons of a kind, since Gassendi thereby introduces an element of idealism which runs counter to his nominalism and empiricism. Gassendi states—in the very chapter devoted to the "pure" operations of the intellect—that "insofar as it is human [intellect], meaning that as long as it is hitched to the body, it has understanding of nothing without being served and provided with images by the Imagination…."[25] If for Gassendi the rational soul, or *forma informans*, is created by God and infused into the body, it is likewise true that this *forma* must undergo "incarnation", so to speak, if it is to be of any practical relevance to us in this life.[26] Much like

---

24 Michael and Michael, "Early Modern Concepts of Mind", p. 42.

25 "Intellectus … prout est humanus, seu quatenus est corpori addictus, nihilque intelligere, nisi Phantasia famulante, speciesque ministrante, potest…" (*SP* II.456b).

26 Here, by comparison, is what Aquinas says on the matter: "For, although the soul is lowest in the order of intellectual substances (as primary matter is lowest in the order of sensible things), it does not have intelligible species naturally impressed on it, as superior intellectual substances have, whereby it can perform its proper operation of intellection; but is in potency to them because it is like a wax tablet on which nothing is written, as is said in *De anima*. For this reason it must receive

---

Aristotle and Aquinas, Gassendi insists on the absence of innate ideas and thereby denies the possibility of intellection independent of empirical reality.[27] In this light, the functions of pure intellection, self-reflection and contemplation of universals that Gassendi describes in his discussion of the operations of the intellect (*SP* II.440ff), are either entirely irrelevant to the process of thought, or somehow still rooted in empirical data, which would contradict Gassendi's statement that they are not dependent on the imagination.

The question here is not only the mind's ability to contemplate universals, but the very nature of these universals. Are they seen in a nominalist light, or are they taken to represent independently existing realities? The suggestion that the mind contemplates universals for which there is no prototype among empirical objects would be alien to Gassendi's epistemology. The intellect is made out to be an incorporeal and pure power of discernment (*subiecto incorporeo; plena, perfectaque intelligendi vis*—II.455a; *mere intelligens ... res*—II.456a), whose relation to the *anima* and imaginative faculties is one of superiority: "[the mind] knows other things besides corporeal, of which there are no images in the Imagination, since these things neither occur, nor even can occur, to the Imagination...."[28] This latter statement is in direct contradiction with Gassendi's view that any and all ideas originate in the senses and are stored in the imagination.[29] Thomas Lennon has compared Gassendi's empiricist and nominalist epistemology to the lower half of Plato's divided line, or the realm of sensory objects and empirically derived ideas, and has rightly indicated that Gassendi "rejects the nonsensuous half of the Divided Line."[30] Introducing notions like contemplation of universals, as well as the recognition of the very

---

its intelligible species from external things through its sensory powers, which cannot perform their proper operations without bodily organs. Consequently it is necessary for the human soul to be united to a body" (Aquinas, *Disputed Question on the Soul*, in *Quaestiones Disputatae* [Turin: Marietti, 1953], vol. 2; translation: J. P. Rowan, *The Soul* [St. Louis, MO: Herder, 1949]).

27 For instance, "Humanus Intellectus, ...quatenus est corpori addictus, nihilque intelligere, nisi Phantasia famulante, speciesque ministrante, potest; ratiocinatione prorsus indiget, ut postquam superficie tenus unamquamque rem noverit, habere introspectam quadamtenus possit" (*SP* II.456b).

28 "Quod vero non propterea eadem cum Phantasia facultas, eaque corporea habenda sit, ex eo iam ostendimus, quod alia praeterea cognoscat [Mens], quorum nullae exstant in Phantasia imagines, quaeque neque cadunt, neque cadere in Imaginationem possunt" (*SP* II.635b).

29 Gassendi's empirical epistemology is vividly presented in *De simplici rerum imaginatione* (*SP* I.92–99), and to a large extent in the very chapters which are devoted to the mind's incorporeality (*SP* II.440ff).

30 Lennon, *The Battle of the Gods and Giants*, p. 111.

---

reason for universals, is akin to imposing the higher half of the divided line, or the purely intelligible realm, onto an epistemology that otherwise makes no provisions for such a radical turn of events. While Gassendi does not deny the existence of general ideas and universals derived from particulars, his stance is similar to Aristotle's for whom universals can neither exist independently from particulars, nor, much less, represent a transcendent reality.

Having explained why the rational soul must be incorporeal, Gassendi affirms that whatever is incorporeal is thereby immortal. The argument from physics consists of two parts: in the first part Gassendi gives a positive proof of matter's corruptibility, and in the second part he introduces and explains the concept of incorporeal substance whose characteristics are the exact opposite of corporeal qualities. The proof of matter's corruptibility closely follows the Epicurean discourse on the disintegration of all atomic composites. Gassendi did not explore the venue that a corporeal soul can itself be immortal, "reassembled" by God on the day of resurrection, or subsisting whole through God's intervention even immediately after death. He clearly dismisses the possibility that matter can somehow be incorruptible by rejecting the Aristotelian notion of incorruptible substance from which the heavenly bodies are allegedly composed (*SP* II.629a). In this discussion of matter's corruptibility Gassendi is in his own element of atomism and proceeds with confidence and persuasiveness, and it may be due to the momentum of the discussion that he fails to realize that he is implicitly denying the prospect of resurrection in the body, advanced as one of the postulates of faith. In any case, Gassendi makes no special provisions for such resurrection, and the thesis of a physical body's irreversible disintegration is not shown to admit of any exceptions.

Likewise, Gassendi's discussion of incorporeal substance and its nature yields controversial conclusions. The discussion proceeds on the principle that what cannot be positively denied, should be assumed to be possible, if not altogether probable: the incorporeality but simultaneous substantiality of the rational soul is to be regarded as a testimony of the limitations of physics and natural reason. This line of reasoning is uncharacteristic of Gassendi. As a mild skeptic, he is the first to acknowledge the limitations of human reason; yet precisely because he is a skeptic, he does not express the need to make up for the fallibility of reason by resorting to doctrines of faith. As for the nature of incorporeal substance, only a negative description can be given: Gassendi presents it as having none of the attributes of matter, such as extension, form, composite parts, faculties, qualities, or other adjuncts. In short, it is simple and undifferentiated substance (*SP* II.629a). However, back in the *Disquisitio* Gassendi had objected to Descartes's similar conception of the mind:

> the question hereafter concerns chiefly the Mind, which you
> make out to be without parts and which, I am guessing, you

would not consider to be changing continuously in the way that light does, but rather to be subsisting unchangingly both in quantity and integrity, in the manner of a rock or a building.[31]

The import of this statement is that the mind (rational soul), according to Gassendi, cannot be in stasis but must engage in some process of becoming, comparable to light renewing itself. Mental operations presuppose a dynamic process or change of state, and human reasoning is discursive by nature, requiring a minimal differentiation into thinking subject and object of thought. None of these requirements can be met if the mind is conceived of as an indivisible, homogeneous and undifferentiated instance of incorporeal substance.

Furthermore, there is the question of how the rational soul "informs" the body rather than simply being present (*est in corpore informans et non simpliciter assistens*); a variation on this same question is how the rational soul conducts itself while in the body (*prout se in corpore gesserit*). Further in the argument Gassendi asserts that the sentient soul (*anima*) serves as the intermediary between the body and the "more divine" soul: thanks to the *anima*, the rational soul is able to join with and cohere with the body ([*corporea anima*] *intercedente divinior illa copuletur, cohaeretur cum corpore—SP* II.627b). The problem is how an incorporeal entity achieves an interface with matter that it may be considered to "inform" matter and act upon it or with it, and this problem remains unsolved in the context of the arguments for immortality. Gassendi is not unaware of the problem: "Indeed, there follows upon this [discussion of incorporeality] the difficulty of how an incorporeal entity is conjoined with the body, that it may be its supporting principle in the highest degree, or its informing form" (*SP* II.443b). His solution is simple, if not altogether simplistic: he states that the link and the liaison between the incorporeal mind and the body, is the sentient soul (*anima*), which is infinitely more subtle in its structure than the body, but retains its fundamentally corporeal nature. This solution echoes a previously advanced idea which is based on Plato's conception of the gradation of Being according to coarseness and subtlety (*SP* II.239b, 258). However, this quasi-Platonic gradation of substance as to crudeness and subtlety, and the presence of an intermediate stage, corresponding to the *anima*, between the metaphysical mind and crude matter, is hardly satisfactory from Gassendi's own standpoint. Such a view obliterates the ontological distinction between matter and non-matter, and ultimately between natural philosophy and metaphysics.

---

31 "et quaestio heic est praesertim de Mente, quam carentem partibus facis, et quam, ut opinor, dicturus non es aliam, aliamque continuo fieri, instar lucis, videlicet; potiusquam eandem numero, individuamque perseverare, instar scilicet lapidis, aut domus" (*Disquisitio* III.346b).

Yet if the Platonic solution is accepted as feasible, it only serves to strengthen the possibility that the mind is corporeal. Since Gassendi does not concede that the rational soul can move by command (*nutu*), and since, moreover, he upholds the Epicurean principle that only a body can move another body, he must be applying Plato's theory on the assumption that there is an affinity, or even homogeneity, between things that are able to impact one another. Therefore, there must be a stage at which the mind is able to "touch" the subtlest kind of matter, in which case the mind itself cannot be very different from that type of matter. On the whole, Gassendi fails to provide an explanation of how the mind can touch even the most ephemeral part of the sentient soul.

Finally, Gassendi's notion of incorporeal substance does little to explain how rational souls can be discrete and individual. Since the incorporeal substance in question is undifferentiated into qualities, attributes or capacities of the kind that describe corporeal substance, the discreteness and individuality of the human soul cannot be the result of its uniqueness: such uniqueness would be precluded by the metaphysical uniformity of rational souls, their lack of distinction from one another. The only other guarantee of discreteness would seem to be the isolation of rational souls from each other, resulting in a kind of monadology. It is not certain whether and how such souls can interact with one another, and whether they run the risk of merging together upon such interaction.[32]

It is no wonder that the theological proofs of immortality are out of accord with Gassendi's natural philosophy, which is founded on a consistently Epicurean framework. Gassendi's stance on natural reason in relation to supernatural issues was developed very early in his philosophical career. In his earliest work, the *Exercitationes* (1624), he calls on his readers to stand up for "true Philosophy" lest it be "extinguished".[33] His concern is that philosophy should not be recruited to serve theology, whether the task is to deliberate on a mere opinion or to provide support for an authoritative statement. Gassendi makes it clear that the kind of homework theology gives to philosophy not only fails to yield anything valuable to theology itself (*SP* II.650a), but also contaminates philosophy and effectively destroys it as a discipline. Thus what I see as Gassendi's failure to make a consistent and convincing case for the rational soul's incorporeality goes to show how deeply embedded Epicureanism

---

32 Gassendi's next series of arguments for immortality proceeds from morality, and includes the argument from God's justice (*SP* I.319ff), from the general consensus regarding immortality (*SP* II.629b–30b), and from the innate yearning of human beings for immortality (ibid., 630b–32a). These arguments are quite representative of the theology of the day, but they are not germane to this paper.

33 "at interim tamen vera Philosophia penitus intercidit: tantoque minus prospicitur, quanto sunt pauciores, qui animadvertant" (*Exercitationes* III.108b).

---

was in his philosophy and how difficult, if at all possible, it was to change some of its postulates without obliterating the entire system. J. J. Macintosh suggests that Robert Boyle, a fervent admirer of Gassendi, "had never quite managed to convince himself that, to borrow Margaret Osler's happy phrase, Gassendi had 'baptized' Epicurus."[34] The reason for this is not only the nature of Epicurean philosophy, but also Gassendi's own failure to convince himself as well as his readers that Epicureanism is amenable to "baptism", or, indeed, that it would profit from such baptism.

Despite concessions to theology in the *Syntagma,* and possibly as a counterbalance to them, the case for matter's inherent and self-sufficient mobility has been strengthened by the formulation of several principles in Chapters I and VIII of Part I, Book IV of the *Physica,* and a partial reiteration of opinions expressed back in the *De Vita et Doctrina Epicuri.*[35] Thus not only have the earlier views on matter survived into the *Syntagma,* but they appear side by side with the "new", theological, position, and thereby weaken its authority.

The import of Gassendi's thesis that the only causality is efficient causality (*SP* I.284a) is that it places a limitation on what can set things in motion. For Gassendi, much the same as for Epicurus, efficient causality is inseparable from matter.[36] Gassendi declares that it greatly pleases him to invoke Lucretius's opinion on the origin of motion in atoms, namely that "the first-beginnings of things move of themselves" (*DRN* ii.132). Gassendi takes a further step and suggests that matter is not simply a self-sufficient principle of motion, but the *only* principle that can impact all things corporeal. He firmly reinstates the Epicurean principle that only a body can produce impact on a body: "since physical actions are corporeal, they cannot be produced by anything except a physical or corporeal principle" (*SP* I.334a–b). Further in the same chapter, Gassendi apparently derides Aristotle for suggesting that God's impact can be "moral" instead of physical. Yet it is Gassendi himself who proposes a very similar solution in the same chapter, saying that God "can act upon and move anything not through any motion on his part, but through his mere bidding (*nutu*), since he is ubiquitous and without limit in power."[37] It is possible to interpret Gassendi's remark on Aristotle as a signal not to take his own words on the subject too seriously, or at least to be aware of the merely

---

34 J. J. Macintosh, "Robert Boyle on Epicurean Atheism and Atomism", in *Humanism and Early Modern Philosophy,* ed. Jill Kray et al. (London: Routledge, 2000), p. 218.

35 René Pintard, *La Mothe le Vayer, Gassendi, Guy Patin* (Paris: Boivin, 1943) suggests that these particular chapters of the *Syntagma Philosophicum* contain a fair amount of the material salvaged from the earlier works on Epicurus.

36 On the revision of the four Aristotelian causes in Epicureanism, see Englert, *Epicurus on the Swerve,* pp. 113ff.

37 "Et de Deo quidem alia ratio est; quoniam infinitae virtutis cum sit, & ubique

nominal status of "moral" causality, or causality by "command". If there is even the slightest doubt that God himself can touch a corporeal universe, what are the chances for an incorporeal mind to successfully command the body to lift so much as a finger?

Finally, Gassendi states in the same chapter that efficient causality cannot come from outside the object in question: "if someone should perhaps say that this power [to act] comes from the agent by whom this form is fashioned, that is not true either, since both the agent and his action, which becomes distinct from him, are external things, and nothing is more internal in a form than its power to act."[38] Here Gassendi shows the inconsistency of the claim that form is incorporeal and passive, and in turn maintains that form is both active and indistinguishable from matter and consists in a particular arrangement of corporeal parts.[39] The significance of the entire context of this discussion is Gassendi's defense of a body's ability to move itself—in other words, rejection of the Aristotelian doctrine that nothing can start its own motion in favor of the Epicurean doctrine of self-moving atoms. Moreover, the above quote is valid in reference to Christian theology as well as Aristotelianism: the "agent by whom the form is fashioned" is evidently the Aristotelian prime mover, but there is nothing to preclude him from being God as well. Since the agent and his action are external to the form, and since they do not set the form in motion, it can be inferred that only an internal cause is to be regarded as efficient. Gassendi does appear to be saying that God is the agent in, and of, the universe, since he apparently permeates it. Yet as long as it is remembered that to "pervade" the universe is not the same as to actually be contained inside the matter of the universe—and God is clearly not immanent in his creation—to this extent God remains separate from and external to the physical source of motion, whereby the only efficient agent becomes matter itself.

3. FROM ATOMS TO AUTONOMY

The principle of matter's self-sufficient internal mobility does not by itself mean that its motion can account for reason and autonomy; it remains to be seen whether matter can move in a way consistent with freedom, that is, neither through necessity, nor by chance. While the operations of the sentient soul—*anima*—are shared by all animals including human beings, the latter must

---

praesens, non ullo sui motu, sed nutu solo agere, & movere quidlibet potest" (*SP* I.334b).

38 "Neque vero est, quod quis forte dicat talem vim esse ab agente, a quo forma educitur, quia & agens, & eius actio, quae sola ab eo prodit, res externa est; & nihil est formae, quam ipsa eius vis agendi intimius" (*SP* I.335b).

39 On this, see also *SP* I.285a: "non sufficit sane dicere [Formam] prodire ex sinu materiae, vel ex certa quadam materiae, partiumque ipsius contemperatione...."

---

possess the capacity of autonomy over and above the common denominator of sensation and fundamental intelligence. Gassendi's discourse on the sentient (and hypothetically intelligent) soul is founded on the atomism of Epicurus and Lucretius, for whom all psychological processes can be expressed in terms of moving atoms—those emitted by external objects combined with those of the sense organs and the mind. While the impacts of *simulacra*—the likenesses of objects of sense perception—serve as the starting point for all psychological processes, they do not determine our responses to them in any rigid way. We are more than the sum of *simulacra* and automatic reflexes to them: our mind is more than a one-way stimulus-response mechanism, but rather an autonomous entity that shapes and controls its own movements, judgments, mores, and passions. In his discussion of freedom, Gassendi establishes, with Epicurus and Lucretius as his primary witnesses, that human beings can override natural necessity insofar as this lies within their power:

> Certainly, while the mind is of such a texture that it can be moved by external causes, it is nonetheless such that it can produce motions from itself, not from external causes, inasmuch as it spontaneously breaks forth in these [motions], which can thereby be called spontaneous and voluntary, and due to which [the mind] can put up a resistance to the impacts of external things, and can be drawn to one thing in such a way that it can likewise be swayed toward another. Thus it can be understood that [the mind] is not bound by necessity alone, but is in a disposition of freedom toward either alternative....[40]

It would be an exaggeration to say that Gassendi had a fully-fledged theory of how atomic motion transforms itself into purposeful and self-initiated actions. Throughout the *Syntagma* he makes sporadic remarks on matter's capability to generate life and even consciousness, and these observations are presented as meditations and remarks on the broader possibility that matter is not only capable of spontaneous and self-initiated developments, but possesses basic self-awareness: "substance not unaware of its workings".[41]

---

40 "Quippe tametsi animus eiusmodi texturae sit, ut possit a causis externis moveri; est tamen etiam eiusmodi, ut motus quosdam a seipso, non a causis externis habeat, ut pote in quos sponte *prorumpat*, quique adeo spontanei, voluntariique dici possint, & propter quos obsistere rerum externarum motionibus valeat, & non ita ad unam feratur, quin deflecti in aliam possit; sicque intelligatur, non unius necessitate alligari, sed ad utramvis liber constitui ..." (*SP* II.839b–40a, italicized by me).

If tangible objects possess secondary properties not inherent in the atoms, can they not likewise be characterized by secondary motions which can only develop among a multitude of atoms? Lucretius indicates that "it is often of great importance with what and in what position these same first-beginnings are held together, and what motions [*quos ... motus*] they impart and receive mutually" (*DRN* i.817–19). Are these motions simply collisions and swerves, and if so, why does Lucretius not indicate as much? Another possibility is that Lucretius is admitting qualitatively new types of motion, which could in theory include the focused, cumulative motion corresponding to freedom. A few lines further, Lucretius reiterates the idea that atoms "move differently [*alio ... modo moventur*] mixed with different elements and in different ways" (i.822), once again implying variety of motion rather than simply indicating that it is gravitation, collision, or swerve. Thus the "third" type of motion which Lisa Sarasohn attributes to Gassendi—the *clinamen* or swerve of the entire mind, translating into autonomy—need not be seen as an invention of his, but instead could very well have been postulated in the works of the Epicureans.[42] Indeed, the soul must be able to initiate locomotion without an external impact, or to resist an external impact, as is clear from Lucretius's description of a staggering person who, through an effort of will transmitting to the body, is able to regain balance after being pushed forward (*DRN* ii.272–283, quoted by Gassendi in *SP* II.839a). Gassendi's own introduction of the rolling motion (*SP* I.277a and I.280b), while it is strange and apparently groundless in terms of physics, makes perfect sense as an atomic metaphor for the mind itself and its capacity for self-initiated motions not requiring external prompting.

Whether a new type of motion can be attributed to individual

---

41 "Nimirum seminalis vis in quadam actuosa, operisque sui non ignara substantia est, cuiusmodi esse solus spiritus potest" (*SP* I.114b). Bloch holds that Gassendi did indeed have a conception of matter that was not only self-moving, but also self-organizing (*La Philosophie de Gassendi*, pp. 252–269).

42 Sarasohn holds that "Gassendi tried to reconcile the contradictory aspects of his version of the Epicurean soul by arguing that Epicurus would have maintained a third kind of motion in the soul, previously identified with the *clinamen*. This third motion is in actuality the result of the mixture of the other varied natural motions of the soul, and it is free [II.839]. Thus, the motion of the soul can be at once natural, voluntary, and free. All motions of the soul, although spontaneously necessitated by nature, combine to form a kind of free motion: The sum is more than the parts" (*Gassendi's Ethics*, p. 140). Sarasohn is referring to Gassendi's use of the terms *declinare* and *flectere* to denote the autonomous motion of the human mind rather than the swerve of an individual atom (*SP* II.839b)—an application that is indeed consistent with Lucretius's own application of *declinare* to the human will at large (*DRN* ii.259-60).

---

atoms (such as the rolling motion proposed by Gassendi), or whether only larger clusters of atoms can develop new types of motion, it is unlikely that the motions and properties of individual atoms have a direct and tangible impact on the sensible level. Rather, their motions produce a cumulative effect whereby the immediate movements of individual atoms are absorbed, mitigated and transformed before they emerge as sensible qualities. In his discussion of efficient causality as intrinsic to the atoms, Gassendi examines a passage by Lucretius which describes levels of distance from the direct power of the atoms and the developments that take place on each level:

> [T]he first-beginnings of things move of themselves; then the bodies that form a small combination and, as one may say, are nearest to the powers of the first-beginnings, are set moving, driven by the unseen blows of these, while they in their turn attack those that are a little larger. Thus the movement ascends from the first-beginnings and by successive degrees emerges on our senses.... [DRN ii.133–139; quoted by Gassendi in SP I.337a]

Gassendi suggests that as colliding atoms form molecules, these latter "carry the impetus of many [atoms]", and "are carried in some direction, but because of mutual cancellation and counteraction of the atoms' motions, the overall movement becomes somewhat slower. As other atoms join with them, the molecules become a little larger and, depending on the motion of the new atoms, themselves move slower or faster."[43] Thus it is not the case that any one atom or even molecule (res seminalis) can have direct, unmitigated impact which is discernible on the sensible level; rather, all such impacts are absorbed and incorporated in the cumulative development that translates into an intelligent or volitional act. Gassendi's terminology in referring to the specifically sentient and intelligent properties is suggestive of the modern term "emergence", which refers to secondary properties of an aggregate that cannot be seen as a mere sum of the primary qualities of its constituents. For instance, Gassendi characterizes the free motion of the human mind by saying that it "bursts forth" (prorumpat—SP II.840a) from its constituent matter.[44] Even in the following statement, which would seem to be a defense of the mind's metaphysical nature, Gassendi uses an

---

43 "ex Atomis invicem concurrentibus, minimulas primum concretiunculas, moleculasve conformari, quae, prout plurium impetus fert, aliquorsum quidem ferantur, sed propter tamen contra-nitenteis, transverseque agenteis, motus efficiatur aliquanto segnior. Accedentibus deinde aliis, moleculas paullo maiores fieri, & pro motu accedentium segnius, celerisve moveri" (SP I.337a–b).

44 Similarly, John Masson indicates that a transformation must take place in order

ambiguous term: "The human mind, or reason, is separated from (*eximetur*) the fabric of atoms, from a corporeal aggregate."[45] *Eximetur* could mean "removed" in the sense of being altogether separate from matter. However, it can just as easily mean "released out of", this time indicating that the mind takes its origin in matter, yet supersedes the mere sum of the qualities and motions of constituent atoms. Another instance clearly states that form (meaning motive and generative force) comes from the heart of matter: "It must also be stated how a certain form emerges from a certain arrangement, and how it never fails to emerge as dominant with regard to its matter...."[46] If this force were of incorporeal origin, and coming from outside, how could it be said to emerge from the matter that it brings into motion?

Therefore, it may be concluded that on some intermediate level, there occurs a transformation of the properties of atomic clusters, so that the tangible result, or the secondary properties of the entire being, be it person, animal, or vegetable, is far more than a sum of the motions of constituent atoms. The significance of such a transformation is not simply an increase in the size of the aggregate, but a proportionate increase in the versatility of its motions and capacities, and quite possibly in the degree of autonomy of the entire being.[47] Factors in the transformation may include atomic shape and size, proportions of different atoms in a body, and mutual arrangements of atoms.

Let us look at the first of these factors: the quality of individual atoms. With regard to the sentient soul, Gassendi writes that it is "itself a body which

---

for the blind swerve to "emerge" as conscious will (*The Atomic Theory of Lucretius* [London: George Bell, 1884], p. 138). Masson's interpretation, however, is based on the assumption that the swerve is indispensable for free will, which is significantly different from Gassendi's position.

45 "Mens, Ratioque humana ab Atomorum contextura, concretioneve corporea eximetur..." (*SP* I.282b).

46 "est in ipsa [re concreta] veluti fons, radixque omnium proprietatum, omnisque actionisque principium; non sufficit sane dicere eam prodire ex sinu materiae, vel ex certa quadam materiae, partiumque ipsius contemperatione; ... sed dicendum praeterea fuerit quomodo ex tali contemperatione talis forma erumpat, quomodo statim suae materiae veluti dominans evadat ..." (*SP* I.285a).

47 Phillip Mitsis draws attention to a principle contained in a passage of *De rerum natura* (ii.308–41). The import of this passage is that the static nature of visible objects can give no indication of the movement of underlying atoms; as a result, we cannot claim that there is an analogy between the invisible and the visible levels of reality (*Epicurus' Ethical Theory* [Ithaca, NY: Cornell University Press, 1988], p. 162). This observation confirms the fact that the properties and motions of larger bodies cannot be the result of simple magnification of the properties and motions of underlying atoms or particles.

---

is nonetheless of the subtlest kind and almost incorporeal (*veluti incorporeum*) by comparison to the rest of the bodily mass ..." (*SP* II.250b). This is a direct correlation to Epicurus's treatment of the kind of matter that makes up the soul: "the soul is a body [made up of] fine parts distributed throughout the entire aggregate, and most closely resembling breath with a certain admixture of heat, in one way resembling breath and in another resembling heat. There is also the <third> part which is much finer than even these [components] and because of this is more closely in harmony with the rest of the aggregate too" (*Letter to Herodotus* 2.63). Lucretius likewise avoids saying that crude atoms can account for intelligence; hence it is the fourth, "unnamed", element which is finer and more mobile than any other, that serves as the building matter of the soul (*DRN* iii.241), but can also be seen as the finest and most active part even of the soul itself—"animae quasi totius ipsa anima" (*DRN* iii.280–281). Gassendi follows in Epicurus's and Lucretius's steps, and posits *materiam tenuissimam* or *florem materiae* as the substance that generates motion in all self-moving natural beings: "in any being, the principle of action and motion is that most mobile and most active part—matter in full bloom, as it were—which is also known as Form, and can be understood as the most tenuous fabric of the minutest and most mobile atoms...."[48] In and of itself, this exceptional quality of the soul-atoms may not be able to remove natural necessity, yet their minuteness and mobility imply that the range of motions they can undertake is greater than that of ordinary, "crude" atoms, and that these motions are less subject to the law of inertia and can be initiated or stopped with greater ease, which would be the first step toward autonomy.

The quality of individual atoms is not the only factor that can contribute to the propensity for freedom in the human soul. Indeed, since the exceptionally fine and mobile atoms are a common denominator of anything that can move of itself, or of its own initiative (Gassendi's example of the boy and the apple indicates that such beings need only possess volition, not necessarily reason or freedom proper—*SP* I.337), it must be determined what features distinguish the human mind and account for its uniqueness. I believe these features rely on two factors: first, the particular arrangement of atoms within the mind, which in turn may account for particular capabilities of the whole, and secondly, the indirectness—mitigation, as it were—of the individual atoms' impact on the overall state of the mind. As I mentioned, the other factor that can help account for freedom in a corporeal mind, and that is a crucial component in the transformation, is the mutual arrangement of parts within

---

48 "in unaquaque re principium actionis, & motus sit pars illa mobilissima, actuosissimaque, & quasi flos totius materiae, quae & ipsa sit, quam Formam solent dicere, & haberi possit quasi tenuissima contextura subtilissimarum, mobilissimarumque Atomorum ..." (*SP* I.337a).

---

the whole. At this point I want to draw attention to the recurrence of the term "form" in Gassendi's discourse on secondary properties, whether these are qualities of living matter in general, or sentient and intelligent properties in particular. The meaning of "form" can be derived from the following: "There is in [the compound object] the source and root of all properties and the principle of all actions. It is not even sufficient to say that these proceed from the heart of matter, or from a certain arrangement of matter and its parts; … it must also be stated how a certain form emerges from a certain arrangement, and how it never fails to emerge as dominant with regard to its matter …" (*SP* I.285a). The context of this discussion is the insufficiency of the material cause alone in accounting for the qualities and actions of matter, but the import of this passage is that form is not only the arrangement of constituent parts, but also the result of that arrangement, and one that supersedes the initial configuration and primary qualities. Gassendi presents it as a foregone conclusion that the qualities and acts of composite bodies proceed from the "heart of matter", while the form itself can be understood as a constellation of properties and functions peculiar to the object or being in question. Thus Gassendi's conception of form is atomistic in its very foundations: it is a mutual arrangement of parts and particles in a larger body, but even more importantly, the mutual arrangement of atoms in the smallest particle.

It is also of great importance that this discussion of form is shortly preceded by a reference to Lucretius to the effect that "every kind grows and is nourished from its own proper material" (*SP* I.284b, referring to *DRN*, i.190). It can therefore be inferred that Gassendi draws on Lucretius's text for his own understanding of form. If we expand the context of Gassendi's reference to *De rerum natura*, we will see that it is part of a broader discussion of the significance of the atoms' mutual positions. Lucretius states that "many bodies [atoms] [are] common to many things, as we see letters to be common to words" (i.195–200). If this is the case, while at the same time there is a certain order to how things come into being, what lies behind the difference of one thing from another, containing the same atoms? Lucretius says, "It is often of great importance with what and in what position these same first-beginnings are held together, and what motions they impart and receive mutually" (i.817–819). For Lucretius such a factor as mutual positions must have been supremely important; the idea is reiterated several times throughout the poem (i.817–19, 908–910, ii.760–762, 1007–1009). The implications of this doctrine for biology and possibly even psychology are immense: Lucretius claims that "the same beginnings constitute sky, sea, earth, rivers, sun, the same make crops, trees, animals, but they move differently mixed with different elements and in different ways" (i.820–822 and ii.1015–1016). While he does not promise to solve the mystery of how exactly organic life arises from inorganic substance, he attributes the differences at least in part to the variety of mutual positions and motions of atoms. If mutual positions of atoms are the crucial factor that accounts for the difference between a lump of coal and a living being, could it not likewise contribute to the transformation from simple life to intelligence, and freedom as a form of intelligence? Lucretius's account at least allows this possibility, while Gassendi's discourse is equally open to such an interpretation.

With particular regard to the human psyche, form can be understood to account for the different actions and functions that a body is capable of, and in the context of the human mind these would be psychological processes, including self-initiated actions and developments in character. These latter can be seen as a function of the arrangement of active, mobile atoms into molecules, and of the further mutual arrangement of these molecules in an aggregate. Just as letters form different words through mere arrangement, so matter, especially *flos materiae*, in various arrangements may account for different functions of the soul and mind, quite possibly including autonomy.

By comparison, here is how Epicurus himself speaks about the properties of the human mind in relation to those of atoms. While he confirms that some people may have a "disordered congenital nature" (meaning that the atoms of their mind move haphazardly), he claims that

> It is not on the atoms that all <the responsibility should be placed for their behaviour …>. Thus when a development occurs which takes on some distinctness from the atoms in a differential way [τροπόν διαληπτικόν]—not in the way which is like viewing from a different distance—he acquires responsibility which proceeds from himself; then he straightaway transmits this to his primary substances and makes the whole of it into a yardstick. That is why those who cannot correctly make such distinctions confuse themselves about the adjudication of responsibilities.[49]

In this passage Epicurus describes a process that qualifies as freedom since the responsibility "proceeds from himself", that is, the person in question. "Differential" means that the development represents a motion—whether visible or on the atomic level—that is much more than, and qualitatively different

---

49 Epicurus, *On Nature* 34.21–22, in David Sedley, "Epicurus' Refutation of Determinism", *Syzetesis: Studi sull'epicureismo Greco e romano offerti a Marcello Gigante* (Naples: Biblioteca della Parola del Passato, 1983). Sedley himself interprets διαληπτικόν as originating separately from atoms, and therefore constituting a non-physical development (pp. 36–38). He concludes that when the self becomes responsible for a new psychological development, "the sort of moral characteristics required in a responsible agent over and above his constituent atoms are ones

from, the mere magnification of the motions of underlying atoms—so much so that this development takes on a life of its own. At the same time, there is no indication that this development originates separately from atoms. Indeed, while the motions of individual atoms are the sole source of the larger body's motion or state, or rather the sole "fuel" of any type of motion, the derivatives of these motions and qualities, or the secondary properties of the larger body, can be infinitely superior in their diversity and flexibility to the primary properties that engendered them. It is remarkable that Gassendi uses an equally ambiguous turn of phrase (*eximetur*) to refer to the unique qualities of the human mind.

The consequences of autonomy for both psychology and ethics cannot be underestimated. Gassendi largely draws on Epicurus's view of psychology in terms of incoming sensations and images: while the impacts of *simulacra*—the likenesses of objects of sense perception—serve as the starting point for all psychological states, they do not determine our responses to them in any rigid way, which means that the mind exerts control over its responses to *simulacra*, and over the opinions, beliefs and feelings that it develops on their basis (*SP* II.833a–b). In other words, rather than exhibiting a merely mechanistic response to external impacts, the mind is able to develop a disposition of selectivity toward these impacts and toward its own responses to them. Drawing on this flexibility of the mind, Gassendi expands on the psychological and ethical consequences of freedom. Using the testimony of Lucretius, he draws attention to the fact that although we may be impacted by an external force, "there is in our breast something strong enough to fight against it and to resist ... by the arbitrament of which, also, the mass of matter is compelled at times to be turned throughout body and limbs, and when thrust forward, is curbed back and settles back steadily" (*DRN* ii.279–83). Elaborating on this, Gassendi himself adds that a person is capable of freedom "not only from external force, but also from vehement passions which the mind or reason is capable of resisting through its freedom" ([*animus*] *non tantum de externa vi, sed de passionibus etiam vehementibus, quibus mens, seu ratio pro sua libertate obsistere potest*—*SP* II.839a). Based on Lucretius's discussion of mental attention and selectivity with regard to incoming *simulacra* (*DRN* iv.802–815), it can be suggested that the images stored in the mind are subject to the same discrimination as *simulacra* arriving from outside, and that therefore there is no essential difference between our ability to filter external stimuli on the one hand, and internal impulses as well as ingrained habits or predispositions, on the other.

---

which differ from the underlying atomic configurations in a much more radical way", and that consequently "matter in certain complex states can take on non-physical properties which in turn bring genuinely new behavioral laws into operation" (p. 39). The problem with such an interpretation is that it challenges Epicurus's thesis that there is nothing in existence besides atoms and void.

It is noteworthy that when Gassendi speaks about the mind's resistance to vehement passions in *De Appetitu, & Affectibus Animae*, he refers to a passage by Lucretius that deals precisely with this ability. Gassendi states that individual temperament results from the person's physiology, or the proportion of different "humors", as well as the nature, shape and arrangement of the atoms that constitute their sense organs and thereby act as gateways for incoming impressions. These physiological factors shape the nature of the soul's dispositions and reactions. However, these factors account only for propensity to act or feel a certain way, not for the actions and dispositions themselves: these are within our power to shape (*SP* II.504a).

By comparison, Epicurus himself describes the most important developments in human nature, and by association the most significant consequence of freedom, in terms of acquisition of new characteristics, or of change of existing ones. In a passage dealing with autonomous developments in human character, he sets the scene by saying that the ingredients of human psychology are "seeds", or atoms, which can be understood as atoms both inherent in the person's makeup, and those arriving from outside as sense perceptions. Epicurus continues by indicating that "that which we develop— characteristics of this or that kind—is at first absolutely up to us; and the things which of necessity flow in through our passages from that which surrounds us are at one stage up to us and dependent on beliefs of our own making" (*On Nature* 34.26). Clearly, what is taking place here is a "filtration" of *simulacra* that impact the senses from inside as well as from outside, and a conscious and voluntary (re)direction of one's desires and impulses toward a certain goal. But what is meant by "these things are at first entirely up to us"? This somewhat cryptic statement acquires clarity and focus when compared with a passage from Aristotle's *Nicomachean Ethics*: "we are in control of our actions from beginning to end, insofar as we know the particular circumstances surrounding them. But we control only the beginning of our characteristics: the particular steps in their development are imperceptible, just as they are in the spread of a disease; yet since the power to behave or not to behave in a given way was ours in the first place, our characteristics are voluntary."[50] Aristotle, of course, does not discuss human psychology in terms of moving atoms; yet in all other respects, the two statements are strikingly similar in their emphasis on character development, rather than specific actions, as the primary manifestation of freedom. Gassendi

---

50 *Nicomachean Ethics*, trans. Martin Ostwald (New York: Macmillan, 1962), Book III. Ch. 6 1114b-1115a. In this instance, Aristotle appears to be using the term "voluntary" as synonymous with freedom per se; another similar instance is the following: "actions concerned with means are based on choice and are voluntary actions" (ibid., 1113b), "choice" (*prohairesis*) being the equivalent of "freedom" in Aristotle's discourse. For direct influences as well as similarities between Aristotle's

makes reference to this very notion in Aristotle's ethics in his description of a physiological process with a point of no return: up to that point, the person has control of their state of health, but their failure to exercise it eventually leads them to forfeit that control and renders the outcome of illness necessary.[51]

As a reviver of Epicurus in the seventeenth century context, Gassendi blazed the trail for subsequent Epicurean scholarship extending into the present day. His work with Epicurean atomism meets two challenges. The first is to maintain the integrity of the fundamental principles of Epicurean physics in an age when atomism all but spelled atheism. The second is to avoid the pitfall of mechanical philosophy which sees matter as inert and entirely dependent on external causality. If the first challenge was the more prominent in Gassendi's time, it is the second one that has extended into the present day and has culminated in such issues as reductionism, which is often (and unjustly) laid at Epicurus's door. The context of the seventeenth century debate on the nature and capabilities of atoms sheds light on the origin of this and other issues which are the subject of today's Epicurean scholarship. (Reductionism, for instance, can be seen as an extension of the highly influential Cartesian reading of atomism informed by the thesis that matter is inherently inert.) Thus Gassendi not only revives atomism, but does so in a manner most consistent with Epicurus: proceeding from the postulate of the inherent mobility of matter. In his accounts of the human mind and will he elaborates on such principles as mutual arrangements of atoms in an aggregate, degrees of distance from the direct power of the atoms, the unique quality of the mind-atoms, and presents a picture not unlike Pietro Pomponazzi's conception of the soul as "the highest material form, attaining in its most elevated operations something beyond materiality."[52]

---

philosophy and that of the Epicureans, see Ettore Bignone, *L'Aristotele perduto e la formazione filosofica de Epicuro* (Florence: La Nuova Italia, 1936).

51 "Id simile esse Aristoteles docet, ut si quis mittat lapiem, quem non valeat retrahere, videlicet, ne mitteret, in eius potestate fuit: aut si quis intemperanter vivens, deinceps necessario aegrotet: nempe in illius quoque potestate, ut temperanter viveret, fuit" (*SP* II.826b).

52 Eckhard Kessler, "The Intellective Soul", in *The Cambridge History of Renaissance Philosophy*, ed. Charles Schmitt, Quentin Skinner, and Eckhard Kessler (Cambridge: Cambridge University Press, 1988), pp. 500–503. Strictly speaking, such a soul can no longer be termed "rational" since the latter becomes the object of Gassendi's discourse on incorporeality and immortality. Yet the capabilities of such a soul go well beyond appetitive and sensory to include imagination, memory and even thought, and quite possibly account for the distinctive human feature of autonomy.

WORKS CITED

Aquinas, Thomas, *Disputed Question on the Soul*, in *Quaestiones Disputatae* (Turin: Marietti, 1953), vol. 2. (Translation: J. P. Rowan, *The Soul*. [St. Louis, MO: Herder, 1949].)

Aristotle, *Nicomachean Ethics*, trans. Martin Ostwald (New York: Macmillan, 1962).

Asmis, Elizabeth, *Epicurus' Scientific Method* (Ithaca, NY: Cornell University Press, 1984).

Bignone, Ettore, *L'Aristotele perduto e la formazione filosofica de Epicuro* (Florence: La Nuova Italia, 1936).

Bloch, Olivier, *La Philosophie de Gassendi: Nominalisme, Matérialisme et Métaphysique* (The Hague: Martinus Nijhoff, 1971).

Englert, Walter, *Epicurus on the Swerve and Voluntary Action* (Atlanta, GA: Scholars Press, 1987).

Epicurus, *On nature*, in *The Hellenistic Philosophers*, ed. A. Long and D. Sedley (Cambridge: Cambridge University Press, 1995), vol. 1, pp. 102–103.

——, *Letter to Herodotus*, in *The Epicurus Reader*, trans. and ed. Brad Inwood and L. P. Gerson (Indianapolis: Hackett Publishing Co., 1994).

Garber, Daniel, "Soul and Mind: Life and Thought in the Seventeenth Century", in *The Cambridge History of Seventeenth Century Philosophy*, ed. Daniel Garber and Michael Ayers (Cambridge: Cambridge University Press, 1998).

Gassendi, Pierre, *Opera omnia* 6 vols (Lyon: Anisson et Posuel, 1658), reprinted Stuttgart-Bad Constatt: Friedrich Frommann Verlag, 1964.

——, *The Selected Works of Pierre Gassendi*, ed. and trans. Craig Brush (New York: Johnson Reprint, 1972).

Kessler, Eckhard, "The Intellective Soul", in *The Cambridge History of Renaissance Philosophy*, ed. Charles Schmitt, Quentin Skinner, and Eckhard Kessler (Cambridge: Cambridge University Press, 1988).

Lennon, Thomas, *The Battle of the Gods and Giants: The Legacies of Descartes and Gassendi* (Princeton, NJ: Princeton University Press, 1993).

Lucretius, *De rerum natura*, trans. W. H. D. Rouse, revised with notes by Martin F. Smith (Cambridge, MA: Harvard University Press, 1982).

Macintosh, J. J., "Robert Boyle on Epicurean Atheism and Atomism", in *Humanism and Early Modern Philosophy*, ed. Jill Kray et al. (London: Routledge, 2000).

Masson, John, *The Atomic Theory of Lucretius* (London: George Bell, 1884).

Michael, Emily and Fred S. Michael, "Early Modern Concepts of Mind", *Journal of the History of Philosophy* 27 (1989), pp. 29–48.

Mitsis, Phillip, *Epicurus' Ethical Theory* (Ithaca, NY: Cornell University Press, 1988).

Osler, Margaret J., *Divine Will and the Mechanical Philosophy* (New York: Cambridge University Press, 1994).

———, "Renaissance Humanism, Lingering Aristotelianism and the New Natural Philosophy: Gassendi on Final Causes", *Humanism and Early Modern Philosophy*, ed. Jill Kray et al. (London: Routledge, 2000).

———, "How Mechanical was the Mechanical Philosophy? Non-Epicurean Aspects of Gassendi's Philosophy of Nature", in *Late Medieval and Early Modern Corpuscular Matter Theories*, ed. Christopher Lüthy, John Murdoch, and William Newman (Leiden, Boston, Köln: Brill, 2001), pp. 423–439.

Pav, Peter Anton, "Gassendi's Statement of the Principle of Inertia", *Isis* 57 (1966), pp. 24–34.

Pintard, René, *La Mothe le Vayer, Gassendi, Guy Patin* (Paris: Boivin, 1943).

Sarasohn, Lisa, *Gassendi's Ethics: Freedom in a Mechanistic Universe* (Ithaca, NY: Cornell University Press, 1996).

Sedley, David, "Epicurus' Refutation of Determinism", *Syzetesis: Studi sull'epicureismo Greco e romano offerti a Marcello Gigante* (Naples: Biblioteca della Parola del Passato, 1983).

David E. White

1. INTRODUCTION

Although separated by two millennia, the philosophies of Epicurus and of Bishop Butler are clearly commensurable. Because of the destruction of all of the manuscript evidence on Butler it is difficult to know exactly what sources Butler used or why he made the changes and additions he did make, but it is nevertheless striking that in the second edition (1729) of his Rolls sermons (1726), he added a preface with three explicit references to Epicurus or the Epicurean philosophy. Thus, at the very least, we can conclude that Butler was conscious that his readers might be interested in how his philosophy compared with that of Epicurus. Knowing that Butler had Epicurus in mind to some degree, and knowing that Butler differentiated between points on which he agreed and those on which he disagreed with Epicurus, we can, without undue speculation, reconstruct a debate between Butler and Epicurus, with each seeking to win the hearts and minds of the audience.

In terms of the general aims and methods of philosophy, there is less separation over two thousand years between the ancient Hellenistic philosopher and the Hanoverian bishop than there is over the two hundred years between Butler and the academic moral philosophers of the twentieth century.

Epicurus reminds us that, "with the knowledge of the heavenly phænomena, both with those which are spoken of in contact with one another, and of those which have a spontaneous existence, as with every other science; it has no other aim but that freedom from anxiety, and that calmness which is derived from a firm belief",[1] and Butler is in complete accord with this sentiment when he tells us our concern in this world is "the science of improving the temper and making the heart better" and that virtue is "demonstrably the happiness of man".[2]

Admittedly, Butler had only the crudest knowledge of the historical-critical methods that are taken for granted by scholars today. He understood Epicurus through the works of Cicero and as closely allied with Hobbes,

---

1 "Letter to Pythocles", in Diogenes Laertius, *Lives and Opinions of Eminent Philosophers*, trans. R.D. Hicks (Cambridge, MA: Harvard University Press, 1965), 10.85.

2 Joseph Butler, *Fifteen Sermons Preached at the Rolls Chapel*, first edition (London: Knapton, 1726), Sermon 15.

but we can count on Butler to provide a clear map of what was of concern to philosophically and theologically inclined readers not only of the early eighteenth century but also well into the nineteenth century.

Sadly, we cannot assume that today's scholars generally know whereof they speak when they claim that Butler's ethics was merely an attempt to identify conscience with the voice of God and required revelation to give it credibility or when they dismiss his *Analogy of Religion*[3] as merely a *tu quoque* against the deists.[4] For example, Kai Nielsen crudely dismisses Butler in favor of Epicurus and Hobbes in his essay "Why Should I Be Moral?"[5] Nielsen, like so many others, pays no attention to what is clear in the text: Butler's whole effort in arguing against Epicurus was to avoid any appeal to religious or theological sentiments that Epicureans would not accept.

If we combine the physics of Newton and the epistemology of Locke with the ethics of Butler, we get what was for a time, at least, Anglican orthodoxy, and what will for all time be a comprehensive Christian philosophy that can at least hold its own over against secularism in the Epicurean tradition. Epicureans were a major target of Christian apologetics for as long as there had been Christian apologetics, and from the first Boyle lecture (delivered in 1692, the year of Butler's birth), Epicurus was attacked over and over by the most prominent intellectual defenders of Christianity in England. It is therefore especially interesting to consider exactly what Butler said for and against Epicurus, since of all the sermons preached in the churches of England throughout history it is only Butler's that are today still routinely studied by students of moral philosophy.

Butler affiliates himself with Epicurus's view that self-love needs to be cultivated, not constricted, but he does differ on three specific points. Butler makes the following claims when explicitly contrasting his system with that of Epicurus or the Epicureans:

1. Self-love is not the whole of virtue and religion.
2. Pleasure is not the whole of happiness.
3. Self-regarding actions are not the whole of actions
   approved by self-love.

Once we know from these explicit references that Butler considered the Epicureans as rivals when he prepared the second edition of his Rolls Chapel

3 Joseph Butler, *The Analogy of Religion, Natural and Revealed, to the Constitution and Course of Nature* (London: Knapton, 1736).

4 For example by Anthony Quinton, "British Philosophy", in *The Encyclopedia of Philosophy*, ed. Paul Edwards (New York: The Macmillan Company and The Free Press, 1967), vol. 1, p. 382.

5 Kai Nielsen, "Why Should I be Moral?", *Methodos* 15 (1963), pp. 275–306.

sermons in 1729,[6] we can also be confident that Butler was implicitly concerned with Epicureans when writing his *Analogy of Religion,* which appeared in 1736. There are three obvious points of comparison between the Epicurean philosophy and the Anglican philosophy as presented by Butler. Contrary to Epicureans, Anglicans maintain:

4. We ought to expect a future life after death.
5. The existence of evil in this world does not provide
   sufficient grounds to deny God.
6. God exists as revealed in the Providence of Nature
   and the Revelation of Scripture.

Since so many commentators have assumed that Butler was drawing on sources of alleged revelation that Epicureans refused to recognize, this paper will avoid any comparison of Butler and Epicurus that does not put them on an equal footing.

The first five issues given in the list above are universal human concerns, and, as already shown, the Epicurean tradition was very much alive in the circles in which Butler lived and moved.[7]

Still, an objection might be raised that Epicurus and Butler are incommensurable not just because of their specific differences over the gods and revelation but more generally because Butler was emphatically a teleological thinker and Epicurus was not.

Getting clear about this objection is essential for making sense of all that follows. Certainly Butler did go on about final causes in nature in a way that could not be accepted by an Epicurean any more than by most philosophers today. Why this is not a problem may be made clear with an example.

Butler repeats teleological commonplaces such as:

Eyes were made for seeing.
Ears were made for hearing.

Clearly Butler thinks that everyone will immediately agree to such statements. But when we examine the context, we see that the reason Butler is so confident everyone will agree is because he has put the emphasis on seeing as opposed to smelling or hearing, whereas the non-teleological party would see "made" as the objectionable word. The non-teleological party would agree that eyes were for seeing as opposed to smelling or hearing, but would resist

---

6   *Fifteen Sermons Preached at the Rolls Chapel,* second edition (London: Knapton, 1729).

7   Howard Jones, *The Epicurean Tradition* (London: Routledge, 1989), ch. 8.

the inference to eyes having been made for that purpose. Butler certainly would insist that eyes were made, he explicitly states that a thousand instances of design prove a designer, but it does not follow that since Butler endorsed this inference he needed it at any particular point in the rest of his argument. There is a great deal that can be said about the eyes and ears that is entirely neutral as regards whether they were made by someone for seeing or whether seeing is merely what they are used for.

So it is in discussing self-love, pleasure, happiness, evil and death. There is a great deal that can be said about them that is entirely neutral as regards whether we are under a divine, providential government in this world and the next, if, indeed, there is a next.

None of this is to suggest that in offering suggestions on how to live better Butler is stepping out of his role as a pastor and as an apologist for Christianity. On the contrary, Butler clearly thought that the best way to live better was to adopt the Christian way of life.

What differentiates Butler from almost all of the long line of Christian critics of Epicureanism, is that Butler came in with a highly optimistic view of human nature.[8] Butler took as obvious what so many other Christian apologists seem to have missed: just as the eyes in the human body are for seeing, so the principle of self-love in human nature is for the promotion of happiness. Explicitly borrowing from the Stoics, Butler believed that the highest rule of ethics is to follow nature. Thus, once one has determined to follow nature, it does not matter whether that nature is ultimately from God in his providence or however else it might have originated.

Contrary to what some have claimed, Butler did not import any theological claims into his ethics in an attempt to legitimate what could not otherwise be defended. Butler saw atheists as bound by the whole of human morality except only for the special regards due to the divine beings and whatever special commands they may have issued through revelation.

The first step in Butler's apologetic is to consider what use might be made of the human nature that is incontestably available to us. After having delivered his sermons "through a course of eight years" as Preacher at the Rolls, Butler took up his duties as Rector of Stanhope and published a selection of just fifteen sermons. Three years later a second edition was called for, and Butler took the opportunity to add a preface. It is in this preface that we find his only explicit references to Epicurus or the Epicurean school of philosophy.

Butler shared with Epicurus a generally empirical orientation. Moreover, the Butlerian and the Epicurean passages in question here do not appeal to any specialized observations or employ any clever logic in deriving conclusions from the observations. Rather, Butler and the Epicurean clash, when

---

8   Ibid., ch. 4.

they clash at all, only in what they claim is obvious to anyone who will reflect on the common examples that are part of everyone's experience.

The passages from Butler, i.e., those in the Preface to the sermons that explicitly mention Epicureans and the corresponding passages cited in Sermon XI, are among the most famous and most celebrated in the whole history of English moral philosophy, but, especially over the last century, they have been read primarily from the psychological point of view. The passages are undoubtedly psychological in their subject matter, but to get clear about what Butler was trying to do, and especially what he was trying to do over against the Epicureans, they might better be read first from the pastoral and apologetic points of view, and in that order. Thus, as we might expect in sermons delivered to a sophisticated congregation, Butler saw that his first aim had to be to make a certain understanding of human nature intellectually respectable in a way that his hearers could use his message to better their lives. Only once both the factual correctness and the practical utility of this view of human nature was made clear to all was Butler ready to make his apologetic move. Throughout Butler's works, we catch little glimpses of the sort of audience he had in mind. Having noted these clues to what Butler was trying to do, we can go on to evaluate how successful his arguments were, first pastorally in giving good advice and then apologetically in moving people in the direction of living the full Christian life.

2. THE HEDONISTIC BASIS OF ETHICS

In paragraph 38 (see the Appendix to this paper), Butler clearly states his pastoral goal as "to obviate that scorn, which one sees rising upon the faces of people who are said to know the world" when mention is made of disinterested action. Butler proposes to obviate this scorn by calling the reader's attention to certain well-known facts of life. The facts that Butler cites are obvious, he thinks, and, specifically when introducing the passage from Cicero on the Epicurean view, he says he finds it "surprising" that anyone would think otherwise. Those who looked at Butler (and the whole long line of clerics and moralists who preceded him) with scorn had, of course, often been given arguments regarding why they should engage in disinterested action. They had been told that virtue required such action. Such appeals seemed irrational since it left them with no reason or motive for the action. Agreeing with the Epicureans, these scoffers found they could not see the point, or even the possibility of an action for which there was no motive. At best they would be acting like unthinking animals. The hope of reward in a future life would supply motive enough, but here again those who scorned found that they could not be moved by hope of reward or fear of punishment in a future life. So, it seemed to them that Butler, or anyone else who hoped to persuade them to pursue disinterested action, would have to provide either a proof, such as Plato claimed to offer, that somehow virtue without reward was to their advantage, or a proof, as many of the Christian apologists claimed to offer, that they could reasonably expect a reward in the next life. They were understandably confident that no such proof would be forthcoming. And Butler did not supply or claim to supply either of these proofs. What Butler did instead was to try to show that the Epicurean case traded on an ambiguity. Butler saw only confusion in "calling actions interested which are done in contradiction to the most manifest known interest, merely for the gratification of a present passion."

For example, desiring to show off I engage in some action that makes me look like a fool. Clearly, that action is in contradiction to self-love. Had I reflected calmly, I would have restrained myself out of self-love and the desire not to appear foolish. We *could* call such an action a foolish but still self-interested action, but it would be clearer and more natural to call the action what it was: an action motivated by pride but disinterested, i.e., not in our own interest.[9] Certainly such a foolish action *could* be called "interested," but only in the trivial sense in which "every action of every creature must" be called interested, "for no one can act but from a desire, or choice, or preference of his own."[10]

Those who love themselves will have no use for this trivialized sense of "self-interest", so they will have to admit that in the substantive and therefore preferred sense of "self-interest" they do act in a way that is contrary to self-interest. The object of self-love is our own happiness. When we act with some other end in view, we may or may not be acting in accord with self-love. Thus, right from the start of his exposition, Butler has broken the back of Epicureanism by showing not what the audience expected, that there is some occult reason for acting contrary to self-interest or that selfless action will be rewarded in a future life, but rather that it is only by semantic confusion that one can deny the existence of selfless action. The actions he first gives as examples are those actions that are clearly motivated from within us to attain some good for ourselves, but they are not in accord with self-interest and therefore cannot be called self-interested in any interesting way, but only according to a trivialized definition of "interested". Thus, Butler's first strike specifically against the Epicureans is not by appeal to the softer side of human nature, and certainly not by the promise of some supernatural reward, but rather by appeal to self-interest.

In a footnote,[11] Butler alludes to two examples from Cicero. Butler seems to anticipate that once he has shown that there certainly are many motives that cannot properly be called interested, the Epicurean will claim to discover amongst the mix of motives that go into producing any action at least some that are selfish. Butler affirms that in countless cases it is impossible to say whether the principle that determined someone to act in a certain way was from self-love

---

9   Appendix, paragraph 35.

10   Appendix, paragraph 35.

11   To paragraph 35 in the Appendix.

or just some particular passion. But, he says, the fact that we cannot make this determination in no way hinders us from distinguishing the concepts of self-love on the one hand and the particular passions on the other, and it would be "absurd" to insist that because we cannot tell them apart in the ordinary course of practice therefore *all* our actions must be motivated in one way or the other. We do act from mixed motives and we cannot, generally, sort them out, but in no sense is there reason to find "nothing but regard for ourselves" at the base of all actions.[12]

3. THE NATURE OF HAPPINESS

There is a sense in which virtue is its own reward, but this is the special case of failure. There is some satisfaction merely in endeavoring to do good without success, but a failed selfish act is only painful.[13]

According to Butler's theory of happiness, happiness consists in the satisfaction or enjoyment of the objects of the various particular affections and passions. But Butler recognizes that appeal to his definition of happiness will have no force against those who maintain the absence of pain is the highest happiness, so he grants the consistency of the Epicurean position. Of course, Butler has no intention, ultimately, of writing off any aspect of human nature, partly just because it is *our* nature and partly because of his belief in a providential design to the world. When writing in opposition to the Epicureans, Butler is content to move on with just the hint that those who follow Epicurus will end up with a bad deal: they will give up too many pleasures that could have been theirs entirely in accord with virtue.

4. SELF-LOVE

Having shown the Epicurean theory to be unreliable or at least highly dubious as a theory of life, Butler next goes on to commend Epicureanism as a vast improvement on the way many lives are lived. Here again, we see how entirely practical and pastoral Butler is.

Butler's thought seems to be that those who follow the Epicurean way successfully will miss many opportunities to do good for themselves and for others since they are blind to the fact that true self-interest includes many actions, such as benevolent actions, that do not fall under their definition of self-interest. Epicureans will also fail in their duties to God, since they do not acknowledge such a being as one would have specific duties toward. And certainly if there is a future life, then the followers of Epicurus will have made no preparation for it. Still, following the Epicurean philosophy may be the right choice for those who, for whatever reason, are not about to accept the full

---

12 Appendix, paragraph 36.

13 Appendix, paragraph 37.

---

religious and moral institution of life. What Butler liked about Epicureanism was the emphasis on the single-minded devotion to what he calls our "chief temporal good". Compared with the "extravagances of mere appetite, will and pleasure", the Epicurean pursuit of rational self-interest is clearly the right choice.[14]

So far, Butler has shown that Epicureanism is out of contention for the preferred philosophy of life. He has shown that certain features of Epicureanism put great strains on credulity. And Butler has done this without making any appeal to specifically religious claims, even those he thinks can be supported by good evidence, let alone those that would require faith. Finally, Butler has placed Epicureanism on a level far superior to the normal run of things, or at least what he took to be the normal run of things. He insists that one could do far worse, as well as far better, than being an Epicurean.

5. DEATH

Butler devotes the long first chapter of part I of his *Analogy of Religion* to his argument for the expectation of a future life. That argument is not directed explicitly against Epicureans, but it does have an interesting application in the critique of Epicureanism.

Most of the arguments by Christian apologists assume that the rewards of heaven and the punishments of hell are affixed by God in response to our actions in this world in much the way some earthly rewards and punishments are affixed to actions by the human governors in this world. Butler uses a different model. Butler takes nature as his guide. According to Butler, we ought to prepare for a future life after death, but our preparation consists in the same sort of moral action that serves us well in this world.

On Butler's theory, therefore, there will be no difference between the apprehension we feel about possibly having done the wrong thing in life and having the consequences catch up with us later in life, and the apprehension we might feel about the same sort of consequences catching up with us after death. There is, therefore, little additional apprehension regarding death by virtue of the belief in life after death. Indeed, if we are comfortable with our actions and morality in this world, then we have nothing to fear from death at all. It may be the Epicurean is no worse off. As long as the Epicurean does nothing different in life because of being confident there is no future life, the consequences will be the same for the Epicurean and for those who follow Butler's advice. Still, the Epicurean runs the risk of acting differently out of confidence that there is no future life and then turning out to be wrong. Since Butler urges acting in anticipation of death in exactly the way one would act in anticipation of continued life in this world, the followers of Butler run no such risk.

---

14 Appendix, paragraph 41.

6. EVIL

Butler was concerned with the problem of evil, and he seems to have understood the problem in something like the terms that Lactantius attributed to Epicurus:

> [1] God, [Epicurus] says, either wishes to take away evils, and is unable; or he is able, and is unwilling; or he is neither willing nor able, or he is both willing and able. [2] If he is willing and is unable, he is feeble, which is not in accordance with the character of God. [3] If he is able and unwilling, he is envious, which is equally at variance with God. [4] If he is neither willing nor able, he is both envious and feeble, and therefore not God. [5] If he is both willing and able, which alone is suitable to God, from what source then are evils? or why does he not remove them?[15]

Butler's reply is again in the skeptical tradition. With the problem put in this form, Butler would probably argue against the truth of step 2. That God is unable to take away all evil does not show that God is feeble. There are things that even an omnipotent being cannot do. Of course, the usual examples of what an omnipotent being cannot do will not work here, unless we can think of an evil whose removal would entail a contradiction. Butler is content to argue against the inference that since we cannot think of any such example there necessarily must not be any such example. He supports this argument with a long explanation of human ignorance.[16]

7. GOD AND REVELATION

As a proof of God's existence Butler appeals to "the general consent of mankind" and Cicero has Velleius the Epicurean give such an appeal in *De Natura Deorum* (I.43–44), but since Butler makes no explicit reference to the Epicurean theology with regard to proofs of existence or of revelation, it is impossible to say exactly what Butler's attitude would have been. Clearly, the Epicureans would have no use for the description that Butler favored most: God is the governor of the universe. When pressed, Butler's final answer seems to be that words simply fail when we attempt to say anything about God.

---

15 Lactantius, *De ira Dei*, trans. William Fletcher in *The Ante-Nicene Christian Library*, ed. Alexander Roberts and James Donaldson (Edinburgh: T&T Clark, 1866–1872), vol. 7, ch. 13.

16 Butler, *Fifteen Sermons*, first edition, sermon 15 and Butler, *Analogy of Religion*, part 1, chapter 7.

Given the traditional Anglican opposition to Epicureanism and to deism, and given that Butler is most often characterized as an opponent of deism, one might expect that Butler would make some reference to Epicurus in his defense of revelation. As is often the case, what one might expect is not what happens. We could speculate that Butler would argue against the Epicureans as he did against the deists that they have already accepted propositions that are as much or more in doubt than the propositions that he needs as premises in his defense of the practice of Christian virtue and piety.

8. CONCLUSION

Of all the "pagan" authors, Epicureans were the ones who drew the most polemical fire from Anglicans in the seventeenth and eighteenth centuries. Butler's reaction to Epicurus is worth reviewing in detail for several reasons. Of all the Anglicans who reacted to Epicurus in the seventeenth and eighteenth centuries, Butler is the only one whose apologetic work continued to be of general interest on through the nineteenth century. Upon his retirement from politics, the first task W. E. Gladstone set himself was to edit the complete works of Bishop Butler. Even today, when some of Butler's work attracts only a few readers, the Preface to the 1729 edition of the Rolls Sermons is still reprinted and studied. It is also well known that Butler had a great influence on Henry Sidgwick and G. E. Moore, and through them on the whole of modern moral philosophy.

What remains a complete mystery is why Butler's only explicit comments on Epicurus are in the 1729 preface, when, as shown above, there is much else in Butler and in the Epicureans that could be compared in a fruitful and non-obvious way.

APPENDIX[17]

[35] The chief design of the eleventh Discourse is to state the notion of self-love and disinterestedness, in order to shew that benevolence is not more unfriendly to self-love, than any other particular affection whatever. There is a strange affectation in many people of explaining away all particular affections, and representing the whole life as nothing but one continued exercise of self-love. Hence arises that surprising confusion and perplexity in the Epicureans[18]

---

17 From the "Preface" to *Fifteen Sermons*, second edition, 1729. The paragraph numbers used here were added by J. H. Bernard for his edition (London: Macmillan, 1900).

18 [Butler's note:] One need only look into Torquatus's account of the Epicurean system, in Cicero's first book *de Finibus*, to see in what a surprising manner this was done by them. Thus the desire of praise, and of being beloved, he explains to be no other than desire of safety: regard to our country, even in the most virtuous character, to be nothing but regard to ourselves. The author of *Reflexions, &c.*,

of old, Hobbes, the author of *Reflexions, Sentences, et Maximes Morales*, and this whole set of writers; the confusion of calling actions interested which are done in contradiction to the most manifest known interest, merely for the gratification of a present passion. Now all this confusion might easily be avoided, by stating to ourselves wherein the idea of self-love in general consists, as distinguished from all particular movements towards particular external objects; the appetites of sense, resentment, compassion, curiosity, ambition, and the rest. When this is done, if the words *selfish* and *interested* cannot be parted with, but must be applied to everything; yet, to avoid such total confusion of all language, let the distinction be made by epithets: and the first may be called cool or settled selfishness, and the other passionate or sensual selfishness. But the most natural way of speaking plainly is, to call the first only, self-love, and the actions proceeding from it, interested: and to say of the latter, that they are not love to ourselves, but movements towards somewhat external: honour, power, the harm or good of another: and that the pursuit of these external objects, so far as it proceeds from these movements, (for it may proceed from self-love) is no otherwise interested, than as every action of every creature must, from the nature of the thing, be; for no one can act but from a desire, or choice, or preference of his own.

[36] Self-love and any particular passion may be joined together; and from this complication, it becomes impossible in numberless instances to determine precisely, how far an action, perhaps even of one's own, has for its principle general self-love or some particular passion. But this need create no confusion in the ideas themselves of self-love and particular passions. We distinctly discern what one is, and what the other are though we may be uncertain how far one or the other influences us. And though from this uncertainty it cannot but be that there will be different opinions concerning mankind, as more or less governed by interest; and some will ascribe actions to self-love which others will ascribe to particular passions: yet it is absurd to say that mankind are wholly actuated by either; since it is manifest that both have their influence. For as, on the one hand, men form a general notion of interest, some placing it in one thing, and some in another, and have a considerable regard to it throughout the course of their life, which is owing to self-love; so, on the other hand, they are often set on work by the particular passions themselves, and a considerable part of life is spent in the actual gratification of them, i.e. is employed, not by self-love, but by the passions.

Morales [Francois La Rochefoucauld], says "Curiosity proceeds from interest or pride; which pride also would doubtless have been explained to be self-love" (page 85, 1725 edition). As if there were no such passions in mankind as desire of esteem, or of being beloved, or of knowledge. Hobbes's account of the affections of good-will and pity are instances of the same kind.

---

[37] Besides, the very idea of an interested pursuit necessarily presupposes particular passions or appetites; since the very idea of interest or happiness consists in this, that an appetite or affection enjoys its object. It is not because we love ourselves that we find delight in such and such objects, but because we have particular affections towards them. Take away these affections, and you leave self-love absolutely nothing at all to employ itself about; no end or object for it to pursue, excepting only that of avoiding pain. Indeed the Epicureans, who maintained that absence of pain was the highest happiness, might, consistently with themselves, deny all affection, and, if they had so pleased, every sensual appetite too: but the very idea of interest or happiness other than absence of pain, implies particular appetites or passions; these being necessary to constitute that interest or happiness.

[38] The observation, that benevolence is no more disinterested than any of the common particular passions, seems in itself worth being taken notice of; but is insisted upon to obviate that scorn, which one sees rising upon the faces of people who are said to know the world, when mention is made of a disinterested, generous, or public-spirited action. The truth of that observation might be made appear in a more formal manner of proof: for whoever will consider all the possible respects and relations which any particular affection can have to self-love and private interest, will, I think, see demonstrably, that benevolence is not in any respect more at variance with self-love, than any other particular affection whatever, but that it is in every respect, at least, as friendly to it.

[39] If the observation be true, it follows, that self-love and benevolence, virtue and interest, are not to be opposed, but only to be distinguished from each other; in the same way as virtue and any other particular affection, love of arts, suppose, are to be distinguished. Every thing is what it is, and not another thing. The goodness or badness of actions does not arise from hence, that the epithet, interested or disinterested, may be applied to them, any more than that any other indifferent epithet, suppose inquisitive or jealous, may or may not be applied to them; not from their being attended with present or future pleasure or pain; but from their being what they are; namely, what becomes such creatures as we are, what the state of the case requires, or the contrary. Or in other words, we may judge and determine, that an action is morally good or evil, before we so much as consider, whether it be interested or disinterested. This consideration no more comes in to determine whether an action be virtuous, than to determine whether it be resentful. Self-love in its due degree is as just and morally good, as any affection whatever. Benevolence towards particular persons may be to a degree of weakness, and so be blamable: and disinterestedness is so far from being in itself commendable, that the utmost possible depravity which we can in imagination conceive, is that of disinterested cruelty.

[40] Neither does there appear any reason to wish self-love were weaker in the generality of the world than it is. The influence which it has seems

plainly owing to its being constant and habitual, which it cannot but be, and not to the degree or strength of it. Every caprice of the imagination, every curiosity of the understanding, every affection of the heart, is perpetually shewing its weakness, by prevailing over it. Men daily, hourly sacrifice the greatest known interest, to fancy, inquisitiveness, love, or hatred, any vagrant inclination. The thing to be lamented is, not that men have so great regard to their own good or interest in the present world, for they have not enough; but that they have so little to the good of others. And this seems plainly owing to their being so much engaged in the gratification of particular passions unfriendly to benevolence, and which happen to be most prevalent in them, much more than to self-love. As a proof of this may be observed, that there is no character more void of friendship, gratitude, natural affection, love to their country, common justice, or more equally and uniformly hardhearted, than the *abandoned* in, what is called, the way of pleasure—hardhearted and totally without feeling in behalf of others; except when they cannot escape the sight of distress, and so are interrupted by it in their pleasures. And yet it is ridiculous to call such an abandoned course of pleasure interested, when the person engaged in it knows beforehand, and goes on under the feeling and apprehension, that it will be as ruinous to himself, as to those who depend upon him.

[41] Upon the whole, if the generality of mankind were to cultivate within themselves the principle of self-love; if they were to accustom themselves often to set down and consider, what was the greatest happiness they were capable of attaining for themselves in this life, and if self-love were so strong and prevalent, as that they would uniformly pursue this their supposed chief temporal good, without being diverted from it by any particular passion; it would manifestly prevent numberless follies and vices. This was in a great measure the Epicurean system of philosophy. It is indeed by no means the religious or even moral institution of life. Yet, with all the mistakes men would fall into about interest, it would be less mischievous than the extravagances of mere appetite, will, and pleasure: for certainly self-love, though confined to the interest of this life, is, of the two, a much better guide than passion, which has absolutely no bound nor measure, but what is set to it by this self-love, or moral considerations.

[42] From the distinction above made between self-love, and the several particular principles or affections in our nature, we may see how good ground there was for that assertion, maintained by the several ancient schools of philosophy against the Epicureans, namely, that virtue is to be pursued as an end, eligible in and for itself. For, if there be any principles or affections in the mind of man distinct from self-love, that the things those principles tend towards, or that the objects of those affections are, each of them, in themselves eligible, to be pursued upon its own account, and to be rested in as an end, is implied in the very idea of such principle or affection. They indeed asserted much higher

things of virtue, and with very good reason; but to say thus much of it, that it is to be pursued for itself, is to say no more of it, than may truly be said of the object of every natural affection whatever.

WORKS CITED

Butler, Joseph, *Fifteen Sermons Preached at the Rolls Chapel* (London: Knapton, 1726 [first edition], 1729 [second edition]).

———, *The Analogy of Religion, Natural and Revealed, to the Constitution and Course of Nature* (London: Knapton, 1736).

———, *Fifteen Sermons*, ed. J. H. Bernard (London: Macmillan, 1900).

Epicurus, "Letter to Pythocles", in Diogenes Laertius, *Lives and Opinions of Eminent Philosophers*, trans. R.D. Hicks (Cambridge, MA: Harvard University Press, 1965), 10.85.

Jones, Howard, *The Epicurean Tradition* (London: Routledge, 1989).

Lactantius, *De ira Dei*, trans. William Fletcher in *The Ante-Nicene Christian Library*, ed. Alexander Roberts and James Donaldson (Edinburgh: T&T Clark, 1866–1872), vol. 7.

Nielson, Kai, "Why Should I be Moral?", *Methodos* 15 (1963), pp. 275–306.

Quinton, Anthony, "British Philosophy", in *The Encyclopedia of Philosophy*, ed. Paul Edwards (New York: The Macmillan Company and The Free Press, 1967).

THE YOUNG MARX ON EPICURUS:
DIALECTICAL ATOMISM AND HUMAN FREEDOM

Paul M. Schafer

Karl Marx's doctoral dissertation on the difference between the Democritean and Epicurean philosophy of nature is an unjustly neglected chapter in the history of ideas. In my view, this is a mistake, for Marx's dissertation, together with the notebooks he prepared in advance of the work, constitutes nothing less than the genesis of his philosophical worldview. Yet there is more to the work than this. No doubt the dissertation contains invaluable resources for the specialist scholar striving to trace the genealogy of Marx's thought. To my mind, however, it is the dissertation's philosophical substance that makes it so interesting. By means of a Hegelian inspired dialectical analysis of Epicurus's natural philosophy, Marx demonstrates the underlying logical continuity between the single elementary atom and the natural world as a whole. Indeed, Marx's analysis follows Epicurus up into the heavens of celestial bodies and down to the world of concrete human thought and action. His study yields a conception of human self-consciousness that is not in opposition to nature, but reflects the rationality disclosed in it. As it turns out, the rational form of human consciousness and the rational form of nature are a logical fit. For the youthful Marx this discovery carried far-reaching conclusions about the nature of human freedom, conclusions that Epicurus could not have accepted.

1. CONTRASTING EPISTEMOLOGICAL MODELS: DEMOCRITUS VERSUS EPICURUS

Marx understood the natural philosophies of Democritus and Epicurus to represent two different modes of comprehending the natural world, not unlike the difference between the epistemological models of modern Empiricism and Rationalism. Though the rudimentary physics of their theories, symbolized by the principle of atoms and the void, is the same, they are "diametrically opposed" in all matters of truth, certainty and human knowledge. The standpoint of Democritus is a kind of mechanistic empiricism, while Epicurus is a dialectical thinker for whom thought takes an active role in the determination of knowledge.[1] To put it a little simplistically, Democritus

---

1 *Karl Marx/Frederick Engels Collected Works,* Vol. 1 (New York: International Publishers, 1975), p. 38. This edition is hereafter referred to as MECW, followed by a volume number. The German edition used is *Marx/Engels Historisch-Kritische Gesamtausgabe,* Erste Abteilung, Band 1, Erster Halbband (Frankfurt: Marx-Engels Archiv, Verlagsgesellschaft M.B.H., 1927), p. 17. This edition is hereafter referred to as MEGA, followed by a volume and part number.

sees the world as an assemblage of parts, an extraordinarily complicated puzzle to be deciphered by the scientific observer. For Epicurus, the world is primarily a construction of the philosophical-scientific observer, whose aim is not so much to decipher a puzzlingly recalcitrant natural substance, but to build a satisfactory (and pleasing) worldview. In this case, the role of thought is active and constructive, and it was this aspect of the Epicurean epistemology that attracted the young Marx.

In Marx's eyes, Democritus is a skeptic and an empiricist, whose position on human knowledge is internally contradictory. On the one hand, he holds that sense perception lacks all objectivity and is utter semblance; it does not touch the true principles of things, the atoms and the void, and, as such, cannot rise above mere opinion to attain anything like sense certainty. For Democritus, as for his Scottish philosophical soul-mate, David Hume, empiricism and skepticism are one and the same. We know only the ideas derived from our sense impressions, but can say nothing certain about the correspondence of those ideas to the actual things. Yet, on the other hand, sense experience is the only true object for thought. Thus, for Democritus, "the world of sensation [is] the real world, full of content."[2] Even though the world of sensation portrays a reality distinct from the true and actual things (atoms and the void) it is filled with value and significance. And it is to this world, the empirical world, that Democritus devoted his life. For Marx, this explains the notorious scientific wanderlust of the man; his lust for knowledge left him no rest—it drove him across the known world, from Persia to Egypt and Ethiopia, across the Red Sea, reportedly even as far as India, in search of positive knowledge.

Epicurus is an opposite kind of figure; he is a dogmatist for whom knowledge is, *by definition*, certain and real. Sensation *is* the standard of certainty and truth. Rather than running away from this fact in search of more and diverse experiences, none of which get any nearer to certainty, Epicurus embraces it. Accordingly, the key to understanding nature is found not in collections of empirical facts, but in the purposive activity of the human mind. Knowledge has as much to do with the state of mind of the perceiver as with the appearances themselves. Moreover, it is not the certainty of things that is paramount, but the peace and serenity of the human mind. Marx puts it best when he describes the Epicurean standpoint as "the serenity of thought satisfied with itself, the self-sufficiency that draws its knowledge *ex principio interno*."[3]

Though Marx did not accept these views without qualification, Epicurus is a philosopher much closer to his own heart than Democritus. Both the idea that sensuous appearance is objective and real, and the idea that thought plays a definitive role in the determination of knowledge had a powerful appeal

---

2   MECW, 1, p. 40; MEGA, I, 1/1, p. 19.

3   MECW, 1, p. 45; MEGA, I, 1/1, p. 24.

---

to the young radical. Though Marx would not go so far as to reduce all knowing to a means to the tranquility of the mind, as Epicurus did, there is no doubt that the Epicurean emphasis on the active and defining role of human thought struck him as a profoundly liberating and modern position.

2. DIALECTICAL ATOMISM

The second and final part of Marx's doctoral dissertation takes up an analysis of the details of Epicurean physics. His aim, in a nutshell, is to delineate the rational form of nature through a careful analysis and criticism of its most elementary material component. Echoing Hegel's exhaustive account of the nature of being in his *Science of Logic*, Marx sought to describe the inner logic of nature from its simplest conception—the atom—to its complete expression in the system of celestial bodies. Indeed, his ambition was to see the universe in a single atom—and not only that, but to grasp the link between nature and human consciousness.

Clearly, such a project is inconceivable within the framework of Democritus's skeptical, empiricist view of knowledge. This approach posits the atom as a kind of raw materiality, a bit of matter within a network of necessary causes and connections. But for Democritus, as we have seen, one's access to this network penetrates no further than the appearances of things. How does one begin to grasp the intrinsic logic linking atoms to their manifestation in time and space and, ultimately, to the heavenly bodies, when one's perception is limited to mere subjective semblance? One cannot. One's best scientific efforts are limited to drawing inferences from the semblances observed. One either begins with uncritical assumptions about the nature of things, or else one admits that the philosophical depths of things are precluded from scientific scrutiny. No doubt the aim of the Democritean philosopher-scientist is to ascertain the causes of the observed appearances. Yet, according to his own natural philosophy, the cause of one phenomenon can only be explained by another phenomenon, and so on. Since one never gets beyond the appearances of things to their rational form, one is left with a strictly mechanistic view of the natural world. According to Marx, this makes Democritus into a classic determinist. Everything is caused by something else, something external to it, and the sequence of causes is endless.

Marx shuns such mechanistic determinism. Like Epicurus, he takes seriously the defining role of human thought in determining the truth of the natural world. Essentially Marx claims that the nature of the atom—its true being—is disclosed only when one thinks about it in the right way. This is so not because the atom is an elusive entity that requires to be somehow harnessed by thought before its secret nature can be revealed. On the contrary, Marx's dialectical account holds that the atom's truth and being *is* what is conceived of it. For Marx—and here the influence of Hegel is decisive—the logic of thinking and the logic of being coincide. *Thinking* about the atom (in the right way, that is, dialectically) is to grasp *the atom.* The consequences of this view are staggering, for it implies that a rigorous examination of atomic being will disclose not only the truth of the atom, but in that truth, the rational continuity of atoms and nature as a whole. Moreover, to the extent that human beings are part of nature, it implies that we too are somehow reflected in the nature of atomic being.

Strictly speaking, *any* way of thinking about the natural world is acceptable to the Epicurean frame of mind. For it is not necessity that characterizes the relation between thought and being, as it is for Democritus, but chance. Accordingly, whatever is abstractly possible, whatever can be conceived about the world, is credible. The only criterion in the determination of knowledge is the effect it might have on our well being. However, as Marx points out, this extreme subjectivism substitutes peace of mind for genuine knowledge: "Epicurus therefore proceeds with a boundless nonchalance in the explanation of separate physical phenomena.... And [he] confesses finally that his method of explaining aims only at the *ataraxy of self-consciousness, not at knowledge of nature in and for itself.*"[4] Though Marx accepts the definitive role of thought in the determination of being, his aim is quite different from Epicurus's. Where Epicurus is a moralist at heart who reduces everything to the well-being of human subjects, the young Marx is a scientist at heart who will settle for nothing less than a systematic knowledge of nature. Consequently, Marx will follow the Epicurean account of the atom only up to a certain point. Let us now turn to the details of this account.

For both Democritus and Epicurus the two basic principles of the physical world are the same: atoms and the void. Both agree that, before all else, the natural world consists of matter (atoms) and the nothingness of abstract space (the void). Furthermore, both define atoms as mobile, not static entities. It is in their account of the nature and origin of atomic motion that the two are distinguished. Marx outlines this difference as follows:

> Epicurus assumes a threefold motion of the atoms in the void.
> One motion is the fall in a straight line, the second originates
> in the deviation of the atom from the straight line, and the
> third is established through the repulsion of the many atoms.
> Both Democritus and Epicurus accept the first and the third
> motion. The declination of the atom from the straight line
> differentiates the one from the other.[5]

Let us begin with the idea that atoms exist in the void of empty space. Though Marx does not explicitly put it this way, the distinction of atoms from

---

4 MECW, pp. 44, 45; MEGA, I, 1/1, pp. 23, 24.

5 MECW, p. 46; MEGA, I, 1/1, p. 25.

---

the void is a quintessentially *dialectical* relation. By "dialectical" I mean both that the logic that defines the relation is binary *and* that it involves an essential negation. Accordingly, the picture we have looks something like this. In its most basic sense, nature is understood as a negative relation between two aboriginal concepts: atoms and the void. To distinguish between atoms and the void, says Marx, is to acknowledge that being, in its most rudimentary sense, is defined by what *is not*. It is only by means of a negative relation to the void that the atom is understood in any positive sense. Before all else, the atom is not-the-void. This initial negation, however, is external to the atom's own being. It is not the atom's own negation that defines it, but the negation of an otherness opposed to it. At this point, then, the atom's being is only relative; its determinateness depends exclusively on something else, on the otherness of the void. As Marx would have it, this is the most basic insight of Greek atomism.

How does the attribution of a falling motion modify this initial understanding of the atom? According to Marx (and Epicurus), not much. Insofar as the atom moves in a straight line its being is still relative, for the uniform motion of falling adds no determinacy to it. Neither solidity nor substance may be attributed to falling atoms, for all individual distinctiveness is washed away in the uniformity of motion in a straight line. Far from distinguishing atoms from the initial, relative being established in their not being the void, motion in a straight line merely emphasizes their utter lack of determinacy. As Marx puts it, "The motion of falling is the motion of non-self-sufficiency."[6]

We seem to be faced with a contradiction. If atoms are understood in this way, then they are devoid of any substance of their own by which we might measure their being or distinguish them as something rather than something else. Insofar as atoms are understood in purely spatial terms—as a spatial point (not-being-the-void) and as motion in a straight line—their being is relative. In not-being-the-void, atoms are understood only in the minimal sense of *not* being nothing. The atom is no more than the-opposite-of-nothing: it is sheer, undifferentiated matter. Yet such a conception is wholly lacking in *form*; and the falling motion does nothing to augment this formless materiality. In fact, whatever minimal determinateness the atom may have possessed by being contrasted to the void is effectively surrendered to the falling motion of the straight line. Conceived in this way, therefore, the atom is devoid of all substantiality. It is, in effect, nothing! As Marx points out, the implication of this conception of the atom could not be graver for our understanding of nature: "The consequence of this for the monads as well as for the atoms would therefore be—since they are in constant motion—that neither monads nor atoms exist."[7]

According to Marx, this must be the conclusion of Democritus, who

---

6   MECW, p. 49; MEGA, I, 1/1, p. 28.

7   MECW, p. 48; MEGA, I, 1/1, p. 27.

---

attributes only the uniform falling motion to atoms. Yet such a conclusion is untenable, for the atom cannot lose its substantiality. It cannot be nothing. Our most basic intuition tells us the opposite: the atom must be the *negation of nothing*, the negation of the abstract space of the void. This dilemma is what must have led Epicurus to the thought of the atom's declination from the straight line. In order for the atom to have genuine self-sufficiency, it cannot be conceived as the immediate negation of abstract space. The negation within it must be made explicit. Accordingly, the truth of the atom is not the uniformity of its motion in a straight line, but the *deviation* from this motion. It is in the negation of its uniform motion that the atom is freed from relative being. For Marx, this deviating motion is the crux of Epicurean atomism.

It is in deviating from the straight line that the concept of the atom is first realized and made complete; for it is only in the motion of declination that its minimal material determination acquires *form*. Marx describes the difference between the two types of atomic motion, and their inherent opposition, in the following passage:

> If Epicurus therefore represents the materiality of the atom in terms of its motion along a straight line, he has given reality to its form-determination in the declination from the straight line, and these opposed determinations are represented as directly opposed motions.[8]

Yet this opposition is now fully determinate; it is, in other words, the atom's *own* opposition. For this reason, the atom is no longer conceived as a mere relative being, determined as the simple negation of the void. The swerving atom is a *self-sufficient* entity that has the source of its being—the negation of the void—not externally, but within itself. As such, according to Marx, it embodies the form of all nature, even of nature's universal manifestation as heavenly bodies: "The atoms are purely self-sufficient bodies or rather bodies conceived in absolute self-sufficiency, like the heavenly bodies. Hence, again like the heavenly bodies, they move not in straight, but in oblique lines."[9] Atoms must not be understood merely as the raw material of nature; in their self-sufficiency, *they embody the form of life itself.* The deviating motion of declination is itself an outward manifestation of the inner logic of the atom: "declination represents the real soul of the atom, the concept of abstract individuality."[10]

The third form of atomic motion, repulsion, is a necessary consequence of the declination of the atom. In swerving, the atom not only negates its relative

---

8 MECW, p. 49; MEGA, I, 1/1, p. 28.

9 MECW, p. 49; MEGA, I, 1/1, p. 28.

10 MECW, p. 50; MEGA, I, 1/1, p. 29.

---

existence by deviating from the motion in a straight line, as we have seen, but it also "abstracts from the opposing being and withdraws itself from it." In the negation of its regular movement within the void, the atom realizes its own existence, abstractly, by relating itself to itself. This realization, moreover, may be viewed in both a positive and a negative sense. The movement of declination negates the atom's simple material determination; yet in so doing, it establishes the atom's own independent being. In this way, the atom realizes itself as a kind of abstract individuality or as what Marx calls being-for-self. Yet implied in the atom's being-for-self is the relation to other selves like itself. For in withdrawing into itself, negating all otherness in the act of self-relation, the atom necessarily establishes a negative relation to that which it negates. To think of the atom as a self-relation in this sense, therefore, requires that we think of the atom in terms of its determinate relationships with other beings like itself, even if these relationships are essentially negative. For the atom cannot realize its self-related identity except in relation to something like itself—another atom. In order to be conceived as an independent, free-standing entity, therefore, the atom must be differentiated from a being that is equally independent and free-standing. In the act of *repulsion* the atom is identified as a positive self-relation through its confrontation with other atoms like itself. Repulsion, says Marx, is the necessary realization of the *lex atomi*—the law of the atom.[11]

This point cannot be overemphasized. In the swerving motion attributed to the atom by Epicurus, and in the corresponding act of repulsion, whereby the atom distinguishes itself by repulsing other atoms from itself, the atom is liberated from external determination and is revealed to be an essentially *self-related* entity. Only when the atom is understood in this sense may it justifiably be designated the elementary particle of life. Understood dialectically, the atom is a dynamic, self-related entity whose form is defined by two intrinsic negations. The atom is not only *not* nothing (through the declination from the straight line), it is also *not* another atom (through the repulsion of other atoms from itself). It is itself—yet not as a clump of raw matter, as a naïve positivist might have it, but as a dynamic self-relation. Only in this sense is the atom a meaningful natural principle, for only as a negative self-relation is the atom distinctively itself: a genuine (if still abstract) individuality.

Marx's dialectical explication of the Epicurean atom is very similar to

---

11 The precise passage from Marx's *Dissertation* runs as follows: "But what is contained herein, namely, [*the atom's*] *negation of all relation to something else, must be realized, positively established.* This can only be done if *the being* [*Dasein*] *to which it relates itself is none other than itself,* hence equally *an atom,* and, since it itself is directly determined, *many atoms. The repulsion of the many atoms is therefore the necessary realization of the lex atomi*" (MECW, 1, p. 51; MEGA, I, 1/1, p. 30).

Hegel's analysis of the concept being-for-self (*Fürsichsein*) in the *Science of Logic*. This is an important observation because, for Hegel, being-for-self is the logical form of human consciousness. According to his analysis, self-consciousness is understood as a being-for-self in that it relates to its object as to its own self; it is, in this sense, a "reflectedness-into-self [*In-sich-Reflektiertsein*]". Being-for-self, in other words, is a mode of being in which the relation to other is no longer external (like the relation of the atom and the void), but has been taken up into the structure of being. As a general category, being-for-self "consists in having so transcended limitation, its otherness, that it is, as this negation, the infinite return into itself."[12] Self-consciousness, according to this logic, is "being-for-self as consummated [*vollbracht*] and posited; the side of connection with an other, with an external object, is removed." Understood in this way, self-consciousness has the presence of infinity within it: it is no longer a product of determinations external to it, but is limited only by its own determinateness.[13]

Marx will draw the same parallel: in his view, the fact that the atom is necessarily characterized as being-for-self demonstrates that the rationality of nature is no different from the rationality of human consciousness. This is evident in the idea of repulsion, which, according to Marx, is "the first form of self-consciousness".[14] Just as self-consciousness, according to the Hegelian analysis, is conceived as a relation of self and other, a dynamic union that has the presence of infinity within it, the atom is a synthesis of self-relation and relation-to-other that is the elementary principle of all nature. This synthesis is made actual in the atom's repulsion, where the negation inherent in its raw identity (i.e., the atom understood as not nothing or not-the-void) is made explicit in the act of differentiating the other atom from itself. In this act the atom is realized,

---

12 G. W. F. Hegel, *Hegel's Science of Logic*, trans. A. V. Miller (Atlantic Highlands, NJ: Humanities Press International, 1969), p. 158. In a related passage, Hegel describes being-for-self as "the polemical, negative attitude towards the limiting other, and through this negation of the latter is a reflectedness-into-self, although *along* with this return of consciousness into itself and the ideality of the object, the *reality* of the object is *also* still preserved, in that it is *at the same time* known as an external existence" (Ibid).

13 In the *Phenomenology*, Hegel describes the negative self-relation of consciousness as a movement of identity and sundering within consciousness: "Infinity, or this absolute unrest of pure self-movement, in which whatever is determined in one way or another, e.g. as being, is rather the opposite of this determinateness, this no doubt has been from the start the soul of all that has gone before ..." (*Hegel's Phenomenology of Spirit*, trans. A. V. Miller [Oxford: Oxford University Press, 1977], p. 101).

14 MECW, 1, p. 52; MEGA, I, 1/1, p. 31.

as Marx puts it, as a synthetic union of matter and form. "In the repulsion of the atoms, therefore, their materiality, which was posited in the fall in a straight line, and their form-determination, which was established in the declination, are united synthetically."[15] Accordingly, the atom is not only mere matter, the raw stuff of nature, nor is it a mere thought, some convenient concept to harness and make known the essence of nature. In the atom, matter and form are united in a dialectical unity that is neither a formal abstraction nor a lifeless immediacy, but a dynamic, self-related being that has the force of life present within it.

At this point Marx turns the analysis against Epicurus. For Epicurus was reluctant to embrace the conclusions implied in his dynamic conception of nature; namely that as a *negative* self-relation the atom is defined by its relation to what it is *not*, that is, to the sequence of logical mediations that give it further and deeper determinacy. The implication of this view is that the atom is fully realized only in the *system* of nature. Marx's own analysis demonstrates that the antinomies between form and matter which characterize the entire development of the atom—from the atom as being-for-self to its qualitative existence to its appearance in the world of space and time—are resolved only in the universality of the heavenly bodies. The truth of the atom lies not in itself, but in the system of nature of which it is a fundamental element.

This account may sound rather bizarre at first; certainly it does not strike us as typically Marxian. Yet even in this examination of Epicurus's philosophy of nature, Marx was working toward a theory of praxis. Like Hegel, however, he realized that before one may speak of praxis or of any philosophy of action, it is necessary to grasp the relation of ideas and reality. If one wishes to speak of the ought, of what one *ought* to do, one must understand the relation of the ought and the is, the relation of reason and reality (or, in this case, of reason and *nature*). What Marx sought to delineate in his analysis of atomic being, therefore, was that reason and nature are not distinct from one another, but that, on the contrary, their relation is *dialectical*. Marx's speculative analysis of the atom demonstrates that nature is *ideal*; or, to put it in the Hegelian language Marx utilized, that the form of nature is the form of consciousness. If this is true, if the rationality of human consciousness is *like* the rationality of nature, then it is possible to work out a theory of freedom that is not antithetical to nature, but is, in fact, rooted in the very logic of nature. As I see it, this is precisely what

---

15   MECW, 1, p. 52; MEGA, I, 1/1, p. 31. By "synthetic unity" Marx seems to have
      in mind the Kantian distinction between analytical and synthetic judgments.
      Whereas an analytical judgment expresses nothing in the predicate which is
      not in already in the concept of the subject, a synthetic judgment is expansive,
      increasing the given cognition. A "synthetic unity" in this sense is a unity larger
      than the sum of its parts (Immanuel Kant, *Prolegomena* [Lasalle, IL: Open
      Court, 1902], pp. 14–16). Cf. Hegel, *Science of Logic*, pp. 786–818.

Marx tried to do, and it led him to formulate a theory of praxis as a necessary correlate to his theory of nature.

3. FROM NATURE TO CONSCIOUSNESS TO FREEDOM

Marx's analysis of the atom sets the terms for a speculative consideration of nature as a whole. Like the atom, nature itself is ideal, a complex system of form and matter governed not externally, but by an immanent, rational necessity. For this reason, nature is not formally distinct from the experience of human beings: the form of consciousness *is* the form of nature. Both are determined by an immanent, dynamic logic. This holds not only for atomic being, but, as Marx contends (against Epicurus), extends to the highest reaches of nature where the abstract form of individual self-related atoms culminates in the unified system of celestial bodies. The heavenly bodies are atoms become concrete and real, the universal in nature. Thus, it is neither the material determination of nature in itself nor the formal determination of abstract individual consciousness that is the governing principle of nature; rather, it is the unity of both in what Marx calls "the absoluteness and freedom of self-consciousness". Against Epicurus, however, it is not the form of individuality, but self-conscious universality—the universal which in free distinction from itself knows at the same time its own concrete affirmation—that expresses the truth of an animate nature as much ideal as it is real. As a whole, then, the natural world is conceived not as alien to the human world, but as bound together with it as an essential moment of the rational activity of free self-consciousness.

This is not to say, however, that human being can be reduced to natural being, or *vice versa*. Though they share the form of self-conscious reason and, as such, are dialectically linked, man and nature are not identical, for their unity is burdened with negation. As we have seen, there is an undeniable parallel between the *lex atomi*, the law of the atom, and the *lex hominis*, the law of the human—both are defined as self-relating, material being. To extrapolate, we may say that to be fully human means not only to exist, to have immediate, material being, but also to be conscious of one's existence. Thus, to exist as a genuinely free individual involves some minimal recognition of one's material determination. Yet implied in such recognition is both an acceptance of one's natural immediacy, and a rejection of the limits imposed by the burden of such immediacy. *To be self-consciously human is to be both for and against nature.* In this sense, the human being is like the atom because it becomes actual only when it frees itself from relative determination and relates itself to itself. Marx puts it as follows: "Thus man ceases to be a product of nature [*Naturprodukt*] only when the other being to which he relates himself is not a different existence but is itself an individual human being, even if it is not yet spirit [*Geist*]."[16] In other

---

16 MECW, 1, p. 52; MEGA, I, 1/1, p. 31.

---

words, in order for humanity to realize the truth of its inner being, it must free itself from determination by external, relative being (as in the declination of the atom), and realize itself as its own proper object (as in the repulsion of the atom from itself). At a very basic level then—what Marx calls abstract individuality—human beings realize the concept of their being and become free only when their relative being and the raw instincts associated with "the power of desire and of mere nature" have been crushed. Only when such dependence on mere nature has been negated and transcended (*aufgehoben*) do human beings arrive on the doorstep of self-consciousness; for it is only then that they are freed to determine themselves in relation to other human beings. Though such self-consciousness is still abstract—it lacks qualitative and historical determination—it nonetheless contains the seed of full spiritual actualization.

4. CONCLUSION

Recognition of the negativity implied in the relation of man to nature is the first step toward a new conception of the activity of philosophy because it redefines the concept of human autonomy. According to the initial position of the youthful Marx, it is impossible to fully understand what it means to be human without grasping the *dialectical* relation of man and nature. In its most basic sense, this means that to exist as a free individual is to recognize both one's material determination in and through nature, and one's formal determination against nature. To be human, in other words, is both to be natural, possessing immediate, material being, and to break away from such material determination in the act of free, self-conscious determination. This second, explicitly negative moment is of special interest, for it is here that we see the origins of Marx's conception of human praxis as a form of activity directed against the external world. In order to realize itself concretely, human self-consciousness must be active in the creation of a world where free interaction between individuals is possible. Just as the atom attains to self-sufficiency only when it declines from the straight line and repels others from itself, human consciousness must be active in the world as praxis and as critique in order to gain autonomy and experience genuine freedom.

WORKS CITED

Hegel, G. W. F., *Hegel's Phenomenology of Spirit*, trans. A. V. Miller (Oxford: Oxford University Press, 1977).

———, *Hegel's Science of Logic*, trans. A. V. Miller (Atlantic Highlands, NJ: Humanities Press International, 1969).

Kant, Immanuel, *Prolegomena to Any Future Metaphysics That Can Qualify as a Science* (La Salle, IL: Open Court, 1902).

Marx, Karl and Friedrich Engels, *Karl Marx/Frederick Engels Collected Works* (New York: International Publishers, 1975), Vol. 1, *Marx: 1835–1843*.

———, *Marx/Engels Historisch-Kritische Gesamtausgabe*, Erste Abteilung (Frankfurt: Marx-Engels Archiv, Verlagsgesellschaft M.B.H., 1927), Vol. 1.

THE FIXATION OF SATISFACTION:
EPICURUS AND PEIRCE ON THE GOAL

David B. Suits

There is probably great value in coming to Epicurus by beginning, as some writers do, with the notion of eudaimonia (perhaps in Aristotle) and then seeing how it is worked out with a hedonist swerve in Epicurus. But I want to look to Epicurus's distant future instead of his recent past. There are some interesting parallels between the ideas of Epicurus and the ideas of C. S. Peirce over two thousand years later. Both of them were empiricists, atomists, and antideterminists. Peirce explicitly agrees with "Lucretius and his great master": "If I make atoms swerve—and I do—I make them swerve but very very little...." This is part of what Peirce calls *tychism*, "the doctrine that absolute chance is a factor of the universe" (6.201).[1]

But in offering some parallels between these two philosophers, I do not mean to say either that Epicurus was a Peircean or that Peirce was an Epicurean.[2] Peirce was critical of two key elements in Epicureanism, namely, hedonism and egoism.[3] And while Epicurus advised us to live a simple life, Peirce was a kind of modern day epicure.[4] Still, there is a particularly interesting parallel between the two thinkers which I want to draw out, because it may be useful in helping us to better understand Epicurus's notions of katastematic pleasure and *ataraxia*.

PEIRCE ON DOUBT AND BELIEF

In "The Fixation of Belief" and "How to Make our Ideas Clear",[5] two articles published in *Popular Science Monthly* in 1877 and 1878, Peirce lays out some important differences between doubt and belief (in the sense of full conviction). Doubt, we are told, is a kind of "irritation" of thought; it is "thought in action", which is a mental struggle to attain belief (or, as he sometimes says,

---

1   All references to Peirce will be by volume number followed by paragraph number from *The Collected Papers of Charles Sanders Peirce*, vols. 1–6, ed. Charles Hartshorne and Paul Weiss, 1931–1935; vols. 7–8, ed. A. W. Burk, 1958 (Cambridge, MA: Harvard University Press).

2   In all of Peirce's *Collected Papers*, Epicurus is mentioned only ten times (and Lucretius five times).

3   On hedonism see 1.603f, 1.614, and 5.559–5.563; on egoism see 2.652f and 5.402 n. 2.

4   An excellent biography is provided by Joseph Brent, *Charles Sanders Peirce: A Life* (Bloomington, IN: Indiana University Press, 1993).

5   5.358–5.387 and 5.388–5.410, respectively. See also 7.313–7.325, and elsewhere.

"the settlement of opinion"). In contrast, belief is "thought at rest"; it is a "calm and satisfactory state", and because it is a kind of satisfaction, "we do not wish to avoid [it], or to change [it] to a belief in anything else" (5.372). The irritation of thought, the goal of which is its own riddance, is termed "inquiry", although Peirce warns us that this term may in some cases seem overly dramatic. The only immediate motive for attaining a belief is the feeling of dissatisfaction which is doubt. Doubt having been destroyed by its own activity, we are in a condition of contentedness which has certain practical consequences, namely, that we are now prepared to act in accordance with the belief, should a suitable occasion for action present itself. This condition Peirce calls habit.

Habits, however, are not guaranteed to be successful. The world is full of surprises, and if an action on the basis of some belief does not do what we expect it to, then we are thrown back into a state of doubt. But doubt is precisely what is irritating, unsatisfactory, full of motive away from itself, and so we seek a new belief. It may be suggested that the reason we were surprised in the first place was that our belief was not true, and so it may be suggested that what we really want, when we are experiencing the irritation of doubt and inquiry, is not simply belief, but rather true belief. "But put this fancy to the test", Peirce says, "and it proves groundless; for as soon as a firm belief is reached we are entirely satisfied...." "The most that can be maintained is, that we seek for a belief that we shall *think* to be true. But we think each one of our beliefs to be true, and, indeed, it is mere tautology to say so" (5.375). In 1903 Peirce added this footnote: "For truth is neither more nor less than that character of a proposition which consists in this, that belief in the proposition would, with sufficient experience and reflection, lead us to conduct as would tend to satisfy the desires we should then have" (5.375 n.2).

The phenomenon of the occasional disintegration of belief back into doubt should lead us to wonder, not how to make beliefs true, but rather how to make beliefs *stable*—we seek the fixation of belief. The problem is that no belief carries with it internal marks which indicate its stability or robustness in the face of challenges, and consequently we are led to a higher order consideration, namely, an examination of the *methods* by which beliefs are formed. We may be able to rank those methods, in hopes of finding and following a method which experience tells us will generate stable beliefs. Peirce discusses four methods of fixing belief, from the simplest and least trustworthy, to the most sophisticated.

The first and most primitive method Peirce calls the method of tenacity, which is "taking as answer to a question any we may fancy, and constantly reiterating it to ourselves, dwelling on all which may conduce to that belief, and learning to turn with contempt and hatred from anything that might disturb it" (5.377). The problem with such a method is that "the social impulse is against it" (5.378): unless we are hermits, we are bound to discover that other people have beliefs different from our own; such a realization will cause us to wonder about our own beliefs.

A better method would therefore be a method of fixing beliefs in a whole community of persons, so that there would be no clash of opinions. Force and indoctrination form the basis of this "method of authority". It is "one of the chief means of upholding correct theological and political doctrines, and of preserving their universal or catholic character" (5.379), and "except the geological epochs, there are no periods of time so vast as those which are measured by" the products of this method (5.380). Still, even given its success in producing very stable beliefs in large communities, no authority can police *all* the beliefs which the people of a community may develop. Moreover, there will always be some communication among communities, and so even in the most authoritative of societies, there will be differences of opinion, and when that happens, there will be some disintegration of belief into doubt for the same reason that belief was not stable under the method of tenacity. Individual beliefs held tenaciously, and popular opinions enforced by a community, will be seen by some people to have been "determined by caprice either of themselves or of those who originated the popular opinions" (5.382). So both of the first two methods suffer because the opinions to which they give rise will be seen to be accidental, and what is accidental is unreliable.

The solution is to find some method which has to do with not only who determines the belief, but also what the content of that belief is. "Let the action of natural preferences be unimpeded, then, and under their influence let men, conversing together and regarding matters in different lights, gradually develop beliefs in harmony with natural causes" (5.382). Under this "*a priori* method", propositions are to be believed because they seem "agreeable to reason". Unfortunately, accident is not fully eliminated, for what is agreeable to one person's reason might not be agreeable to another's, and what is thought reasonable in one era might be discounted in another. This method "makes of inquiry something similar to the development of taste; but taste, unfortunately, is always more or less a matter of fashion", and so this method, while it "eliminates the effect of some causal circumstances, only magnifies that of others" (5.383).

The fourth method of fixing belief is a solution to the problems (principally the problem of the accidental character of belief) of the first three. The method of science postulates an external permanency "upon which our thinking has no effect" (5.384) but which has regular and predictable effects on our experiences. To the extent that our beliefs are in harmony with these external permanencies, then to that extent the action of the world upon us occasions no doubts, either about individual beliefs, or about the method used to attain them. We are satisfied with our beliefs, and when they are products of a reliable method, we can be confident that we will *remain* satisfied (excluding error in the use of the method, and excluding those questions for which we have not yet found an answer).

Louis Loeb points out that the first three methods are ultimately unsatisfactory because they generate beliefs which have been determined by something extraneous to the facts. "This argument", he says, "*presupposes* that belief characteristically aims at the truth. Were this not the case, the line of reflection Peirce describes would not be unsettling. Peirce endorses the presupposition: 'A Man … wishes his opinions to coincide with the facts, and … there is no reason why the results of those three first methods should do so.'"[6]

But we ought to ask "Why would one wish one's opinion to coincide with the facts? What would be the advantage?" I take it that the introduction of the notions of "fact" and "coinciding with" is motivated by the failure of the first three methods. But the failure is not a failure to produce beliefs which coincide with the facts; it is not as though all along one were aiming at the facts. Rather, the failure is simply a failure to produce stable beliefs. That is to say, if one could, somehow, be confident that one's present beliefs would remain forever stable, then one could have no motive to seek something other or better. There is no criterion for judging the matter other than belief itself—that is, satisfaction itself. The only further issue, then, is whether the satisfaction will continue, and it is *that* concern which motivates the desire that beliefs "coincide with the facts". The assumption is that by introducing the notion of fact—that is, of "some external permanency"—one will have a basis for a method for ensuring stability; "the only rational ground for preferring the method of [scientific] reasoning to the other methods is that it fixes belief more surely" (7.325).

Let the foregoing serve as a brief summary of the purpose and methods of fixing belief. I have mentioned Peirce's views in psycho-epistemology because I think there is a pleasing and useful parallel with some of Epicurus's ideas concerning pleasure and tranquillity in psycho-ethics. In order to draw the analogy out, we need to understand something of Epicurus's notion of katastematic pleasure.

KINETIC AND KATASTEMATIC PLEASURE

The difference between kinetic and katastematic pleasure is mentioned without elaboration in Diogenes Laertius X.136. "Kinetic" implies motion or change. Thus, kinetic pleasures are pleasurable changes. It is not that whenever there are changes, we take pleasure in them; rather, there is a kind of pleasure— kinetic pleasure—one of whose characteristics is that we experience a change of state. Whenever we undergo some pleasant change, such as satisfying a desire, the pleasure is of the kinetic type. If "kinetic" refers to change, then "katastematic" refers to non-change, or, we might say, a condition of satisfaction. Katastematic pleasure, then, is characterized by our remaining in a state. Or one could also say that kinetic pleasures are characterized by engagement in some activity, specifically some activity either away from something or towards something,

---

6   Louis E. Loeb, "Sextus, Descartes, Hume, and Peirce: On Securing Settled Doxastic States", *Noûs* 32 (1998), pp. 205–230, at p. 208.

either case implying a kind of struggle (although, as we will see later, the word "struggle" is a bit too dramatic). Katastematic pleasures, on the other hand, are pleasures we take in, or because of, or during our relative inactivity—that is to say, in our not having to struggle away from anything or towards anything. I will elaborate on these ideas below. But we may as well admit at once that the distinction is vague.

If I have a headache, I take some aspirin, and not long thereafter I feel the pain receding. Eventually I am no longer in pain. Now, it is one thing to experience the headache's going away, when I am still in some pain, and another thing to be in a state without a headache at all. There is, then, the kinetic pleasure of the headache's going away, and there is the katastematic pleasure of not having a headache.

In addition, there are, I perceive, two kinds of katastematic pleasure. The distinction has been hinted at now and again in the literature, but I want to make it explicit. (1) The headache has just now finally disappeared, and so I am in a state of *relief* from pain; I am in a state of having become satisfied. (2) It would usually be odd to say, some days later, that I am in a state of relief from a headache, and so katastematic pleasure of the second kind is a condition wherein I do not even consider the headache—I neither have a headache nor attend to the memory of it; I am in a state not unlike a person who never had a headache at all.

So it is also with mental disturbances. Suppose I am troubled in mind; I am worried about something—my job performance, perhaps. Now my attitude begins to change, either on account of my awareness of some change in the world (perhaps my employer praises me or gives me a raise), or in some change in my desires (perhaps I no longer care to please my employer). In any case, my anxiety recedes. This is one kind of kinetic pleasure. Once the anxiety has vanished, I am in a state of relief from that anxiety. This is a katastematic pleasure of the first sort—a state of having been satisfied. And eventually not only am I not concerned about my job, I am not even attending to having been relieved of the former anxiety, and so I have attained a katastematic satisfaction of the second kind: a state of not being anxious, but also of not having just been relieved of anxiety.

Epicurus's notions of pleasure in motion and pleasure in rest have their analogs in Peirce's concepts of doubt and belief. "Thought in action [doubt] has for its only possible motive the attainment of thought at rest [belief]; and whatever does not refer to belief is no part of the thought itself" (5.396). To adopt Epicurean terminology, we might say that *kinetic* thought has for its sole motive *katastematic* thought. In addition, belief (katastematic thought) involves the creation of some habit—a readiness for action—such that there can be *variations* of a habit without changing its nature: "If beliefs do not differ in this respect, if they appease the same doubt by producing the same rule of action, then no mere differences in the manner of consciousness of them can make them different beliefs, any more than playing a tune in different keys is playing different tunes" (5.398). Again, "the whole function of thought is to produce habits of action; and … whatever there is connected with a thought, but irrelevant to its purpose, is an accretion to it, but no part of it" (5.400). Those comments by Peirce are echoes of Epicurus: "As soon as the feeling of pain produced by want is removed, pleasure in the flesh will not increase but is only varied".[7]

I suggest, then, that Epicurean katastematic pleasure is analogous to Peircean belief as habit.[8] When doubt and inquiry have come to an end, we have attained the calm state of belief. But this state of mind is not nothing. That is, it is not simply the absence of doubt (which might also describe a dead person). Rather, it is the undisturbed *working* of habit—our going through our activities without concern or question.

I take Epicurus as claiming that our hedonistic goal is to attain the fixation of katastematic satisfaction of the second sort, in both body and mind. Satisfaction in the body is called *aponia*; satisfaction in the mind is called *ataraxia*. We are ideally to be like the gods, who are neither being relieved of pain, nor in a state of just having been relieved of pain. This is so, because the gods are not the sort to have been in pain in the first place.

John Cooper says that "it seems possible, or even likely, that in his own writings Epicurus was not always careful to make it clear that what he intended as the goal of life was, as we could put it, a certain state of consciousness caused or occasioned by the complete absence of pain and distress."[9] I am not at all convinced that "state of consciousness" is apt. Cooper takes Epicurus to mean that our highest good is a perception or consciousness of not being in pain or distress; this is important, he says, in order to avoid ancient criticisms of Epicurus that he makes our highest good to be like being dead (or at least asleep).[10] On my view, however, Epicurus identifies our highest good with some aspect of second order katastematic satisfaction, which is not so much a pleasurable state of consciousness (that is, a pleasurable perception of our condition), nor a condition of perfect quiescence, but rather a style of living wherein there are no serious problems. For example, since we are animals, we must periodically eat, and Epicurus recommends that we adopt a life style wherein easily obtained food is satisfactory for us; we ought not to yearn for richer foods, or a greater

---

7 *Kuriai Doxai (KD)* 18. All references to Epicurus's works will be to *The Epicurus Reader: Selected Writings and Testimonia*, trans. Brad Inwood and L. P. Gerson (Indianapolis: Hackett Publishing Company, 1994).

8 There is also an alluring parallel between Peircean habit and Epicurean *prolepsis*.

9 John M. Cooper, *Reason and Emotion: Essays on Ancient Moral Psychology and Moral Theory* (Princeton: Princeton University Press, 1999), pp. 496–497.

10 D. L. II.89.

---

variety of foods, or foods which will bring discomfort later on, or foods which are difficult to get. The result is that we are *easily satisfied*, and the result of being easily satisfied is that we can turn our attention to (or rather keep our attention on) other things without worry or concern about food: we are in a condition to exercise a healthy body and mind without the distractions of discomforts, nor even the threat of discomforts, *nor even the distractions of recently having been in discomfort.*

Here are two more everyday examples. In riding a bicycle, small variations—leaning slightly this way or that—are necessary in order to keep the bicycle on a straight track. But these small corrections are (after we have developed the habits necessary for riding bicycles) automatic, easy, and unnoticed. Walking, too, is usually no struggle (hence not a *problem*) if we have no physical impediments. An infant is clumsy at walking; we adults do it effortlessly, not even noticing that walking consists in rhythmically falling forward and catching ourselves. Our habits are so stable (because so successful) that no attention need be given to them.

As Peirce says, "Belief is not a momentary mode of consciousness; it is a habit of mind essentially enduring for some time, and mostly (at least) unconscious; and like other habits, it is (until it meets with some surprise that begins its dissolution) perfectly self-satisfied" (5.417). Self-satisfied, but usually not self-aware. The function of a habit is that it prepares me for action in a situation where my attention dwells elsewhere. In this it may be distinguished from policy, which is a regular way of acting which *is* self-aware; that is, when I act out of policy, I attend to the policy in order to determine the action, whereas in acting from habit, I am attending to the goal of the action, or to some other concern, and the habit takes care of the details.

But both habits and policies reduce the burden of doubt. When Epicurus recommends that we submit all choices to scrutiny,[11] we need not take him to mean each and every choice of each and every action on each and every occasion, because that would create a practically insuperable barrier to a serene life. It is true that when a habit or policy is in development, we do have to attend to it. But once in place, habits and policies help keep us satisfied, and only when something new or surprising presents itself will we have to pause for a reevaluation.

Neither kinetic pleasures which are relievings of pain nor katastematic pleasures of the first sort are ideals, because both require us to have been in pain. Both kinetic pleasure and the first stage of katastematic satisfaction can be brought about by putting oneself in pain and then relieving oneself of the pain. But purposefully putting oneself in pain for the sake of relief of that very pain is something Epicurus nowhere recommends. He does say that not every

---

11 *Let Men* 132, *KD* 22, 25, *Vatican Saying* (*VS*) 71.

---

pain is to be avoided; there are times when accepting a pain might be prudent. However, that is not because it is pleasurable to be relieved of such a pain, but rather because sometimes putting up with a present pain can make a future katastematic satisfaction of the second kind more likely or more robust. If, for example, I know that certain diseases can be painful, and if I now put up with the minor pain of being inoculated against such diseases, then I am acting out of prudence: I accept a present discomfort for the sake of a future second order katastematic pleasure, namely, never having been in pain brought about by those diseases.

But there is a problem here. We often do seek kinetic pleasures and katastematic satisfactions of the first sort. It seems to be a natural preoccupation with us, for we invent problems to solve; we play games. If there are no challenges, we quickly invent some. We enjoy the kinetic pleasures and the katastematic satisfactions of the first sort which accompany such activities. We even endure the pains of love because of the immense kinetic pleasures and first order katastematic satisfactions which great passions promise. Yet Epicureans "do not believe that the wise man will fall in love.... 'Sexual intercourse', they say, 'never helped anyone, and one must be satisfied if it has not harmed.'"[12] It is difficult to know how far Epicurus went with such advice. Did he recommend that we avoid playing games? Might he have come close to extolling the virtues of something like Stoic detachment? There seems to be something superhuman—even godlike—in an existence which is characterized purely by second order katastematic contentedness. I suspect that if Epicurus would have recommended that we eschew purposely posing pains for the sake of the pleasures of their own riddance, then he would have done so only in those contexts where they create a risk to long-term contentment. In other contexts, such activities might in fact be beneficial. Consider Phillip Mitsis's claim that on Epicurus's view "kinetic pleasures are a matter of rational indifference to our overall happiness."[13] I disagree. First of all, the process of being relieved of some pain is one kind of kinetic pleasure, and it is only by being relieved of pain that we can attain a painless life (unless we start out life in a painless state, and unless nothing comes along to disturb that state). Second, once we are in a stable condition, we need not be indifferent to kinetic pleasures, as long as such pleasures do not pose an undue risk of pain. It may in fact be necessary to have kinetic pleasures. I am, for example, healthy and without fear or anxiety. But I might exercise in order to challenge my body somewhat, in order to keep it healthy. I might pose puzzles and problems to solve, in order to keep my mind active. I can certainly take kinetic pleasure in such physical and mental

---

12 D.L. X.119.

13 Phillip Mitsis, *Epicurus' Ethical Theory: The Pleasures of Invulnerability* (Ithaca: Cornell University Press, 1988), p. 49, n. 99.

---

problem-solution changes, especially when I know that such activities do in fact encourage *aponia* and *ataraxia*.

EPICURUS AND THE FIXATION OF SATISFACTION

Peirce says that "If the premisses [of an inquiry] are not in fact doubted at all, they cannot be more satisfactory than they are" (5.376). Had Epicurus written an analogous claim for his ethics, it might be this: Katastematic pleasure cannot be more satisfactory than it already is. But Peirce adds this footnote:

> We have to acknowledge that doubts about them may spring up later; but we can find no propositions which are not subject to this contingency. We ought to construct our theories so as to provide for such discoveries; first, by making them rest on as great a variety of different considerations as possible, and second, by leaving room for the modifications which cannot be foreseen but which are pretty sure to prove needful. [5.376 n. 1]

A parallel Epicurean footnote might be something like this:

> We have to acknowledge that any satisfactory condition may later on be interrupted by pain or anxiety—there can be no condition not subject to such contingencies (i.e., we are humans, not gods). We ought to achieve *ataraxia* so as to anticipate such possibilities; first, by becoming satisfied in as great a variety of cases or conditions or desires as possible, and second, by leaving room for different ways of satisfying each of our needs which are pretty sure to arise later on (i.e., don't commit to only one way of satisfying a need).

As Mitsis says, "by claiming that kinetic pleasures are mere variants and readily substitutable for one another, Epicurus greatly decreases the vulnerability of our pleasures. If I can achieve the same katastematic satisfaction from a wide range of goods, then I greatly increase my ability of avoiding the frustration of my desires."[14] We might say that redundancy decreases risk, hence increases reliability.

According to Peirce, different beliefs are satisfactions with respect to various habits of action. An epistemological contentment is a kind of confidence that one's method (the method of science, if Peirce is right) is bound to produce stable beliefs on any subject to which it is applied—in the long run. That is, the

14 Ibid., p. 49.

method of science will be able to satisfy our doubts. An analogous claim can be made for Epicurus: different katastematic pleasures are satisfactions with respect to various habits of action. Consider a calm, steady, satisfied state of mind with respect to, say, food. One is not now hungry, and one is confident of having food available when needed. One can also be satisfied with respect to thirst, etc. So each of these is a separate contentment. Overall contentment—*ataraxia*—involves the confidence that one will be able to deal with any minor disturbance which comes along. So one can have episodes of katastematic pleasure without having tranquillity. Tranquillity requires not only stretches of time free from pain and anxiety, but also a confidence that such states will continue. Issues of long-term stability are found throughout Epicurus.[15] So the question is not merely present satisfaction, but a confidence that it will continue. And that confidence will rest upon a secure method for attaining satisfaction.

Epicurus, like Peirce, is a fallabilist. Although there is no final guarantee of success, we can hope for a reliable method which tends to work for satisfaction. If Epicurean satisfaction is anything like Peircean satisfaction, then we ought to be able to describe various methods of fixing Epicurean satisfaction, and I want to see how far the parallel with Peirce can be sustained. What kinds of methods available in ancient Greek culture might do as analogs for Peirce's four methods?

Let us start, as Peirce did, with the least reliable method, tenacity, which is this: once a belief has been achieved—no matter how—you are to maintain that doxastically calm state by refusing to let anything disturb it. I wonder if Stoic detachment might provide an ethical parallel. The ideal Stoic will remain unperturbed in the face of external circumstances, no matter what, because he is detached from all externals: he does not rely on them, he has no hopes for them, he has no expectations regarding them. It is not as though the Stoic sage hides from externals; rather, he makes himself into a pure spectator of them.

Peirce says that "the social impulse is against" the method of tenacity. One's beliefs are bound to clash with other people's beliefs, unless one is a hermit. Analogously, the Stoic ideal might be called into doubt, unless one is successful in being an emotional hermit, utterly unconcerned with the goings on of the world. It seems to me though that one's natural, animal condition is against it. Perhaps Epicurean gods, being physical but not quite animal, are exempt from the attachments—emotional, sexual and others—which humans are drawn to. But humans are in fact not gods, and so however much they try to keep their souls isolated from the world, they are going to be moved by hunger, thirst, pain and sometimes anxiety about what the world will bring next.

---

15 *Let Men* 128, 129, 131, 132, 134f; *KD* 7, 10, 11, 14, 16, 21, 26, 29, 30, 31, 32, 33, 40; *VS* 33, 34, 39, 44, 54, 71, 77, 81. See also *KD* 38.

According to Peirce, the method of authority is a way of fixing belief in a community, and he uses politico-religious power as an example of how long-term, society-wide beliefs might be maintained (by indoctrination—especially of the young—and otherwise by force). For a good example of the recommendation of the method of authority in ancient Greece, we can look to Plato. In *Republic* we are warned that citizens must be made to act together in both belief and sentiment (462a–b). And Plato's *Laws* recommend the regulation of "everything, public and private" (780a), from universal education—the caprice of individual householders is seen as destructive of the community of spirit and character (book seven)—to the punishment of impiety because of the infection which would spread to others if a person is allowed to express impious beliefs (book ten).

Epicurus does not share Plato's zeal for social reform. Rather, we are to "live unknown" and retreat from public life.[16] Epicurus has a distrust of the crowd[17] and advises that we free ourselves "from the prison of general education and politics".[18] There are parallels in Epicurus with Peirce's complaints about the method of authority. For example, in *KD* 36 we find that what is just depends on "the peculiarities of a region", so that what is just is not the same for everyone; and in *KD* 37 we find that a law which is not "in accord with what is useful in mutual associations" is not just.

We move, then, to the *a priori* method, which Peirce says is characterized by letting "the action of natural preferences be unimpeded".

> Systems of this sort have not usually rested upon any observed facts, at least not to any great degree. They have been chiefly adopted because their fundamental propositions seemed "agreeable to reason." This is an apt expression; it does not mean that which agrees with experience, but that which we find ourselves inclined to believe. [5.382]

An analog for the *a priori* method might be Cyrenaicism, in which "natural preferences" would be our natural inclination to avoid every pain and pursue every pleasure. And for Peirce's mention of "agreeable to reason" we could substitute "agreeable to feeling". The latter phrase would not refer to that which agrees with experience (that is, agrees with prudence, for prudence is acting on reasonable expectations built up on the basis of experience), but rather that which we find ourselves inclined to experience (namely, immediate pleasure and the avoidance of immediate pain). But lack of prudence is precisely

---

16 Plutarch, *Against Colotes* 1127de.

17 *VS* 29, 59, 67, 81.

18 *VS* 58. Cf. *VS* 76.

---

the failing of Cyrenaicism. When we are motivated by pain, for example, we are not moved *merely* to rid ourselves of the present pain. And that is because we—we rational animals—are strategizers; we use pleasure and pain as guides to our actions, but neither occurrent pleasure (that is, pleasurable sensation) nor relief from pain is the final goal of action, just as when we are driving down the road, the curb on one side and the center line on the other might be used as guides, but they are not the ends that we seek.

What does it mean to say that pleasure and pain are guides for our choices? They are indicators, telltales, signals, but they are signals of two different types. Pleasure is a signal that we are proceeding correctly, and pain that we are proceeding incorrectly. But even here we must be cautious, because we are not to order our choices by means of these guides alone; the world is far too complex—and, as actors in the world, we are far too complex—to be guided solely by such primitive signals. We must supplement them with prudence, i.e., "sober calculation which searches out the reasons for every choice and avoidance",[19] which teaches us that some pains are acceptable if they are part of the way to greater pleasures or to lesser pains, and that some pleasures ought to be passed over if they give rise to future pains. Humans, that is, can (and *must*) strategize, for if we fail to do so, we may be unpleasantly surprised by pain. In a chess game (as in any other situation of strategy), we ought not to choose the move which gains us the most at the moment, but rather the move which gains us the most overall (i.e., which brings us closer to the goal). In business, I might have to spend money in order to make money. In sports, I might have to practice to the point of fatigue in order to be strong enough to win. In a maze, I might have to go east, south or west in order eventually to exit at the north.

In general, a situation of strategy is a situation in which there is a goal but no immediate and evident access to it, and so what appears to be a route to a goal may not be a route to the goal at all, and what appears not to be a route to the goal may be a route after all. That is, we can err. The having of pleasure does not present itself as a situation of strategy, which is why pleasure is said to be intrinsically good. But the having of pain is a situation of strategy, because something must be done about it. Pleasure, by itself, does not motivate; pain does.[20] But if all routes to goals were direct, then there would be no need to

---

19 *Let Men* 132.

20 The issues here have partly to do with developmental psychology. It seems to me that in unsophisticated organisms, the motivation of pain is precisely and only to its own riddance, and when a mind becomes complex enough to strategize, then even in the absence of pain, it can appreciate the absence of pain as a goal, and so prudence is a defense against possible future pain. This, by the way, is in contrast to Cicero, who, in opposition to Epicurus, claims that "the 'static' condition of feeling no pain exerts no driving power, supplies no impulse to the will...; it is the

strategize. A puzzle is a situation of strategy in which all moves to the goal (and there might be alternative sets of moves) can be discovered in advance: there is an *a priori* method of strategizing. A game, however, is a situation of strategy in which not all moves to the goal can (at least in practice) be calculated in advance. Life, we might say, is like a game we are playing: we must strategize a way to goals, but we are not guaranteed that any strategy will succeed; we must induce, and not deduce, our way.[21]

But Cyrenaicism seems not even to see a puzzle, much less a game. "For with the body we can perceive nothing except what immediately affects it in the present, but with the mind we can also perceive past and future."[22] And the Cyrenaics hold that "bodily pleasures are much better than those of the soul."[23] So Cyrenaicism recommends that we follow whatever is agreeable to present sensation.

The issues of prudence and strategy take us to the fourth method of fixing satisfaction. If the first three methods are unreliable, then we seek something better. "To satisfy our doubts, therefore, it is necessary that a method should be found by which our beliefs may be determined by nothing human, but by some external permanency—by something upon which our thinking has no effect" (5.384). And this is the foundation for the method of science. By analogy, we might think of Epicurus as saying: To reach *ataraxia*—to hold our satisfaction stable—it is necessary that a method should be found by which our satisfaction may be determined by nothing human, but by some external permanency. Epicurus does not make a claim quite like this, but he does have a theory of external permanencies—namely, the atoms—and the atomic theory is the basis for a method of fixing satisfaction. Not only *can* knowledge of the world help us reach tranquillity, but its *only* useful function is as an instrument for tranquillity. "First of all, do not believe that there is any other goal to be achieved by the knowledge of meteorological phenomena, whether they are discussed in conjunction with [physics in general] or on their own, than freedom from disturbance and a secure conviction, just as with the rest [of physics]."[24] And similarly for Peirce: "The only justification for reasoning is that it settles doubts, and when doubt finally ceases, no matter how, the end of reasoning is attained" (7.324). Consequently, "unless investigation is to lead to settled opinion it is of no service to us whatever" (7.334).

---

positive sensation of pleasure and delight that furnishes a motive" (*De Finibus* II.32, Rackham translation).

21 Yet if there is one single aspect which characterizes much of the history of ethical theories, it is, I think, this: that they try to turn the strategies of life into puzzles.

22 *De Finibus* I.55. Cf. *Tusculanae Disputationes* 5.96, *KD* 18, D.L. X.31f, 137.

23 D.L. X.89.

24 *Let Pyth* 85. See also *KD* 10, 11.

In respect to that final method of fixing satisfaction, we can find an additional parallel between Epicurus and Peirce concerning the *social* nature of satisfaction. For both Peirce and Epicurus, a community of like-minded persons is useful (but perhaps not strictly necessary) in reaching tranquillity. On Peirce's view, one is concerned to rid oneself of the dissatisfaction of doubt. But as it turns out, he recommends a method of satisfying our doubts which is social in a very important way: in its assumption of external permanencies, the method of science posits an independent reality, but our beliefs about that reality are not guaranteed to be true, except in the indefinitely long run:

> The real, then, is that which, sooner or later, information and reasoning would finally result in, and which is therefore independent of the vagaries of me and you. Thus, the very origin of the conception of reality shows that this conception essentially involves the notion of a COMMUNITY, without definite limits, and capable of a definite increase of knowledge. [5.311][25]

Of course, a hermit *could* follow the scientific method, but a person could do even better—could have a better chance at producing stable beliefs—in the company of other investigators. And similarly for Epicurus: an egoistic hedonist might achieve *ataraxia* in isolation from others, but he has a better chance if he has the support of friends, because "a life without friends is full of dangerous traps and fear."[26] In *Let Men* 135 we are advised to enlist a "like-minded friend" to help practice Epicurean precepts. And "of the things which wisdom provides for the blessedness of one's whole life, by far the greatest is the possession of friendship."[27]

CONCLUSION

For Peirce, a condition of doubt is an irritation which ends in the satisfaction of belief, whereas for Epicurus, a condition of pain is an irritation which ends in the satisfaction of katastematic pleasure. For Peirce, meta-considerations about the stability of belief lead us to reflect on the methods by which belief might be attained. For Epicurus, meta-considerations about the stability of katastematic pleasure lead us to reflect on the methods by which satisfaction might be attained. For Peirce, the method of science is offered as the most reliable of the methods. For Epicurus, it is prudence, or "sober calculation which searches out the reasons for every choice and avoidance and drives out

---

25 See also 2.220, 2.654f.

26 *De Fin* I.66.

27 *KD* 27. See also *KD* 40, *VS* 23, 34, 52, 78.

the opinions which are the source of the greatest turmoil for men's souls."[28]

I mentioned earlier (note 20) that we are, at a basic level, motivated not by pleasure, but rather by pain. But consider this comment: "And he [Epicurus] uses as a proof that the goal is pleasure the fact that animals, as soon as they are born are satisfied with it but are in conflict with suffering by nature and apart from reason."[29] If we may read "pleasure" as "katastematic pleasure", then I understand the matter this way: we are naturally motivated only when we are in pain, or when we perceive some lack, or anticipate some risk of pain or disturbance. But when we are not in pain, or when we do not perceive a risk, we are not motivated. Our *telos*, as lack of disturbance, fits this description. When we do not have it, we are motivated towards it, and when we do have it, we are satisfied, and so we are not motivated (to leave it).

But why wouldn't our *telos* be, more precisely, *lack of motivation*? Well, it might be—but not under ordinary circumstances. As animals, we cannot be completely free of motivation, because we live in a world of contingencies, most of which cannot be anticipated. We do not live undisturbed in the *intermundia* as the gods do. We might indeed give Stoical advice a try, detaching ourselves from the contingencies of the external world. But we ought to wonder whether that really can be accomplished by us *animals*, and whether, even if we did succeed for a while, doing so would put us at risk of pain later on.

This point did not go unnoticed by the skeptics. For Sextus Empiricus, the goal of *ataraxia* was unattainable precisely because we are animals: cold and thirst, for examples, are unavoidable.[30] Epicurus, on the other hand, seems at one point to say that perfection is attainable:

> He who has learned the limits of life knows that it is easy
> to provide that which removes the feeling of pain owing to
> want and *make one's whole life perfect*. So there is no need for
> things which involve struggle. [*KD* 21; emphasis added]

But what are "the limits of life"? I presume that they refer to what is humanly possible to achieve. We are not gods, and so we are subject to the contingencies of the particular physical world we live in; and we are also subject to error. Still, when one has set up reasonable defenses, one has done all that can be done, and one can be confident that the defenses will be sufficient against the usual disturbances of life: "it is easy to provide that which removes the feeling

---

28 *Let Men* 132.

29 D.L. X.137.

30 For a useful discussion of parallels between the thought of Peirce and the skeptics—and Descartes and Hume as well—see Loeb, "Sextus, Descartes, Hume, and Peirce".

---

of pain owing to want." That, in human terms, must count for making our lives "perfect", even though, relative to the gods, we lack some of their perfections.

But what is this living perfection, if we are from time to time still faced with desires which must be satisfied, so that *ataraxia* is never fully fixed? And will that give us cause for despair? Let us look to the analogy with Peirce, who mentions a trivial case of indecision: whether to pay a cab fare with a nickel or with five pennies (5.394). But is this flicker of hesitation an example of the irritation of doubt? Peirce cautions us that the term "doubt" in such a case is somewhat inapt—"too strong for my purpose". Still, it is the same *kind* of thing as any other hesitation or uncertainty; perhaps it is only a matter of degree of doubt, or degree of importance of the issue. What do such minor disturbances say about belief as a calm, steady, satisfied condition? And then what would such cases of small disturbances tell us about *ataraxia* as tranquillity? On Epicurus's view, tranquillity is not—as some critics objected—equivalent to sleep, or fitting only for a corpse. Rather, it is the undisturbed functioning of a healthy organism. But then how should we understand "undisturbed"? Is *ataraxia* upset because when I reach for a glass of water to take a sip, I am not yet in a condition of having had the sip? Perhaps it is, but in such a case the term "disturbance" (*taraxia*) would be too strong for Epicurus's purpose. Still, it is the same kind of thing as any other disturbance; perhaps it is only a matter of degree of disturbance, or degree of importance of the issue.

It seems to me that there are three, interrelated, key factors. (1) In simple cases such as the examples above, the degree of importance is certainly very small. That is, before the desire is fulfilled (or the belief achieved), any disturbance (or any doubt) is very small. (2) Any disturbance about not yet having the sip of water (or any hesitation about how to pay the cab fare), is easily put to rest, and without conscious struggle, by anyone who has had experience with glasses of water (or nickels and pennies). And (3) *one can therefore be confident of imminent success*, either in the manner one has chosen to follow, or in some easily available alternative.[31]

---

31 My thanks to Christine Sage Suits and Dane Gordon for their helpful comments and suggestions on an earlier draft of this paper.

Brent, Joseph, *Charles Sanders Peirce: A Life* (Bloomington, IN: Indiana University Press, 1993).

Cicero, *De Finibus*, trans. H. Rackham (Cambridge, MA: Harvard University Press, Loeb Classical Library, 1914).

Cooper, John M., *Reason and Emotion: Essays on Ancient Moral Psychology and Moral Theory* (Princeton: Princeton University Press, 1999).

The Epicurus Reader: Selected Writings and Testimonia, trans. Brad Inwood and L. P. Gerson (Indianapolis: Hackett Publishing Company, 1994).

Loeb, Louis E., "Sextus, Descartes, Hume, and Peirce: On Securing Settled Doxastic States", *Noûs* 32 (1998), pp. 205–230.

Mitsis, Phillip, *Epicurus' Ethical Theory: The Pleasures of Invulnerability* (Ithaca: Cornell University Press, 1988).

Peirce, Charles S., *The Collected Papers of Charles Sanders Peirce*, vols. 1–6, ed. Charles Hartshorne and Paul Weiss, 1931–1935; vols. 7–8, ed. A. W. Burk, 1958 (Cambridge, MA: Harvard University Press).

THEOLOGICAL PARADOX IN EPICURUS

Marianna Shakhnovich

Epicurus's philosophical heritage continues to attract the attention of scholars. Research in the field of Epicureanism is relevant because Epicurus is one of the most mysterious thinkers in the history of philosophy. Controversy over the essence of his doctrine has persisted uninterrupted through more than two thousand years.

In this presentation we want to examine some important problems in the contemporary study of Epicurus's philosophy of religion.

The first that needs to be discussed is the problem of the reception and the influence of Epicurus's philosophy of religion. Debates on how to evaluate these have taken place since ancient times. Usually, the Epicurean tradition is linked with the denial of creationism, providentialism and immortality, with the development of natural science and secular morals. Epicurus's influence on the philosophy of religion in modern thought can be compared with that of Aristotle on medieval Christian theology. The Enlightenment is called "new Epicureanism". In Russia, in the 18th century, Epicurus's philosophy played an important role in the formation of atomistic materialism and free thinking.[1] The reception of Epicurean doctrine in Old Russia is a vivid example of the interpretation of Epicurean philosophy of religion in medieval culture.

An educated person in Kievan Rus' possessed a certain amount of knowledge both of classical mythology (the earliest source of which was the translations of the Byzantine chronicles of George Hamartols and John Malalas[2]) and in the so called "Hellenic wisdom" of classical philosophy. Though the study of Greek philosophy was not encouraged by the Orthodox Church, the names and sometimes the apophthegms of Pythagoras, Anaxagoras, Democritus, Zeno, Socrates, Plato, Aristotle and Epicurus were mentioned in translations and in original ancient Russian texts.

---

1 Marianna Shakhnovich, *Sad Epicura. Filosofia Religii Epicura i Epicureyskaya Traditsiya v Istorii Evropeyskoy Mysli.* [*The Garden of Epicurus: Epicurus's Philosophy of Religion and Epicurean Tradition in the History of European Thought*] (St. Petersburg: St. Petersburg State University, 2002), pp. 211–222.

2 "Die Chronik des Georgios Hamartols in altslavischen Übersetzung", *Slavische Propyläen* 135 (Munich: W. Fink Verlag, 1972). E. M. Shustorovich, "Drevneslavianskiy Perevod Chroniki Ioanna Malali. (Istoria izuchenia)" [Old Russian translation of the Chronicle of John Malalas. (The History of Research)], *Vizantiysky vremennik* 30 (1966), pp. 136–152.

The Russian reader of the end of the 10th century could find information on Epicurus and his disciples in the New Testament in the book of *Acts,* described as opponents of Christianity: "While Paul was … in Athens, he was greatly distressed to see that the city was full of idols.… A group of Epicurean and Stoic philosophers began to dispute with him".[3]

An anti-Epicurean stance was characteristic of the Christian tradition on the whole, both in Western and the Byzantine patristic literature. Selected works of Byzantine Church fathers began to spread through ancient Russia at the end of the 10th century. Works by Athanasius of Alexandria, Cyril of Jerusalem, Basil the Great, Gregory of Nazianzus, Gregory of Nissa, John Chrysostom, and John of Damascus were translated into Old Russian. Works by Pseudo-Dionysius the Areopagite were read. Various selections from Irenaeus, Eusebius of Alexandria, Eusebius of Caesarea and Augustine were also known among the Orthodox clergy. Although these works contained mainly theological ideas, they were at the same time important sources of knowledge of the philosophical thought of pagan antiquity.

Among these works was the *Haexameron* of Basil the Great, in which Epicurus was not named specifically, but atomistic natural philosophy was criticized.

The most significant influence on the transmission of the ancient Greek philosophers belongs to *Melissa*, the Byzantine florilegium. A version of *Melissa* was translated in Southern Rus' at the end of the twelfth century (not later than 1220) and called in Russian *Pchela*.[4] This compilation was attributed to Maximus Confessor (seventh century). Among the texts of *Pchela*, which were chiefly ethical in character, one could find sayings of Homer, Hesiod, Pythagoras, Plato, Aristotle, Democritus, Aeschylus, Euripides, Isocrates, Herodotus, Demosthenes, Xenophontes, Sophocles, Plutarch, Lucian and Epicurus. A reader at that time, educated in the patristic tradition, could probably not distinguish between Epicurus's and Democritus's concepts in natural philosophy, but, thanks to the gnomologium *Pchela*, he, undoubtedly, was acquainted with Epicurus's original ethical and theological doctrines.

Comparison of quotations attributed to Epicurus in the most ancient surviving Russian manuscript of *Pchela* with Greek texts attributed to him have shown that, first, the ancient Russian *Pchela* has nine quotations from Epicurus on the life of the sage and on God; second, in addition to other sources, Epicurus's sayings compiled by his disciples were used as the basis of the original Byzantine *Melissa*; and third, that in the *Pchela* Epicurus, known as an atheist, was introduced without criticism, though some citations were slightly

---

3   New Testament, *Acts,* 17:16–18.

4   "Melissa. Ein byzantinischen Florilegium, griechisch and altrussisch", *Slavische Propyläen* 7 (Munich: W. Fink Verlag, 1968).

paraphrased and one of them acquired Christian overtones.[5]

The second problem is that of properly understanding and evaluating Epicurus's philosophy of religion. According to Denis Diderot no philosophical system is less understandable and more slandered than Epicurus's.[6] His critics called him pig (Augustine, *Enarrat. psalmi*, 73, 25), his followers, the savior who brought the truth (Lucretius, *De rerum natura*, V.1–90). Since ancient times the Garden of Epicurus was described as a den of iniquity (D.L. X.6), but his followers and even some of his opponents considered him to be a person of high morals (Seneca, *De vita beata*, 13, 2–4; *Ep.* XII, XIII, XXI, XXXIII). Epicurus wrote that one could be satisfied with little (D.L. X.130–131), but he was described as the advocate of depravity and gluttony (Jerome, *Contra Jovin.* II, 36; Theophilus, *Ad Autolycum* III, 6; Clement of Alexandria, *Strom.* II, 23; Augustine, *Epist.* 8, 14; *Contra Acad.* III, 18, 41). He was proclaimed "the open atheist" *(offen Atheist)*[7], but he affirmed the existence of gods (*Principle Doctrines*, I). His denial of providence was used as the basis for criticism of Christianity, but some modern scholars consider him to be a Christian before Christ.[8] He called for studying nature, but he was included among the opponents of science.[9] His followers claimed that he was a great philosopher, an original thinker, a rationalist and an optimist; his opponents described him as a rude ignoramus, a weak compilator, a mystic and a pessimist.[10] Truth be told, it is difficult to find another philosophical doctrine which provoked such contradictory references and strong reactions.

The paradox of Epicurus's philosophy of religion is that although he was known as an atheist, he claimed the existence of gods, and theology played an important role in his philosophical system.

From the middle of the second century B.C. there was a fairly generally used list of ancient atheists, which was introduced by the Alexandrian poet and philosopher Clithomachos of Carthage. He wrote a treatise *On Disbelief in Gods*, devoted to the famous Greek *atheoi*. He used the views of earlier authors for his classification, among them Posidonius. Clithomachos's list in its turn was used by Cicero (*ND* I, 42, 117–119), Sextus Empiricus (*Adv. Math.* IX, 50–58),

---

5 Shakhnovich, *Sad Epicura*, pp. 202–211.

6 *Encyclopédie, ou Dictionnaire rasonneé* (Paris: n.p., 1755), vol. 5, p. 176.

7 Karl Marx, Friedreich Engels, *Die deutsche Ideologie* (Berlin: Dietz, 1960), p. 134.

8 Norman W. De Witt, *Epicurus and his Philosophy* (Minneapolis: University of Minnesota Press, 1954); George A. Panichas, *Epicurus* (New York: Twayne Publishers, 1967); Adelaide D. Simpson, "Epicureans, Christians, Atheists in the Second Century", *Transactions of the American Philological Association* 72 (1941), pp. 372–381.

9 Benjamin Farrington, "Epicureanism and Science", *Scientia* 48 (1954), pp. 62–72.

10 Shakhnovich, *Sad Epicura*, pp. 222–227.

Pseudo-Plutarchus (*Plac. Phil.* 880 D–E = *Aetius Plac. Phil.* I, 7, I), Lactantius (*Div. Inst.* I, 2, 1–2) and others.[11] In all of these lists, in addition to Epicurus, we can find the names of three sophists—Protagoras, Prodicos, Critius—and then the names of two cyrenaics—Theodorus, Euhemerus—as well as that of Diagoras. Their doctrines differed greatly.[12]

It is interesting that Epicurus himself considered these philosophers, in contrast to himself, actually to be atheists, and in the twelfth book of his *On Nature*, he drew a line between his ideas and theirs. He criticized Prodicos, Critius and Diagoras for their attitude towards the gods and asserted that they were insane and furious in their insanity.[13] Philodemus repeated these words in his book *On Piety*, defending himself and his disciples from accusations of atheism.[14] Diogenes of Oinoanda maintained the same statement and criticized those who denied the existence of the gods.[15]

In our book *The Paradoxes in Epicurus's Theology*[16] we have compared his "atheism" with the doctrines of those thinkers who were mentioned in the canon of ancient atheists and with the ideas of Democritus, because many authors (from Cicero to church fathers) considered his views to be similar to Epicurus's. Comparing his philosophy of religion with the concepts of Democritus, the sophists, Diagoras, Theodorus and Euhemerus gave us the opportunity to conclude that Epicurus affirmed the error of the traditional opinion of the gods, and in contrast to other thinkers mentioned in the list of atheists, stated their real existence.

From this point the third acute problem appears. What is the essence of Epicurean theology?

In order to answer this question we had to reconstruct the theology of Epicurus on the basis of the few remaining original texts. We tried to dissect particular features of Epicurus's theology. The foundations of the argument for historical or psychological evidence of the existence of God lay in Epicurus's theology. According to his system, the argument was proved by the concept of πρόληψις (preconception), which was the central notion of his epistemology.

---

11 Marek Winiarczyk, "Der erste Atheistenkatalog des Kleitomachos", *Philologus* 20 (1976), pp. 32–46.

12 Paul Decharme, *La critique des traditions religieuses chez Grecs, des origins au temps de Plutarque* (Paris: A. Picard et fils, 1904), pp. 393–411.

13 Epicurus, *Opere*, ed. Graziano Arrighetti (Turin: Giulio Einaudi, 1973), fr. 27.

14 Philodemus, *On Piety*, part I, ed. Dirk Obbink (Oxford: Clarendon Press, 1996), fr.19.

15 Diogenes of Oinoanda, *The Epicurean Inscription*, ed. with intro., trans. and notes by Martin Ferguson Smith (Naples: Bibliopolis, 1993), fr. 16.

16 Marianna Shakhnovich, *Paradoxi Teologii Epicura* [*The Paradoxes in Epicurus's Theology*] (St. Petersburg: St. Petersburg Philosophical Society, 2000). (In Russian.)

The theory of προλήψις provides the opportunity to explain the presence of the concept of the gods: there is knowledge of the gods, hence the gods exist.

Epicurus was the successor of the eleatic school in the interpretation of the attributes of the gods. His gods had two attributes: blessedness, connected with ethics, and immortality, connected with his ontology and epistemology. The notion of ἰσονομία (equal distribution) lies at the basis of the notion of the gods: the existence of the mortal was the condition for the existence of the immortal.

The most difficult text to analyze is the scholia to "Principal Doctrines, I" (D. L. X.139) about the concept of god:

Εν ἄλλος δέ φησι τοὺς θεοὺς λόγῳ θεωρητούς, οὓς μὲν κατ'ἀριθμὸν ὑφεστῶτας, οὓς δέ κατὰ ὁμοείδειαν ἐκ τῆς συνεχοῦς ἐπιρρύσεως τῶν ὁμοίων εἰδώλων ἐπὶ τὸ αὐτὸ ἀποτετελεσμένων, ἀνθρωποειδεῖς.[17]

Elsewhere he says that the gods are contemplated by reason, and that some exist "numerically" while others are similar in form, because of a continuous flow of similar images to the same place; and that they are anthropomorphic.[18]

This passage has been the subject of dispute for many centuries. Some scholars asserted that the author of the scholia mixed the types of images of the gods and the types of gods, others argued that Epicurus himself stated that there were two species of divinity. Rudolf Hirtzel argued that the images κατὰ ὁμοείδεαν were of democritian shape and are different from those in the intermundia. He thought that it was Cicero who mixed the species of the gods in Epicurus and Democritus.[19] Hermann Diels, Knut Kleve, and Graziano Arrighetti considered that from the scholia it can be determined that Epicurus had a theory of two species of images of gods: the first, which reaches individual human beings and makes singular impressions, and the second, which occurs only in general notions of the gods.[20] Olof Gigon took the passage literally and stated that according to Epicurus there are two types of gods: the gods existed in

17 Epicurus, *Opere*, fr. 5-I.

18 *The Epicurus Reader*, ed. and trans. Brad Inwood and L. P. Gerson (Indianapolis: Hackett Publishing Company, 1994).

19 Rudolf Hirzel, *Untersuchungen zu Ciceros philosophischen Schriften*, Bd I. (Leipzig: S. Hirzel, 1877).

20 Hermann Diels, "Ein Epikurus Fragment über die Götterverehrung", *Sitzungsberichte der Preuss. Akademie der Wissenschaften* 37 (1916), pp. 886–909; Knut Kleve, "Gnosis Theon. Die Lehre von der naturlichen Gotteserkenntnis in

single form (Olympic) and others in innumerable quantity.[21] Phillip Merlan and Dietrich Lemke ascribed the type κατὰ ὁμοείδεαν to the Epicurean gods and the type κατ'ἀριθμὸν to the individual gods of popular religion.[22] Adam Krokevich and Carlo Diano affirmed that in this passage the images which were perceived as *the single* and *the general* were described.[23]

We think that a solution to this textological problem is in the epistemological aspect. To our mind, this scholia tells not about the types of gods, but about the origin of the gods and the possibility of their cognition. We can find the same comparison in Aristotle's *Metaphysics*: "Some things are single in number, others in shape. Those which have the same matter are single in number, those who are formed in the same way have the same shape."[24] In our scholia we can find two different species of gods: one species is similar to human beings, another, to the gods. In Epicurus there are two streams of atomic images proceeding from opposite directions. According to the principle of isonomia, one stream of images, κατ'ἀριθμὸν, which is similar to human beings, forms the atomic gods, while another stream of eidola, κατὰ ὁμοείδεαν, similar to gods, falls down from the intermundia, creating the notion of the gods in human beings. From human beings, as well as from other objects, there is a constant tiny atomic flow. Those atomic eidola create the gods in the intermundia, and this is why the gods are anthropomorphic. The gods are similar to a waterfall: the shape is constant, but the drops of water constantly change.

Epicurus thought that the gods of traditional religion were fictitious, and he proclaimed the falsity of Olympic mythology, but it was impossible for him not to admire the images of the gods, in which beauty, wisdom and kindness were embodied. Cicero wrote that Epicurus affirmed the existence of the gods because there had to be a nature so perfect that it would be impossible to find more perfect.[25] The Epicurean gods are fundamentally different from the gods of traditional religion, because the Epicureans did not feel themselves dependent on them. Thus, their gods differ from the gods of the other ancient

---

der epikureischen Theologie", *Symbolae Osloensis* 19 (1963); Graziano Arrighetti, "Sul problema dei tipi divini nell'Epicureismo", *La Payola del Passato* 8 (1955), pp. 327–356.

21 Olof Gigon, *Epikur. Von der Ueberwindung der Frucht* (Zürich: Artemis Verlag, 1949).

22 Phillip Merlan, *Studies in Epicurus and Aristotle* (The Haque: Martius Nijhoff, 1960); Dietrich Lemke, *Die Theologie Epikurs. Versuch einer Rekonstruktion* (Munich: Beck, 1972).

23 Adam Krokiewicz, *Hedonizm Epicura* (Warsaw: Pax, 1961); Carlo Diano, *Epicuri Ethica* (Florence: in aedibus Sansonianis, 1946).

24 Aristotle, *Metaphysics*, 1016b 31.

25 Cicero, *De natura deorum* II, 17.46.

philosophers. They play the role of ethico-aesthetical ideal.

The irrelevant gods of Epicurus are the ideal for the Epicurean who strives for ataraxy. The atomic gods are *dei otiosi* who do not need any victims and who do not interfere in anything. The idea of such gods is connected with the Epicurean doctrine of personal irrelevance and noninterference. This is the result of a spiritual crisis of the Hellenistic period stimulated when everyday life is threatened, when it becomes necessary to escape and the individual tries to find peace for his soul in the face of a horrible cataclysm.

The concept of the gods was an integral part of Epicurus's philosophy of religion and was an implicit, immanent element of his philosophical system connected with his physics and epistemology. The attitude to the gods as ideal models gave birth to Epicurus's understanding of piety, expressed through imitation of, and dialogue with, the gods. In the book *On the Modes of Life* Epicurus wrote that one ought to pay homage to the gods not to escape their anger, but because the nature of the gods is higher than our own.[26] From the point of view of his opponents, he was an atheist, because he did not believe as the majority did, but from his point of view he gave his disciples the pure concept of god, which encouraged them on their way to moral perfection. This is why Lucretius proclaimed Epicurus to be the savior of mankind.

The main principles of Epicurus's philosophy of religion serve as the basis for its ethical doctrine. The essence of this doctrine was the theory of four truths, the knowledge of which marked out a path to achieving happiness. Epicurus provided his followers with a four-fold remedy: the fear of gods is vain, because they don't interfere with human life; the fear of death is vain, because death is nothing to us (when we are, death is not come, and when the death is come, we are not); evil is either of short duration or is easily supportable; pleasure is at the disposition of all (D. L. X.139–140).[27] At this point the fourth problem in the investigation of Epicurean doctrine appears, the problem of secular morals.

The history of philosophy of religion and ethics can hardly be separated from the history of the Epicurean tradition. Among the followers of Epicurus we can mention the great Roman poets and the Russian poet Alexander Pushkin, Spinoza, as well as the young Schelling, Thomas Jefferson, and the founder of Moscow University, Mikhail Lomonosov, and many others.[28] We can join in the opinion of Karl Jaspers that in everyone's life there are some moments when Epicurean philosophy can be a shelter from weakness, can offer help in living

---

26 *Epicurea*, ed. Hermann Usener (Stuttgart: Teubner, 1966), fr. 13.

27 Principal Doctrines, I–IV.

28 Mario Capasso, "Studi su Epicuro: Parte seconda. La fortuna dell'epicureismo", in *ΣΥΖΗΤΗΣΙΣ, Studi sull'epicureismo Greco e Romano*, vol. 2, Rassegne Bibliografiche (Naples: Gaetano Macchiaroli, 1982), pp. 492–505.

---

through difficulties, and can give knowledge of how to master fear. And in this sense, Epicurus's doctrine is always up to date.[29]

WORKS CITED

Arrighetti, Graziano, "Sul problema dei tipi divini nell'Epicureismo", *La Payola del Passato* 8 (1955), pp. 327–356.

Capasso, Mario, "Studi su Epicuro: Parte seconda. La fortuna dell'epicureismo" in *ΣΥΖΗΤΗΣΙΣ, Studi sull' epicureismo Greco a Romano*, vol. 2. Rassegne Bibliografiche, pp. 447–518 (Naples: Gaetano Macchiaroli, 1982).

Decharme, Paul, *La critique des traditions religieuses chez Grecs, des origines au temps de Plutarque* (Paris: A. Picard et fils, 1904).

De Witt, Norman W., *Epicurus and his Philosophy* (Minneapolis: University of Minnesota Press, 1954).

Diano, Carlo, *Epicuri Ethica* (Florence: in aedibus Sansonianis, 1946).

"Die Chronik des Georgios Hamartols in altslavischen Übersetzung", *Slavische Propyläen* 135 (Munich: W. Fink Verlag, 1972).

Diels, Hermann, "Ein Epikurus Fragment über die Götterverehrung", *Sitzungsberichte der Preuss. Akademie der Wissenschaften* 37 (1916), pp. 886–909.

Diogenes of Oinoanda, *The Epicurean Inscription*, ed. with intro., trans. and notes by Martin Ferguson Smith (Naples: Bibliopolis, 1993).

Encyclopédie, ou Dictionnaire rasonneé (Paris: n.p., 1755).

Epicurea, ed. Hermann Usener (Stuttgart: Teubner, 1966).

Epicurus, *Opere*, ed. Graziano Arrighetti (Turin: Giulio Einaudi, 1973).

---

29 Karl Jaspers, *The Great Philosophers* (New York: Harcourt, Brace & World, 1993), vol. 3, pp. 109–111.

The Epicurus Reader, ed. and trans. Brad Inwood and L. P. Gerson (Indianapolis: Hackett Publishing Company, 1994).

Farrington, Benjamin, "Epicureanism and Science", *Scientia* 48 (1954), pp. 62–72.

Gigon, Olof, *Epikur. Von der Ueberwindung der Frucht* (Zürich: Artemis Verlag, 1949).

Hirzel, Rudolf, *Untersuchungen zu Ciceros philosophischen Schriften*, Bd I. (Leipzig: S. Hirzel, 1877).

Jaspers, Karl, *The Great Philosophers* (New York: Harcourt, Brace & World, 1993).

Kleve, Knut, "Gnosis Theon. Die Lehre von der naturlichen Gotteserkenntnis in der epikureischen Theologie", *Symbolae Osloensis* 19 (1963).

Krokiewicz, Adam, *Hedonizm Epicura* (Warsaw: Pax, 1961).

Lemke, Dietrich, *Die Theologie Epikurs. Versuch einer Rekonstruktion* (Munich: Beck, 1972).

Marx, Karl and Friedreich Engels, *Die deutsche Ideologie* (Berlin: Dietz, 1960).

"Melissa. Ein byzantinischen Florilegium, griechisch and altrussisch", *Slavische Propyläen* 7 (Munich: W. Fink Verlag, 1968).

Merlan, Phillip, *Studies in Epicurus and Aristotle* (The Hague: Martius Nijhoff, 1960).

Panichas, George A., *Epicurus* (New York: Twayne Publishers, 1967).

Philodemus, *On Piety*, Part I, ed. Dirk Obbink (Oxford: Clarendon Press, 1996).

Shakhnovich, Marianna, *Paradoxi Teologii Epicura* [*The Paradoxes in Epicurus's Theology*] (St. Petersburg: St. Petersburg Philosophical Society, 2000). (In Russian.)

——, *Sad Epicura. Filosofia Religii Epicura i Epicureyskaya Traditsiya v Istorii Evropeyskoy Mysli* [*The Garden of Epicurus: Epicurus's Philosophy of Religion and Epicurean Tradition in the History of European Thought*] (St. Petersburg: St. Petersburg State University, 2002). (In Russian with English summary.)

Shustorovich, E. M., "Drevneslavianskiy Perevod Chroniki Ioanna Malali. (Istoria izuchenia)" [Old Russian translation of the Chronicle of John Malalas. (The History of Research)], *Vizantiysky vremennik* 30 (1966), pp. 136–152. (In Russian.)

Simpson, Adelaide D., "Epicureans, Christians, Atheists in the Second Century", *Transactions of the American Philological Association* 72 (1941), pp. 372–381.

Winiarczyk, Marek, "Der erste Atheistenkatalog des Kleitomachos", *Philologus* 20 (1976), pp. 32–46.

Daniel C. Russell

"Every friendship", Epicurus tells us, "is worth choosing for its own sake, though it takes its origin from the benefits it confers on us" (*Vatican Sayings* [*VS*] 23).[1] Here we find in a single saying two main lines of Epicurus's thought about friendship: (1) a real friendship must be something that the friends pursue for its own sake, and (2) much of the point of friendship is what the friends gain from the friendship. The first line sounds much more edifying than the second, but to say that some of the point of a friendship is what the friends stand to gain from it is not to say that friendships are mercenary. It is rather to say that there is such a thing as an "economy" of friendship.[2] We don't always look at friendships for what we might get out of them, but we do recognize that part of what is good about friendships is that there usually is something to get out of them. Moreover, friendship need not be "selfless"; however devoted I am to my friend, my interests count too. Friendships have principled limits, and friendship is a kind of balance—a balance of both interests and motivations.

However, although my interests have to be part of the balance, it is of course possible for them to tip the balance, and in this respect Epicurus's account of friendship appears notoriously unstable. For Epicurus, the overarching goal that holds together all of the wise person's pursuits—what the ancients call a *telos* or "final end"—is the agent's own pleasure, understood as tranquility or peace of mind. But if the goal that holds together all of my pursuits is my own tranquility, how can I also value my friends for their own sake? How can I both *do everything for the sake of my own pleasure*, and *do some things for the sake of other people*?

I would like to focus on this problem as it arises from a number of key texts in which Epicurus puts forth his account of friendship, and in doing so I think we shall find quite a new way of understanding friendship in Epicurean philosophy. The biggest obstacle to understanding Epicurus's account of friendship, I maintain, is the rather natural assumption that if I have a final end (such as tranquility), then all of my other goals are rational only if I pursue them for the sake of my final end. I argue that that assumption is false, and I show why

---

1   All translations are from Brad Inwood and Lloyd Gerson, *Hellenistic Philosophy*, 2nd ed. (Indianapolis: Hackett, 1997). I accept, as do Inwood and Gerson, the emendation of *aretē* ("Every friendship is *a virtue*") to *hairetē* ("Every friendship is *worth choosing*").

2   I owe the phrase to Elizabeth Giles.

its falsity matters for understanding Epicurus on the value of friends and the nature of goals.[3]

One main line of thought about friendship in Epicurus is the following:

A. *We need friends because we need security.*

> The same understanding produces confidence about there being nothing terrible which is eternal or even long-lasting and has also realized that security amid even these limited bad things is most easily achieved through friendship. [*Key Doctrines (KD)* 28]

> [Epicurus claimed the wise man would have friends] so that he might have someone to attend him when sick, and to help him when he is thrown into prison or is impoverished.... [Seneca, *Letters* 9.8]

> We do not need utility from our friends so much as we need confidence concerning that utility. [*VS* 34]

> The constant friend is neither he who always searches for utility, nor he who never links friendship to utility. For the former makes gratitude a matter for commercial transaction, while the latter kills off good hope for the future. [*VS* 39]

Friends help us to ward off difficulty and they assist us when we face difficulty, and the confidence we have in their friendship is a source of confidence about the future. In fact, a good friend is one who (*inter alia*) recognizes these very facts about friendship. This should bring to mind the economy of friendship mentioned above. It is also connected to another main line of thought in Epicurus:

B. *The goal of all action, to which every choice must be referred, is one's own pleasure, understood as tranquility.*

> If you do not, on every occasion, refer each of your actions

---

3 It is worth pointing out that the interpretation of Epicurus I shall offer here is—like any alternative interpretation—an inference to the best explanation of Epicurus's whole view. There are no "smoking gun" texts that settle the issues for us all on their own.

to the goal of nature [sc. tranquility], but instead turn prematurely to some other criterion in avoiding or pursuing things, your actions will not be consistent with your reasoning. [*KD* 25]

The unwavering contemplation of [the differences between necessary and groundless desires] enables one to refer every choice and avoidance to the health of the body and the freedom of the soul from disturbance, since this is the goal of a blessed life. [*Letter to Menoeceus (Men.)* 128]

Epicurus is clearly unflinching about this principle, but here Epicurus's economy of friendship begins to seem precarious, since it is unclear how he can *also* say that:

C. *A good friend is not mercenary.*

Indeed, while Epicurus says in *VS* 39, above, that the real friend will link friendship to utility, he also says that the real friend does not always search for utility. Does that mean that the real friend will sometimes refer his actions to some other criterion than his own tranquility, and thus will sometimes go *against* proper reasoning, as Epicurus understands it in *KD* 25? This should make us a bit more suspicious, then, about Epicurus's initially sensible-looking claim that:

D. *Friendship is good for its own sake, but begins from benefit.*

Every friendship is worth choosing for its own sake, though it takes its origin from the benefits it confers on us. [*VS* 23]

Is Epicurus claiming that friendship starts with proper reasoning, but then, in growing beyond concern for one's own benefit, comes to stand in opposition to proper Epicurean practical reasoning?

So exactly what value will friends attach to each other, if they reason as Epicureans? Epicurus's answer appears to be a ragbag of ideas about friends and goals. According to Epicurus, the ultimate standard of all value is to be my own pleasure (as in B), and yet he *also* says that I must not value my friend entirely for the sake of my own pleasure, but also for his or her own sake (as in C and D).[4] In that case valuing a friend *for his own sake*—and not just for

---

4 Julia Annas, *The Morality of Happiness* (Oxford: Oxford University Press, 1993), p. 240, puts the point thus: "If we did not allow that pleasure was our ultimate

---

Daniel C. Russell

the pleasure the friendship brings—seems to be a moral "loose end":[5] it is my valuing something that I take to be a good *in itself*, and thus not only because it promotes my tranquility. In *that* respect the value is detached, or "loose", from my final end. Thus if friendships really have only hedonistic and mercenary value, then it will be irrational to love a friend for his own sake;[6] and to the extent that friends love each other for each other's sake, to that extent their love is loose from, not referred to, the goal of pleasure. This problem I shall call the "Loose Ends Problem".

The specter of the Loose Ends Problem makes it rather surprising to find Epicurus praising friendship to the heavens:

E. *Friendship is the greatest source of blessedness in life.*

Of the things which wisdom provides for the blessedness of one's whole life, by far the greatest is the possession of friendship. [*KD* 27]

Friendship dances around the world announcing to all of us that we must wake up to blessedness. [*VS* 52]

The noble man is most involved with wisdom and friendship, of which one is a mortal good, the other immortal. [*VS* 78]

If Epicurus really means this, then it seems that not just any pursuit, but one of our *most important* pursuits in life is a loose end, and thus a serious embarrassment to Epicurus's theory of value and practical reasoning. Consequently, although our sources say clearly that Epicurus was a devoted friend, we may worry with Cicero that the real question is whether such practices are consistent with Epicurus's theory, and they don't seem to be.[7]

Notice the assumption that is at the core of the Loose Ends Problem, viz. that Epicurus's notion of a final end *does* make valuing a friend for his own

---

reason for seeking friendships, then pleasure would not be complete, and thus not our final end. If we treated friendship purely instrumentally, we would be allowing not *friendship* into our lives, but something else."

5 I owe the term to David Schmidtz, "Choosing Ends", *Ethics* 104 (1994), pp. 226–251, who characterizes a loose end relative to a scheme of practical reasoning as a terminal end not justifiable within that scheme, but nonetheless held by an agent employing that scheme.

6 See Suzanne Stern-Gillet, "Epicurus and Friendship", *Dialogue* 28 (1989), pp. 275–288, at pp. 280–282.

7 See Cicero, *De Finibus* (*Fin.*) II.80–81. See also Plutarch, *Against Colotes* 1111b.

sake a loose end. That assumption is also ubiquitous in modern approaches to Epicurus's account of friendship. One very common approach is to tinker with the notion of friendship, so that, on the one hand, a friendship can be itself a sort of pleasure,[8] or so that, on the other, friendship never really accrues the kind of value that would make it a loose end. Hence John Cooper, for example, argues that friendships, for Epicurus, are more or less a way of simply passing the time in the company of others in order to avoid boredom; David O'Connor argues that the thesis of *VS* 23 is that a good Epicurean will choose *friendships* for their own sakes, as opposed to valuing the *friends* themselves; Tim O'Keefe argues that loving a friend is less a matter of placing a certain kind of value on the friend than it is a range of behaviors with respect to the friend.[9] However, the more we dilute the value friends place on each other for each other's sake, the harder it is to understand the joy that Epicurus says we derive from the very memory of our friends, even after they have died—and surely the harder it is to see how the recollection of times spent with a dear friend could make the last day of Epicurus's life a "blessedly happy day", despite the most agonizing pains of urinary blockages.[10] One finds solace in the memory of a *friend*, not in someone with whom one passed the time or to whom one acted in a friend-like way, without having valued him for his own sake. We must refuse to dilute the value that Epicurus seems to place on friends, not so that we may smuggle in our own assumptions about what friends are,[11] but because a diluted conception of

---

8   Stern-Gillet, "Epicurus and Friendship", pp. 283f suggests this, following Andre-Jean Festugière, *Epicurus and His Gods*, trans. C. W. Chilton (Oxford: Blackwell, 1955); however, as Phillip Mitsis, *Epicurus' Ethical Theory* (Ithaca: Cornell University Press, 1988) points out, this strategy seems to require "a conflation of pleasure and its sources … [and] a slide from 'sources of happiness or pleasure' to 'parts of happiness or pleasure'" (pp. 114f).

9   See John M. Cooper, *Reason and Emotion: Essays on Ancient Moral Psychology and Ethical Theory* (Princeton, NJ: Princeton University Press, 1999), pp. 509f; David O'Connor, "The Invulnerable Pleasures of Epicurean Friendship", *Greek, Roman, and Byzantine Studies* 30 (1989), pp. 165–186; and Tim O'Keefe, "Is Epicurean Friendship Altruistic?" *Apeiron* 34 (2001), pp. 269–305. Marianna Shakhnovich has reminded me that for the Epicureans "friend" can often mean simply "fellow Epicurean" (O'Connor, "Invulnerable Pleasures", also makes this point). While "friend" does have this titular role in Epicureanism, still I do not think that it can have had *only* that sort of role, as I argue below; I shall also argue that the assumption that "friend" would *need* to be merely titular for the Epicureans is false.

10   See Plutarch, *A Pleasant Life* 1105e, Diogenes Laertius, *Lives of Eminent Philosophers* x.22.

11   An important pitfall to avoid; see especially O'Connor, "Invulnerable Pleasures", who shows convincingly that many ancient criticisms of Epicurean friendship

---

friendship will not match what Epicurus says about the roles that friends can play in a good life.

Be that as it may, notice that the assumption underlying these approaches to Epicurean friendship is that if we do *not* dilute Epicurus's conception of friendship in some such way, it would be inconsistent with his theory of value and practical reasoning. Indeed, Phillip Mitsis, who argues against tinkering with the notion of friendship, nonetheless concurs that

> Epicurus, then, must either modify his account of *eudaimonia* [happiness] and rational agency or weaken his commitment to friendship. By doing neither he is forced into an inconsistency. He defends the pursuit of *aponia* [removal of all pain] and *ataraxia* [removal of all anxiety] based on his model of happiness as the satisfaction of desire. But in trying to add friendship as an additional requirement for happiness, he undermines this defense.[12]

Consequently, Mitsis says, Epicurus needs to explain the value of friendship for non-hedonic reasons, yet doing so would force him to take back his claim that pleasure is the standard of all value. Epicurus is simply trying to have his cake and eat it too.

Alternatively, Julia Annas argues that the value Epicurus places on friendship requires a "two-level view" of practical reasoning:

> In making and keeping friends, we do not refer every act of friendship to increasing our overall pleasure; rather, we accept as our aim that of having genuine other-concern for our friends. But the aim of this whole policy, of having friends rather than coping with life in some other way, is guided by the aim of increasing our pleasure. Thus pleasure is our aim when we are thinking of the policy as a whole; but it is not our aim in individual acts of friendship, which are aimed at the friend's good for its own sake.[13]

Unfortunately, as Annas points out, Epicurus rules out a two-level view when he says—as we have seen (*KD* 25, *Men.* 128)—that we must on every occasion refer our actions to our goal of tranquility. Now, "on every

---

misfire, since they rely on an ideal that is connected to a set of values which Epicureans simply do not share.

12 Mitsis, *Epicurus' Ethical Theory*, p. 125.

13 Annas, *The Morality of Happiness*, p. 240.

occasion" is ambiguous: it may mean either that we must refer each *action* to the goal of pleasure, or simply that we must refer all of our serious *values* to the goal of pleasure.[14] In either case, however, Epicurus's point is that we cannot compartmentalize concern for our friends—whether in the individual actions we do for them[15] or in the value we place on them—from our concern for our own pleasure, as a two-level view would have us do. Moreover, a two-level view would not really solve Epicurus's problem anyway. To construct a two-level view is to recognize that these levels are going to conflict, and so the two levels will be very unstable, and irrational to adopt.[16] Once again, then, we find the assumption that valuing a friend for her own sake is a moral loose end, given Epicurus's hedonist conception of our final end.

However, that assumption is false. I maintain that for Epicurus friends value each other for each other's sake, *and* that this view is perfectly consistent with Epicurean hedonism. The key lies in understanding just what it means, for Epicurus, to "refer" our actions, values, and projects to the final end of tranquility. On my view, valuing something for its own sake is, for Epicurus, consistent with referring our choice of it to our final end of living tranquilly. In other words, from the claim that

(A) Everything I do, I refer to the goal of pleasure

it does not follow that

(B) Everything I do, I do for the sake of pleasure.[17]

That inference is invalid, and its invalidity matters.

Let's approach the Loose Ends Problem again from a different angle. We may say that for the hedonist all goods form a network in which all goods besides pleasure must be appropriately connected to pleasure. Consequently,

---

14 Annas, *The Morality of Happiness*, pp. 240f, takes the former reading, O'Keefe, "Is Epicurean Friendship Altruistic?", the latter.

15 As Robert Sharples, *Stoics, Epicureans, and Sceptics: An Introduction to Hellenistic Philosophy* (New York: Routledge, 1996), puts it, for Epicurus "a present action cannot be detached from the motive of pleasure altogether and interpreted entirely in terms of concern for others" (p. 120).

16 Annas, *The Morality of Happiness*, p. 241. See also Mitsis, *Epicurus' Ethical Theory*, p. 113 for a similar problem in another strategy. However, see O'Keefe, "Is Epicurean Friendship Altruistic?", for a fresh defense of a two-level view in Epicurean practical reasoning.

17 It is worth pointing out that it is just this sort of inference that Butler denies in *Sermon* XI (I thank David Suits and Dane Gordon for bringing this to my

---

anything without the appropriate connections to pleasure cannot be within the network, and therefore cannot be a good. Some of the value of friendship, of course, is clearly located within such a network: friends bring us a kind of security, and security is necessary for pleasant peace of mind since without security we worry. But according to Epicurus this does not exhaust the value of friendship, since we also pursue friendship for its own sake. So the question is whether friendship, *as a thing worth pursuing for its own sake*, can be brought within the network.

To answer that, we need to step back and ask just what it means for some good to be "appropriately connected" to pleasure. Now the connection that most naturally suggests itself is, roughly, some sort of "maximizing": a good is appropriately related to pleasure, in this case, insofar as it increases the sum, quality, duration, and/or intensity of our pleasures. Somewhat notoriously, however, Epicurus eschews any such conception of pleasure maximization as a driving force in a hedonist theory.

This is so because for Epicurus the pleasure that is our final end is "katastematic" pleasure. Katastematic pleasures are opposed to what Epicurus calls "kinetic" pleasures, which are the ordinary phenomenal experiences of pleasure, what we might think of as pleasant excitations or "titillations".[18] Katastematic pleasure, by contrast, is not an active phenomenal state, but a quiet tranquility or peace, which consists in the absence of all mental and physical pain. As Epicurus is said to have written, "freedom from disturbance and freedom from suffering are katastematic pleasures; and joy and delight are viewed as kinetic and active."[19] Moreover, our final end is katastematic

---

attention). Referring all one's actions to one's own happiness, he argues, does not imply doing all things for the sake of one's own private interests—indeed, he argues that the latter may be a barrier to happiness:

> a person may have so steady and fixed an eye upon his own interest, whatever he places it in, as may hinder him from *attending* to many gratifications within his reach, which others have their minds *free* and *open* to.... [I]f there be any guess to be made from appearances, surely that character we call selfish is not the most promising for happiness.... Happiness consists in the gratification of certain affections, appetites, passions, with objects which are by nature adapted to them. Self-love may indeed set us on work to gratify these; but happiness or enjoyment has no immediate connection with self-love, but arises from such gratification alone. Love of our neighbour is one of those affections. [*Fifteen Sermons Preached at the Rolls Chapel*, 2nd ed. (London: James and John Knapton, 1729), §§9, 16; italics in original]

18 See Athenaeus, *Deipnosophists* 12, 546ef.

19 Diogenes Laertius, *Lives* X.136.

pleasure, since "The removal of all feeling of pain is the limit of the magnitude of pleasures."[20] For this reason, while every kinetic pleasure is a good in and of itself—indeed, our understanding of pleasure as a thing to be pursued depends on our apprehension of the goodness of every pleasure[21]—still we do not always pursue every kinetic pleasure, since doing so indiscriminately can lead to considerable pain or anxiety.[22] Our goal, in other words, is not some qualitative experience, but a condition in which no physical and mental needs are unmet. Such a condition, clearly, does not admit of "maximization" or increases in "intensity". Of course, it is possible for someone in this condition to partake in pleasures that are qualitative experiences, but Epicurus claims that such added pleasures serve not to increase one's overall pleasant katastematic condition, but only to "vary" or "adorn" it.[23] Difficult as this idea is, what is clear is that Epicurus rejects a maximizing conception of katastematic pleasure.

So Epicurus needs another way to characterize how some goods are directly connected to our goal by promoting it in various ways: friends, for instance, are a source of confidence and security, and it is this sort of security which allows the mind to be at ease; political office, as well as a retiring disposition and material prosperity, also do the same.[24] One kind of appropriate connection in Epicurus's hedonist network of goods, then, is that between our tranquility and things that provide the means, such as security, that make that tranquility feasible. Things that promote pleasure do so not by increasing or maximizing our pleasure, but either by being sources of kinetic pleasures that vary katastematic pleasure, or by making katastematic pleasure possible.

Kinetic pleasures also reveal a third type of network connection for Epicurus. Kinetic pleasures are not goods just because they vary our katastematic pleasure; rather they are goods in themselves, being themselves types of pleasure. We might worry that this lands Epicurus with a clumsy proliferation of final ends: our final end is katastematic pleasure, yet every kinetic pleasure is an end in itself; so what exactly is our goal, katastematic pleasure, or all of these kinetic pleasures? Epicurus avoids this problem by noting that while every kinetic pleasure is good for its own sake and worth pursuing, nonetheless we cannot plan our lives around episodic experiences of kinetic pleasure. What emerges as our final end from among a host of things good for their own sake must be something that meets our need to put together a coherent life. Kinetic pleasures cannot meet that need by themselves, so we must have some single final end to regulate how, when, and where we are to partake of kinetic pleasures.

---

20 *KD* 3; see also *Men.* 127–132, Lucretius, *On the Nature of Things* II.1–61.

21 For kinetic pleasures as basic goods, see Athenaeus, *Deipnosophists* 12, 546ef; for the apprehension of pleasure as to-be-pursued, see Cicero, *Fin.* I.30–33.

22 See *Men.* 129–130, *KD* 8, *VS* 73.

23 See Cicero, *Fin.* I.37, 38; see also Cicero, *Fin.* I.56; *KD* 18.

24 See *KD* 6, *KD* 14.

Daniel C. Russell

Katastematic pleasure, rather than kinetic pleasure, can be our final end because unlike kinetic enjoyment it is a goal that affords a perspective on the way one lives one's life as a whole, and that is important because it is from such a perspective that I am most susceptible to mental anguish—which is far worse, Epicurus says, than bare physical pain.[25]

Naturally, this regulating by the final end of katastematic pleasure involves forgoing some kinetic pleasures and even enduring some pains. This regulating does not, however, amount to an abandonment of hedonism, for the simple reason that *the overarching final end that does the regulating is itself a hedonistic end,* namely katastematic pleasure or tranquility. By contrast, if one were to pursue kinetic pleasure for its own sake, but only as regulated by moral virtue (say) as a final end, then one would not be a hedonist. For purely hedonistic reasons, then, an agent who sees herself as someone with a life to live must adopt katastematic pleasure as her overarching final end, and that final end must regulate the other sorts of ends she can pursue.

This is very important for our purposes: on Epicurus's view, kinetic pleasures are goods in and of themselves, and yet they need not promote or augment the final end of tranquility, or produce the security it requires. So for Epicurus kinetic pleasures are goods that we pursue for their own sakes, *without being loose ends,* because our pursuit of them is always regulated by our over-arching need for tranquility. Therefore there is a further kind of network connection by which kinetic pleasures are "referred" to our final end of katastematic pleasure: in particular, the kinds of kinetic pleasures we can pursue, and the ways in which we can pursue them, are regulated by our need for tranquility, even though we pursue the kinetic pleasures that we do strictly for their own sake.

I spoke above about the final end's role of "regulating" one's kinetic pleasures; what is this "regulative" network connection? The final end's regulating of kinetic pleasures involves the requirement that, for any kinetic pleasure I may pursue for its own sake, I must determine whether or not it can be pursued in a way that is consistent with my overarching final end of living tranquilly. For instance, taking a second dessert may bring kinetic pleasure, and thus considered all by itself it is a good and is worth pursuing for its own sake. But in making an all-things-considered judgment to pursue it or avoid it, I must consider the pain it may bring later on; perhaps I will feel uncomfortably full, or even upset about my eventual weight gain. If that is the case, then given my overarching goal of tranquility, I should forgo the second dessert, all things considered.

I maintain more generally that for *anything* I might pursue, even if I pursue it for its own sake, I must determine whether it is rational from my perspective as a continuing agent to pursue it. And so I maintain *not* that

---

25 See Diogenes Laertius, *Lives* X.137; Cicero, *Fin.* I.55–56.

friendships are kinds of kinetic pleasures, but that the "regulative" network connection that exists between kinetic pleasures and tranquility is *the same kind of network connection that exists between friendship and tranquility*: for any friendship I may pursue or maintain, I must determine whether I can do so *and* lead a tranquil life. Furthermore, the regulative connection would be sufficient to make friendship, understood as something to pursue for its own sake, appropriately connected to the final end of tranquility. There is no reason, that is, why a hedonist of the sort that Epicurus is would have to believe that the only things good for their own sakes are pleasures. Hedonism need not be a form of value monism—the view that only pleasures are good for their own sake; hedonism can also be a thesis about our final end—the view that our final end is a kind of pleasure. Indeed, for the ancients, unlike most modern philosophers, hedonism is understood primarily as a view about our final end. And surely someone counts as a hedonist who believes that pleasure is the overarching goal that unifies all of her pursuits, that is, that pleasure is her final end. On the view I have sketched, pleasure can be our final end in exactly that sense, even if there are things other than pleasure—such as friendship—that we pursue for their own sakes. Epicurean hedonism is not the thesis that all intrinsic goods are pleasures, but the thesis that pleasure is our final end. Indeed, even from Epicurus's insistence that "pleasure is the starting point and goal of living blessedly", and is "the starting point for every choice and avoidance", it follows that pleasure is our final end, and that all of our choices are referred to that end, but it does *not* follow that only pleasures are goods.[26] If pleasure is the final end that regulates all of my pursuits, then I can be a hedonist even while I pursue certain goods, such as friendships, for non-hedonic reasons.

Moreover, we have good reason to think of final ends, in the ancient conception, as regulative ends. As David Sedley notes, the main sense of *telos*, even in Plato and Aristotle, is not a goal to be aimed at, but rather a "supreme fulfillment" of the life one leads.[27] The difference is this: a *telos* understood as a goal one aims at serves as a final end inasmuch as all of our other activities are directed at promoting that goal; a *telos* understood as a supreme fulfillment, on the other hand, gives us a specification of what the goodness of a life consists in—not what was acquired in the life, but how the agent went about living it. In

---

26 See *Men.* 128–129, 130; see also *Fin.* I.29–30. For the debate between Epicureans and Stoics over pleasure as our final end, see Diogenes Laertius, *Lives* VII.85–86, Seneca, *Letters* 121.8–9.

27 David Sedley, "The Ideal of Godlikeness", in *Plato 2: Ethics, Politics, Religion, and the Soul*, ed. Gail Fine (New York: Oxford University Press, 1999), pp. 309–328, at p. 321. Sedley also notes that Cicero's book on goals is titled "De Finibus Bonorum et Malorum", and observes that while "evils" cannot be said to have a goal that they aim at, they can be said to have a supreme fulfillment.

---

this latter sense, to say that a life achieves the final end is not to say that its final end is some distinguishable end that the activities of that life have promoted or attained, but rather that there is some good-making quality of that life to which we can appeal in explaining why all of the activities of that life compound into a life that is good.[28] Hence, Sedley says, "When Epicurus (*Letter to Menoeceus* 128) calls health and tranquility 'the *telos* of the blessed life', he means its supreme fulfillment, not the goal it aims at." Indeed, this must be so, given that Epicurus thinks that death is nothing to us, since it cannot interfere with our achieving our final end (see especially *Men.* 124–127, *KD* 19): if our final end were a goal that we aim at, then death could keep us from hitting it, simply by cutting short our time; but death cannot keep us from having lived in a tranquil manner. Consequently, the fact that a regulative end may be a way in which one engages in all of one's activities, rather than some further goal that one's activities are regarded as promoting, does not prevent a regulative end from being a final end or *telos*. On the contrary, that seems to be precisely how final ends were understood to work in ancient ethics.

To sum up, a good will fall within Epicurus's hedonist network of goods if it is either a kinetic pleasure that varies katastematic pleasure, or a good that will promote or facilitate katastematic pleasure, *or* a good the pursuit of which is successfully regulated by the final end of katastematic pleasure, that is, if it is the kind of thing one can pursue in a way consistent with one's goal of living a tranquil life. The connection between tranquility and friendship, I maintain, is the regulative connection: I refer my activities with respect to friendship to my final end of tranquility insofar as I engage in those activities only if it is possible for them to be part of a tranquil life. In that case, my own pleasure is still my final end, and as such it organizes all of my life's endeavors around a central hedonistic end—and that is all that being an Epicurean hedonist requires. At the same time, friendship is thus brought within the hedonist network of goods because full-blooded friendship is regulated by my final end of tranquility, and in that case I can *both* be a hedonist *and* value friends for non-hedonistic reasons.

If we think about a final end as regulative, we can see why Epicurus would take friendship to be such an important part of the happy life. According to Epicurus (as we saw in E), we pursue friendship for its own sake because doing so is crucial for happiness. One achieves happiness just in case one lives tranquilly, but although it is the tranquility of our action which accounts for the happiness of our lives, nonetheless tranquility is not *itself* an activity in its own right. In other words, our happiness consists in the way in which we do the things we do, namely with tranquility. But tranquility itself is not an activity, but a peaceful state of mind of the one acting. To live a happy life, then, *there must*

---

28 See Annas, *The Morality of Happiness*, p. 34 for further discussion of this difference in understandings of a final end.

---

be activities that one engages in in a tranquil way. Our happiness consists in the tranquility with which we live, but in order to live in a tranquil way there must be things that we *do* with our lives. Nor is it enough merely that we do just any old thing, but it matters what kind of things we do: the things we do must be meaningful, they must be things we can live for. We can fill our lives only with activities that can actually *fill up* our lives.[29] Indeed, this is a perfectly general fact about happiness as a goal; as David Schmidtz has recently remarked,

> If my student says she wants to be a professional philosopher, it sounds like she has something to live for. But if she says that all she wants is to be happy, it sounds like finding something to live for is precisely what she needs.... Although she values happiness, the fact remains that she will become happy not by adopting happiness as an end, an item to pursue, but only by adopting, pursuing, and achieving other ends, items worth pursuing for their own sake.[30]

And Epicurus could hardly make it clearer that friendship is exactly this sort of thing. Our reasons for pursuing a friendship outgrow our reasons for initiating it, and yet we can still be hedonists, not because we aim only at pleasure, but because pleasure always has the last word in determining what pursuits we really can engage in.

A regulative end, therefore, has three main roles. For one thing, a regulative end functions as a necessary condition on what a person pursuing that end can engage in. But more than that, a regulative end also gives a specification of the goodness of a good life, that is, it tells us what the goodness of a good life consists in. Finally, and perhaps most importantly, a regulative end also entails positive requirements on what sorts of other ends one must adopt, and how one must adopt them, in order to fulfill one's regulative end. One's theory of value, and one's account of what choices and pursuits are rational, are determined by what one specifies as the final end that regulates all of one's values, choices, and pursuits. Epicurean hedonism is the view that the goodness of a good life consists in the tranquility with which it is lived, and thus that we must specify our final end as tranquility, and that we must refer our actions to this end by allowing this end to regulate them.

It is important to note what I have shown, and what I have not. For one thing, I have *not* shown that friendship is, for Epicurus, compatible with tranquility full stop; it may *still* be the case that friendship involves the sort

---

29 This point is sometimes overlooked; indeed, I think that Cooper, *Reason and Emotion*, overlooks it in construing Epicurean friendships as time-fillers, as it were.

30 Schmidtz, "Choosing Ends", p. 249 n. 34.

---

of pain, inconvenience, and sacrifice that always makes it a bad bargain if one's final end is tranquility, *and* it may still be the case that friendship always threatens the self-sufficiency of the happy life by extending one's interests too deeply into relationships that are too far beyond one's control. Moreover, for all that I have said here the virtues *could* turn out to be the sorts of things one can value for their own sake, *pace* Epicurus;[31] on my view, showing that the virtues, as Epicurus understands them, are not valuable for their own sake would require showing, as I have not, that those virtues are not the sorts of things that a tranquil person could value for their own sake (and so my view does at least offer a distinctive form that such an argument would need to have). What I *have* shown, though, is that from

(A) Everything I do, I refer to the goal of pleasure

it does not follow that

(B) Everything I do, I do for the sake of pleasure.

And that is enough to solve the Loose Ends Problem. Epicurus can claim consistently that our final end is our pleasure, that all of our choices must be referred to pleasure, *and* that we value some things besides pleasure for their own sakes.

As I think it did for Epicurus, the notion of a regulative end should help us to see how one's own happiness or *eudaimonia* can be the final end that continually unifies all of one's interests and projects, even if the value of those interests and projects is not derivative from one's own happiness. And that would be a real help, as it would illuminate the richness and variety of other-regarding values that can be rationally and consistently incorporated into a life that is aimed at an agent-centered goal.[32]

---

31 I thank Michael Taber and Mark Wheeler for raising this point.

32 I thank Julia Annas, Mark LeBar, and Tim O'Keefe for their comments on an earlier version of this paper; special thanks to Tim for graciously sharing a manuscript of his (then) forthcoming article on Epicurean friendship. I also thank the participants in the RIT conference for their comments, especially Marianna Shakhnovich, Michael Taber, and Mark Wheeler. Finally, I am greatly indebted to Dane Gordon and David Suits for their generosity and hospitality, for their editorial assistance, and for making the RIT conference a great success.

WORKS CITED

Annas, Julia, *The Morality of Happiness* (Oxford: Oxford University Press, 1993).

Butler, Joseph, *Fifteen Sermons Preached at the Rolls Chapel*, 2nd ed.
    (London: James and John Knapton, 1729).

Cooper, John M., *Reason and Emotion: Essays on Ancient Moral Psychology
    and Ethical Theory* (Princeton, NJ: Princeton University Press, 1999).

Festugière, Andre-Jean, *Epicurus and His Gods*, trans. C. W. Chilton
    (Oxford: Blackwell, 1955).

Inwood, Brad and Lloyd Gerson, *Hellenistic Philosophy*, 2nd ed. (Indianapolis:
    Hackett, 1997).

Mitsis, Phillip, *Epicurus' Ethical Theory* (Ithaca: Cornell University Press, 1988).

O'Connor, David, "The Invulnerable Pleasures of Epicurean Friendship",
    Greek, Roman, and Byzantine Studies 30 (1989), pp. 165–186.

O'Keefe, Tim, "Is Epicurean Friendship Altruistic?" *Apeiron* 34 (2001),
    pp. 269–305.

Schmidtz, David, "Choosing Ends", *Ethics* 104 (1994), pp. 226–251.

Sedley, David, "The Ideal of Godlikeness", in *Plato 2: Ethics, Politics, Religion,
    and the Soul*, ed. Gail Fine (New York: Oxford University Press,
    1999), pp. 309–328.

Sharples, Robert, *Stoics, Epicureans, and Sceptics: An Introduction to Hellenistic
    Philosophy* (New York: Routledge, 1996).

Stern-Gillet, Suzanne, "Epicurus and Friendship", *Dialogue* 28 (1989),
    pp. 275–288.

EPICURUS ON FRIENDSHIP:
THE EMERGENCE OF BLESSEDNESS

M. R. Wheeler

PART 1: THE PROBLEM

As is familiar, Epicurus was a normative hedonist in the sense that all of our choices and actions should aim at pleasure, even if in fact some don't.[1] For Epicurus, happiness, the blessed life, is the life of pleasure, and pleasure is the only good choiceworthy for its own sake. Yet, Epicurus claimed that friendship, too, is intrinsically good:

> All friendship is choiceworthy for its own sake, though it starts from the need of help.[2]

For a normative hedonist, the claim that friendship is an intrinsic good generates a problem: How can friendship be choiceworthy for its own sake when only pleasure is?

Most have thought this an intractable problem for the Epicurean, but some have attempted to resolve it by claiming that friendship itself is the highest pleasure. According to Festugière, for example, "the exchange of thoughts and the support derived from mutual affection no longer serve only to give mutual strength during the pursuit of abstract learning, they are the end in themselves; in these heart to heart exchanges lies that peace of the soul which is perfect happiness."[3] More recently, Stern-Gillet has argued that "fully fledged Epicurean friendship is not so much a source of pleasure-to-come as pleasure itself."[4]

---

1 Here I generalize Cooper's account of normative hedonism according to which "all our choices and actions ought to be aimed at attaining and then preserving in our lives a secure, constant, uninterrupted enjoyment of the pleasure that is given by the absence of pain from our bodies and of distress, anxiety, agitation, and disturbance of any kind from our minds" (John M. Cooper, *Reason and Emotion* [Princeton, NJ: Princeton University Press, 1999], pp. 495–496). Cooper's account leaves out kinetic pleasures as possible ends-in-themselves.

2 *Sententiae Vaticanae* (hereafter "*SV*") XXIII. Following Usener, Festugière, Stern-Gillet, Rist, and Mitsis, I read *SV* XXIII with *hairetē* and not *aretē*.

3 A. J. Festugière, *Epicurus and His Gods*, trans. C. W. Chilton (Cambridge, MA: Harvard University Press, 1956), p. 37.

4 Suzanne Stern-Gillet, "Epicurus and Friendship," *Dialogue* 28 (1989), pp. 275–288, at p. 283.

Unfortunately, neither Festugière nor Stern-Gillet provide us with an account of how this is supposed to work. As Mitsis notes, Festugière "does not explain how we are to understand these claims in a hedonist context."[5] Stern-Gillet, recognizing clearly the problem "as to whether Epicurus's hedonism can survive the ascription of some kind of intrinsic value to friendship",[6] leaves it obscure how an Epicurean would account for the simultaneity of friendship and pleasure.

I think something like the proposal made by Festugière and Stern-Gillet is correct: friendship—while not strictly identical with happiness or the greatest good—is identical with a kind of katastematic pleasure and, hence, choiceworthy for its own sake. Mitsis—in his book *Epicurus' Ethical Theory: The Pleasures of Invulnerability*—charged Epicurus with an incoherent account of pleasure and friendship.[7] Against Mitsis, I will argue that Epicurus can maintain his normative hedonism while promoting friendship as an intrinsic good. Friendship is a kind of pleasure; aiming at friendship, it turns out, is aiming at katastematic pleasure.[8]

PART 2: CONCEPTUAL PRELIMINARIES AND WORKING ASSUMPTIONS

Even if, following Rist, we think that few persons valued friendship "so highly as Epicurus, or analyzed it so uncompromisingly", the extant remains do not provide us with anything like Epicurus's complete philosophical analysis of friendship.[9] Yet we must work with some analysis or other, and preferably one plausibly attributed to Epicurus. I will use Aristotle as a guide in considering Epicurus's theory of friendship. Since, for Epicurus, every benefit is strictly reducible to pleasure, the relevant Aristotelian concepts are friendships based

---

5   Phillip Mitsis, *Epicurus' Ethical Theory* (Ithaca, NY: Cornell University Press, 1988), p. 114.

6   Stern-Gillet, "Epicurus and Friendship", p. 282.

7   As Mitsis put it, "Like Mill, Epicurus believes that we can value something for its own sake apart from its instrumental contribution to our satisfaction. This position is inconsistent with the claims of his hedonism, but it shows that any hedonist who wants to give a plausible account of happiness must appeal to intrinsically desirable sources of value and concede that the achievement of happiness is not entirely in our own hands" (Mitsis, *Epicurus' Ethical Theory*, p. 128).

8   My strategy can be seen, in part, as a response to Cooper's view that "it is one thing to say that pleasure is the only thing that is good in itself (and pain the only bad in itself), and quite another to say that living pleasantly (that is, in the constant and secure enjoyment of the highest pleasure) is the correct goal for the blessed and happy life" (Cooper, *Reason and Emotion*, p. 495).

9   John M. Rist, "Epicurus on Friendship", *Classical Philology* 75 (1980), pp. 121–129, at p. 121.

---

on pleasure and those based on virtue; I'll call the first kind of friendship a "hedonistic friendship" and the second kind a "true friendship". For our purposes, I need only work with the following partial concepts, derived from Aristotle's complete analyses:

(F1) x and y are true friends only if (1) x has goodwill for y for y's sake and (2) y has goodwill for x for x's sake.

(F2) x and y are hedonistic friends only if (1) x has goodwill for y for the sake of x's pleasure and (2) y has goodwill for x for the sake of y's pleasure.

We may not require much to be persuaded that Epicurus embraced a hedonistic conception of friendship. An Epicurean has goodwill for her friend, at least in part, for the sake of her own pleasure. Following Cicero, we might go so far as to charge Epicurus with a strictly hedonistic conception of friendship and, hence, with having missed the very essence of friendship. As he puts it, the hedonistic system Epicurus promotes "undermines the very foundations of friendship".[10] Nevertheless, there are good reasons for thinking that Epicurus championed the ideal of true friendship. The following quotes suggest this:

> He is no friend who is continually asking for help, nor he who never associates help with friendship. For the former barters kindly feelings for a practical return and the latter destroys the hope of good in the future." [*SV* XXXIX]

> All friendship is desirable in itself, though it starts from the need of help. [*SV* XXIII]

From what Torquatus claims in *De finibus*, I, xx, 66–70, it seems clear that the Epicureans both promoted true friendship and recognized the altruism entailed by it. Moreover, it would be odd, given his biography, were Epicurus to have rejected the concept of true friendship or failed to grasp its essentially altruistic nature.

In what follows, I make a number of assumptions for which I will offer no arguments. I assume that when Epicurus speaks of friendship, he means true friendship, and that he maintains neither an associationist nor a contractualist view of friendship (relying upon arguments made by Mitsis for this latter claim).[11] I assume that Epicurus is committed to emergentism—both

---

10 *De fin.* II, xxv, 80.

11 Mitsis, *Epicurus' Ethical Theory*, chapter 3.

---

with respect to social and psychological facts—and that he maintains neither a dualist, a supervenience, a reductive physicalist, nor an eliminitivist materialist view. I assume that friendship is among the external goods subject to fortune, and I take Epicurus to be a psychological egoist in the sense that we can understand an agent's actions only in terms of the agent's interests.

PART 3: RESOLVING THE PROBLEM

How can Epicurus claim that friendship is a katastematic pleasure? If the pleasure of friendship is something separate from friendship, then Epicurus cannot claim consistently that friendship is choiceworthy in itself. Can Epicurus coherently claim that the pleasure of friendship isn't separable from friendship?

Epicurus posits a strong relation between pleasures and actions. The activities of the virtues and their associated pleasures are inseparable and mutually entailing, as Annas has noted.[12] In the *Kuriai Doxai*, Epicurus claims that

> It is not possible to live pleasantly without living prudently and honourably and justly, [nor again to live a life of prudence, honour, and justice] without living pleasantly. And the man who does not possess the pleasant life, is not living prudently and honourably and justly, [and the man who does not possess the virtuous life], cannot possibly live pleasantly.[13]

And in his *Letter to Menoeceus*, he admonishes his pupil that:

> The virtues are by nature bound up with the pleasant life, and the pleasant life is inseparable from them.[14]

I accept Mitsis's view according to which "Epicurus analyzes pleasure not primarily as a subjective state of consciousness or mental event but rather as the overall healthy condition or functioning of a natural organism."[15] Pleasure is not primarily a subjective state of consciousness. Following Mitsis, we can distinguish between the empiricist view of pleasure and the dispositionalist view of pleasure. According to the empiricist view, activities give rise to feelings that are separate from the activities themselves and of a kindred nature.[16] For

---

12 Julia Annas, "Epicurus on Pleasure and Happiness", *Philosophical Topics* 15 (1987), pp. 5–21, at p. 11.

13 *Kuriai Doxai* V.

14 *Letter to Menoeceus* 132–133.

15 Mitsis, *Epicurus' Ethical Theory*, p. 8.

16 Ibid., p. 21.

Epicurus, all of the kinetic pleasures are felt pleasures of this kind. According to the dispositionalist, pleasure cannot be separated from activities. Rather, pleasure is, as Mitsis puts it, "some further description of the manner in which someone realizes a perceived good, engages in an activity, or perhaps attends to that activity."[17] The katastematic pleasures are the primary kind of pleasures, and these are to be understood dispositionally in terms of activities. In making sense of Epicurus's view of friendship, I will adopt a dispositionalist account according to which every katastematic pleasure is a state identical with certain kinds of activities, states that cannot be separated from these activities.[18]

Friendship and pleasure are not strictly identical; this much is clear. If they were, then there could be no pleasure without friendship. On the face of it, this is implausible, and more so when considered in the context of Epicurus's theory of pleasure. The solitary derive kinetic pleasure when relieved of the cold, satisfied by food, warmed by wine; and the kinetic pleasures of sex can be shared without friendship; more generally, the satisfaction of most, if not all, of the natural desires necessary for survival produces kinetic pleasure independent of friendship.

If friendship is a kind of katastematic pleasure, then although not every state of katastematic pleasure need be identical with friendship, every friendship is identical with some state of katastematic pleasure. Every pleasure or pain—for Epicurus—is a certain state of the body or soul. As is familiar from the *Letter to Herodotus*, "the soul is a body of fine particles distributed throughout the whole structure [i.e., the body]"; it possesses "the chief cause of sensation"; and, when the body is dissolved, "no longer has the same powers nor performs its movements, so that it does not possess sensation either". The body, too, has sensation, by virtue of its relationship with the soul atoms. For Epicurus, then, every pleasure is a state of some set of body or soul atoms.

We recall that x and y are friends only if (1) x has goodwill for y for y's sake and (2) y has goodwill for x for x's sake. Friendship is a certain kind of social relation involving the souls of two friends; more specifically, friendship is a reciprocal social relation essentially involving the souls of at least two friends. The set of atoms involved in the relation of friendship is some union of sets of

---

17 Ibid.

18 So, whereas for Cooper, living pleasantly "means living constantly, securely, and uninterruptedly in a condition of the highest pleasure, which itself is explained as the pleasure that one experiences when one is completely without pain in the body (or, equivalently sometimes, when one is in a state of bodily health) and without suffering any mental disturbance" (*Reason and Emotion*, p. 495), on the view to be developed here living pleasantly means living constantly, securely, and uninterruptedly in a condition free from bodily and mental disturbance, which condition itself is the pleasure one experiences living that way.

---

atoms composing both friends, some of which atoms are soul atoms.

Friendship, of course, is more than the mere union of two sets of atoms. The reduction of the relation of friendship to a mere set theoretical relation among microphysical atoms is neither desirable nor necessary. According to Emergentism, social and psychological states are novel properties that emerge in the world as a function of the (usually complex) relations among aggregates of basic physical particles. Friendship, on this view, is an emergent property realized when two human beings—each taken separately an aggregate of atoms exhibiting a high degree of structural complexity and emergent properties—develop a reciprocal relation that, once developed, is a new aggregate of ultimately physical parts. Among the essential parts of this new aggregate are the souls of the friends, and from this whole emerges the reciprocal social relation of friendship. Katastematic pleasures, too, are emergent properties. If every friendship is a katastematic pleasure, then each instance of the emergent property of friendship must be identical with some instance of the emergent property of katastematic pleasure. Emergentism makes this a coherent possibility.

Emergentism allows for the theoretical possibility that friendship is a kind of pleasure and, hence, allows the normative hedonist to claim that friendship is choiceworthy for its own sake. But of course, theoretical possibility is one thing, plausibility another.

PART 4: AN OBJECTION—THE INSTRUMENTAL VALUE OF FRIENDSHIP

I have described how Epicurus can make sense of the claim that friendship is choiceworthy for its own sake, and not merely as a means to pleasure. Do I mean to imply—contrary to what is apparent from the texts—that friendship isn't a means to pleasure? No. Friendship, though choiceworthy for its own sake, is also an instrumental good. Of some pleasures produced by friendship—those for which it *is* strictly an instrumental good—the pleasure clearly is separate. In some cases, friendship may merely be a means to kinetic pleasure. We have already noted that Epicurus believes that friends help each other in times of want. Ultimately, of course, help must come in the form of satisfied desires, and the relevant desires to consider are those the satisfaction of which contributes either to survival, health of the body, or freedom from disturbance of the mind. Textual evidence shows that friendship will enable us—in some cases—to satisfy natural needs for survival.[19] In these cases, the

---

19 A friend may help me when I am hungry; I may call upon her to send me preserved cheese (Diog. Laert., X. 11). A friend may help me when physically ill; pleasurable conversation with my friend, or even the pleasure of the memory of past conversations, can balance the pain arising from the disease in my stomach (Diog. Laert., X.22).

---

friendship serves merely as a means to securing certain sensual pleasures. In other cases, friendship may be a means to certain katastematic pleasures, if for example friendship is a means to the katastematic pleasure of philosophical comprehension.

PART 5: ANOTHER OBJECTION—THE INSTRUMENTAL VALUE OF THE OTHER VIRTUES

It is widely believed that Epicurus demoted the traditional virtues to merely instrumental goods. Julia Annas has argued against this view, claiming that in general "virtue can be sought and valued for its own sake."[20] Annas recognizes that her interpretation conflicts with Epicurus's explicit and often repeated commitment to the merely instrumental value of the traditional virtues. If Annas can overcome these textual difficulties, she would need to explain still how each of the virtues is choiceworthy for its own sake, given that only pleasure is an intrinsic good. The account I have sketched above makes this possible. I do not think, however, that the textual difficulties can be overcome, and my view doesn't entail that all of the traditional virtues be kinds of katastematic pleasure. Epicurus assigns merely instrumental status to most of the traditional virtues; on the account sketched above, all of the traditional virtues are emergent properties; those which have merely instrumental value aren't identical with a kind of pleasure. Of course, if I am correct, then at least one of the traditional virtues—friendship—has more than instrumental value. This would be a difficulty only if Epicurus had failed to treat friendship differently from the other traditional virtues, but he does. Epicurus assigns a special status to friendship, consistently treating friendship separately from the other traditional virtues and never derogating it to a merely instrumental status. In the letter to Menoeceus—where Epicurus addresses at some length the merely instrumental character of the virtues—he doesn't mention friendship, and as we know he explicitly assigns it intrinsic worth.

PART 6: NON-SOLIPSISTIC PLEASURE?

In general, we conceive of pleasure solipsistically: I feel my pleasures, you feel yours, I have access only to my pleasures, you only to yours. My view entails that at least some pleasures are non-solipsistic; they are literally shared. Specifically, my view entails that at least one kind of pleasure is identical with a kind of social relation. *Prima facie*, this is nonsense.

If—following the empiricist account—we conceive of pleasure solely in terms of a positive feeling had by some consciousness, and feelings are private, monadic properties had by a consciousness, then it is nonsensical to claim that pleasure is a social relation. The katastematic pleasures—as I conceive of them

---

20 Annas, "Epicurus on Pleasure and Happiness", p. 12.

here, *pace* Cooper—are not feelings, except in the negative sense that they are defined in terms of the lack of disturbance of the soul or pain. Annas's way of putting the matter is helpful:

> Pleasure as our final good *is* the condition of unimpeded natural activity, not the pleasure felt as lack or need is removed.[21]

Annas here contrasts the felt kinetic pleasures with the katastematic pleasures identical with natural activities. Recall that on the dispositional view of pleasure, every pleasure is identical with some activity or other.

This much is relatively uncontroversial, I think. More difficult is the claim that some states of consciousness are essentially relational. Some states of consciousness, such as veridical perceptual states, are essentially relational in the sense that my private consciousness must be related to something else in order to be in that state. But, for friendship to be a social relation identical with pleasure, it must be possible for the katastematic state of my soul and the katastematic state of your soul not only to be produced by our friendship but to be constituted by the relational activity of our friendship. This is possible because the katastematic state of pleasure that is friendship is the natural and unimpeded activity shared by friends, an intimate activity of friends living together.

I don't pretend to think that I can prove Epicurus maintained such a view; I have surely gone beyond what the texts directly support. Nevertheless, Epicurus could maintain such a view, and if he did it would help to make sense of more than just the intrinsic value of friendship. Philodemus informs us that, according to Epicurus, the gods have friendships.[22] This is puzzling. We know that Epicurus's gods are fully self-sufficient, and if every pleasure is a purely solipsistic state of the soul, no god would need a friend to achieve complete happiness. If, as seems reasonable, we suppose that complete happiness presupposes friendship, and if friendship is essentially relational in the strong sense just described, then every god would need a friend in order to achieve complete happiness.

PART 7: MAKING SENSE OF ALTRUISM

An additional benefit of the view offered here is that it allows Epicurus to make sense of the altruistic aspect of friendship. How can I, a psychological hedonist, justify my goodwill for my friend for my friend's sake? Stated in hedonistic terms, how can a psychological egoist justify acting on behalf of her friend's pleasure for the sake of her friend's pleasure? Torquatus had mentioned

---

21 Ibid., p. 13.

22 Philodemus, *De Dis* 3, fr. 84, col. 1, 2–9.

---

two conditions for true friendship: (1) that I treat my friend's pleasure as my own and (2) that I treat my friend exactly as myself. Cicero rightly noted that (2) is too weak; what we need is the stronger claim that (3) I treat my friend as an end-in-herself. Taking (1) and (3) as conditions on the altruistic nature of friendship, I will argue for two claims. First, I will argue that friendship is a relation between friends such that I have pleasure in the friendship if, and only if, my friend has pleasure in the friendship. Second, and less problematically, I will argue that friendship is possible only if I treat my friend as an end-in-herself.

Since friendship is a kind of pleasure and I have a friendship with you just in case you have a friendship with me, I have the pleasure of our friendship just in case you have the pleasure of our friendship. Epicurus apparently recognized this affective affinity between friends when he claimed that:

> The wise man is not more pained when being tortured [himself, than when seeing] his friend [tortured].[23]

But what does it mean, then, to say that I treat my friend's katastematic pleasure as my own? It means that I treat the friendship my friend has for me as the friendship I have for my friend; it means that I treat the activity of friendship undertaken by my friend with me as the activity of friendship undertaken by me with my friend; and this makes perfect sense given the reciprocal nature of the activity of friendship. Hence, we can satisfy Torquatus's first condition on altruistic friendship.

Cicero's condition—that we treat our friends as ends-in-themselves— makes clear that friendship is essentially altruistic: you and I are friends only if I have goodwill for you for your sake and you have goodwill for me for my sake. If friendship is a kind of pleasure, then it is an essentially altruistic kind of pleasure. As noted in discussing the friendships among the gods, a completely pleasurable life requires friendship:

> Of the things wisdom acquires for the blessedness of life as a whole, far the greatest is the possession of friendship. [*Kuriai Doxai*, XXVII]

The very nature of friendship entails that I have a completely pleasurable life only if I have goodwill for you for your sake and you have goodwill for me for my sake. If I am an Epicurean hedonist, then of course I choose the completely pleasurable life, and if that is my choice, then I choose to have goodwill for my friend for my friend's sake. How does this fit into Epicurus's psychological egoism? As in Aristotle, Epicurean altruism will retain

---

23 *SV* LVI–LVII.

---

ultimate reference to an agent's self-interest: it is in my interest to be altruistic: it is in my best interest to have goodwill for my friend for my friend's sake. In the case of friendship, my friend's interests are my interests.

PART 8: DEATH

"Death means nothing to us"—so, famously, wrote Epicurus to Menoeceus. It is clear that Epicurus viewed death as inevitable and, hence, so too the death of our friends. No less clear is the fact that he recognized the risk of pain involved in friendship. Since friendship is essential for a completely pleasurable life, and it involves the risk of our friend's betrayal and death, friendship threatens our self-sufficiency by exposing us to the risk of unhappiness. Others have discussed the relation between friendship and self-sufficiency, and I think that for the Epicurean sage—unlike the Stoic wise man—the good of friendship with its attendant risk trumps the virtue of self-sufficiency. But how can we claim that death is nothing to us when death threatens either to deprive us of our friends or our friends of us? Once our friend has died—though it may be that "sweet is the memory of a dead friend"[24]—he or she no longer exists and, therefore, cannot remain a friend. Doesn't the death of our friends threaten our happiness, and in this way become something for us? Knowing that I will die and, hence, cause my friends to suffer, isn't my death also something for me to fear insofar as I fear harming my friends?

Recent philosophers—hoping to demonstrate that death should mean something to the Epicurean—have developed a battery of arguments for and against the so-called deprivation thesis according to which a person's death does or doesn't deprive her of possible pleasures and pains. These arguments focus on whether or not the individual who dies is deprived of pleasures and pains that they themselves could have had, were they not to have died. I will consider another version of the deprivation thesis, one that focuses not on the consequences of death for the person who dies but on the consequences for bereaved friends. Modifying Fred Feldman's formulation of the deprivation thesis for the case of friendship, we get:

> (Friendship Deprivation Thesis) My death is bad for my friends if, and only if, the welfare level of my friends at the nearest world at which I don't die is greater than their welfare level at the nearest world at which I do die.[25]

---

24 Plutarch, *contr. Ep. beat.* 28, 1105d.

25 I base this on the analysis found in Fred Feldman, "Some Puzzles About the Evil of Death", *Philosophical Review* 100 (1991), pp. 205–227.

If death is nothing to us, and hence never bad for us, it follows from this thesis that my friends are never worse off by my having died than they would be were I to have survived. This seems wrong, and if false—given the additional and plausible premise that I should fear my death if it is bad for my friends—I should fear my death. How might Epicurus respond?

In the first place, it must be borne in mind that only the Epicurean sage achieves the recommended equanimity with respect to death. Secondly, it is clear that the Epicurean sage will not suffer extremely from the death of a friend. Epicurus sometimes suggests that we won't suffer at all from the loss of our friends,[26] but other passages, however, suggest a more moderate view:

> Let us show our feeling for our lost friends not by lamentation
> but by meditation. [*SV* LXVI]

It is clear that—in any case—the Epicurean sage will not suffer overmuch at the passing of a friend.

Nevertheless, if we assume that my friends will suffer even a little bit when I pass away and we assume that a completely happy life is only possible with friends, then there are many cases to consider in light of the Friendship Deprivation Thesis, and the cases are fairly complicated. Thankfully, we needn't work through all of the permutations to discover Epicurus's best response to all of them: for my death to mean nothing to my surviving friends, each must have at least one friend remaining after I have died (else complete happiness isn't possible), each must be wise enough to know the true nature of death (insuring that all know of the certainty of death and none suffer for fear of my plight after death), and every nearby world is a world in which each loses at least one friend (insuring that in every nearby world each friend will suffer from the loss of a friend). Since it is plausible that every nearby world is a world in which everyone loses at least one friend, my bereaved friend in this world—being otherwise

---

26 Some quotes seem favorable to this line of interpretation:

> As many as possess the power to procure complete immunity from
> their neighbors, these also live most pleasantly with one another,
> since they have the most certain pledge of security, and after they
> have enjoyed the fullest intimacy, they do not lament the previous
> departure of a dead friend, as though he were to be pitied. [*SV* XL]

And more dramatically:

> When it is time for us to go, spitting contempt on life and on those
> who here vainly cling to it, we will leave life crying aloud in a glorious
> triumph-song that we have lived well. [*SV* XLVII]

Such remarks might lead us to think that, for Epicurus, the death of a friend is
no cause for pain. This might seem a flaw in the theory, but that is another issue.

self-sufficient as a sage, and having secured the blessing of friendship through another—will neither be better off nor worse off by my having died.

CONCLUSION

Epicurus said that "the greatest blessing is created and enjoyed at the same moment."[27] I have argued that friendship is a relational activity between friends the being of which is a katastematic pleasure: the very activity of friendship is its enjoyment.

WORKS CITED

Annas, Julia, "Epicurus on Pleasure and Happiness", *Philosophical Topics* 15 (1987), pp. 5–21.

Cooper, John M., *Reason and Emotion* (Princeton, NJ: Princeton University Press, 1999).

Feldman, Fred, "Some Puzzles About the Evil of Death", *Philosophical Review* 100 (1991), pp. 205–227.

Festugière, A. J., *Epicurus and His Gods*, trans. C. W. Chilton (Cambridge, MA: Harvard University Press, 1956).

Mitsis, Phillip, *Epicurus' Ethical Theory* (Ithaca, NY: Cornell University Press, 1988).

Rist, John M., "Epicurus on Friendship", *Classical Philology* 75 (1980), pp. 121–129.

Stern-Gillet, Suzanne, "Epicurus and Friendship", *Dialogue* 28 (1989), pp. 275–288.

---

27 *SV* XLII.

DEATH AS A PUNISHMENT:
A CONSEQUENCE OF EPICUREAN THANATOLOGY

Stephen E. Rosenbaum

The basic, controversial principle of Epicurean ideas about death is that, if death is nonexistence, then "death is nothing to us." Although there is relatively little accord about how to understand the principle and even less agreement about its plausibility, people are at least familiar with it. There is, I suspect, substantially less familiarity with the Roman Senate's debate about how to punish the Cataline conspirators. Having been led by one Cataline, a number of Roman citizens tried to overthrow the legitimate republican government of Rome, but were thwarted and captured. The Senate subsequently considered their punishment, whether to exile them and confiscate their property, along with deprivation of citizenship, or put them to death.

Julius Caesar argued in the Senate that the conspirators' punishment should not be death, on the ground that "death is the end of all suffering" and that they deserved something worse.[1] He might have said, in our idiom, that death was too good for them. The Senate rejected his reasoning, and voted to put the conspirators to death. I want in this paper to explore, or perhaps reconstruct, the reasoning implicitly lying behind Caesar's thinking about the death penalty, and urge that although he suffered a political defeat, the idea he advocated is far more interesting and fruitful than one might at first imagine.

I want to investigate the idea, perhaps first noticed by Caesar, that Epicurus's basic idea about death implies that death is not a punishment, or at least not as severe a punishment as commonly believed. This exploration will, importantly I think, help us reflect on the exact nature of the death penalty, on the extent to which death can be much of a punishment and on the nature of punishment itself. Perhaps it will as well lead us to think more extensively about Epicurus's view of death and its implications. Because I shall focus on the nature of the death penalty, with Epicurean thanatology in the background, as the logical inspiration for it, as it were, I shall clarify to some extent the principal Epicurean idea about death.

To explicate the background of the discussion, it will help to begin with Epicurus's apparently startling expression of his idea about the value of death

---

1 Sallust, *The Cataline Conspiracy*, trans. S. A. Handford (Baltimore: Penguin, 1967): "As regards the penalty you proposed, it would be relevant to observe that to men in grief and wretchedness death comes as a release from suffering, not as a punishment to be endured, because death terminates all suffering ..." (LI.16–24).

for people. "Death is nothing to us", he declared famously.[2] Most simply put, he thought that one's own death is not and cannot be bad for one. However bad our deaths might be for others, they cannot satisfy the fundamental requirement for having value for us, namely that we be capable of being affected by our deaths, in the sense that one's death is one's nonbeing.

We ought at the outset to recognize ambiguity in the term "death", and then clarify the meaning of the term in this context, because without that clarification, one could easily think that, contrary to his claim, it is possible for us to be affected by our deaths. Epicurus did not mean by "death" the manner of one's dying or the process of one's dying, because his basic reasoning would then have made no sense, since our deaths in this sense can cause us pain and can thus affect us. Nor did he mean the "moment of death", captured in the expression, "his death occurred at 10:01 P.M." Since his reasoning was directed against the fear of death, where that fear in Epicurus's thinking seems to have been associated with the fear of an unpleasant afterlife, or possibly with the fear of not being alive, one would not expect him to have been particularly concerned about the moment of death. He meant the condition of being dead, one's state after one dies. So, he thought that one's being dead, that condition, could not be bad for the one in that condition.

A brief review of Epicurus's main argument why "death is nothing to us" will help illuminate the point about the meaning of "death". "When we exist", he reasoned, "death is not yet present, and when death is present, then we do not exist. Therefore, it is relevant neither to the living nor to the dead, since it does not affect the former, and the latter do not exist."[3] This statement could apply only to the state of being dead. Moreover, when Epicurus said that "good and evil require sentience" and that "death is the absence of sentience", he can only be understood to mean by "death" the condition of being dead.[4] So, by "death is nothing to us", Epicurus meant to declare that one's own condition of being dead is not bad for one.

Epicurus's view is likely to strike many as absurd, because it appears to conflict so completely with the common sentiment that death is one of the worst fates, as it were, that could befall an individual. Indeed, many philosophers have argued against this view in a variety of ways, because it contradicts a fundamental "intuition". For my purposes here, it will not be useful extensively to describe, classify, and discuss all of the objections against Epicurus's basic thesis about death, because I want to focus on the implications of that thesis for the death penalty and the way we think about the death penalty. Nevertheless, it is important to describe the most common objection to Epicurus on death,

---

2   Diogenes Laertius, *Lives of the Eminent Philosophers*, X.125.

3   Ibid.

4   Ibid., 124.

because that objection lays the basis for an objection to the idea that the death penalty is not much of a penalty.

The most widespread philosophical objection to Epicurus on the idea about death has its roots in Aristotle's puzzling remarks about death. Many contemporary thinkers argue that Epicurus's argument is beside the point, because death is bad for people because it is a deprivation. It is a deprivation, even if people cannot experience it, and is thus bad for people, even without being able to be experienced. Such an idea has roots in Aristotelian comments about death. Aristotle adopted a view about the value of death for those who die different from Epicurus's, as do most contemporary thinkers who have taken positions on the issue, and so there seems to have been dialectical opposition between the Epicurean idea and the Aristotelian and the neo-Aristotelian view (as I shall call them) of many contemporary thinkers.[5] Aristotle believed that death is bad for those who die, perhaps the very worst thing that could happen to them, for he said that "death is the most terrible of all things, for it is the end, and nothing is thought to be any longer good or bad for the dead."[6] Aristotle's declaration is based on a different conception of value from that of Epicurus. The Aristotelian view is not that the condition of being dead is bad for those who die, which would contradict Epicurus's view. Rather, adopting a different theory of value and viewing expansively the categories of thing that can bear value for people, his thesis is that *the fact* that one dies is bad for one. Aristotle's different theory of value permits propositions to have value for individuals, even when those propositions do not entail the existence of some state or condition of which the individuals which they are about can be aware, and do not entail the existence of some cause of such a state or condition. This idea opposes the implicit Epicurean concept of value, according to which value (good and bad) must be essentially linked to concrete conditions of people, effects on people, and the causes of those conditions or effects.[7]

A few examples of these different notions of value would be useful for understanding one basic difference between those who support the Epicurean view and those who reject it and for understanding one objection to questioning the death penalty as a punishment. Someone's pain or the cause of such pain can be bad for someone, according to a concrete notion of value, of the kind

---

5   I have discussed extensively the two different views of value in my "Appraising Death in Human Life: Two Modes of Valuation", *Midwest Studies in Philosophy* 24 (*Life and Death: Metaphysics and Ethics*), ed. Peter French and Howard K. Wettstein (Oxford: Blackwell Publishers, 2000), pp. 151–171.

6   Aristotle, *The Complete Works of Aristotle*, vol. 2, ed. Jonathan Barnes (Princeton: Princeton University Press, 1984), p. 1760; *Nicomachean Ethics*, III, 6 (1115a, 8–27).

7   Epicurus said that "all good and bad lie in sentience [… agathon kai kakon en aisthesei …]" (Diogenes Laertius, X.124).

Epicurus relies on. Also the fact that someone is in pain can be bad for someone, because it is related appropriately to a concrete state or condition of the person. With a different concept, however, which I'll call Aristotelian, a fact might be bad for someone, without being logically linked to conditions of which they might be or become aware. For example the fact that after one's death, one's descendents suffer reverses, can be bad for a person, although one can never be affected by the reverses or be aware of them. While this point may seem only remotely related to a discussion of Epicurus's view of death and how it impinges on the death penalty, it will form later the basis of an objection to my initial views about Epicurus's views of death and the death penalty.

What is the argument that Epicurus's idea about death should make one question the severity of the death penalty, and how should we reconstruct Caesar's thinking? We should begin by asking what a penalty is, or what a punishment is. The classical conception is that punishments are harms, or bads, done to someone in a certain context. It is unnecessary now to describe completely or fully the context, because that is not related to the argument. It is clear however that it involves laws and actions by official bodies. This concept is manifest in the writings of Bentham, Mill, Sidgwick, Hart, and others, although it is for the most part merely implicit.[8] Anyhow, for the sake of the argument, I assume for the time being this conception of punishment. I will later urge that one could obviously avoid the conclusion by adopting a different concept of punishment.

The argument continues by focusing on the nature of the death penalty. What exactly is the death penalty? It seems that the death penalty must in some sense be death, caused by those responsible for administering punishments. Just as the punishment of imprisonment is incarceration, so also the punishment of death is death. If the death penalty is death, however, in what sense should we understand "death"? In light of the three notions of death by which I earlier explicated Epicurus's view of the value of death for people, we should consider the condition of being dead, the process of dying, and the moment at which a person becomes dead. If the death penalty is the state of being dead, commencing at the

---

8 See, for examples of works in which the view is evident, Jeremy Bentham, *An Introduction to the Principles of Morals and Legislation* (London: The Athalone Press, 1970), p. 158; John Stuart Mill, *Utilitarianism* (Indianapolis: The Bobbs-Merrill Co., Inc., 1957), pp. 74–76; Henry Sidgwick, *The Methods of Ethics* (Chicago: University of Chicago Press, 1907), pp. 72, 281. The view is also expressed in contemporary sources: H. L. A. Hart, *Punishment and Responsibility: Essays in the Philosophy of Law* (Oxford: Oxford University Press, 1968), p. 4; and a bit less clearly, Richard Wasserstrom, "Capital Punishment as Punishment: Some Theoretical Issues and Objections", *Midwest Studies in Philosophy*, ed. Peter French, et al. (Minneapolis: University of Minnesota Press, 1982), pp. 476–478.

time the person killed becomes dead, I do not see that it can be a punishment, in light of Epicurus's persuasive view that being dead is not bad for the dead. If the death penalty is the moment at which one becomes dead, I also don't see how that could be bad for the person killed, since the moment of death would seem to be bad just because it leads to being dead. What would be bad about the moment of death if people survived it? If being dead is not bad for people, why would the moment of death be? Of course, some think of the moment of death as being the first moment of the condition of being dead, and so it could not in this case be bad for someone, again, assuming the Epicurean idea of death. The death penalty might on the other hand be a particular process of dying. Is the process of dying the punishment? At least as we think of the death penalty, the process is not that to which one is sentenced. One might administer death in any number of different ways. The various ways, lethal injection, lethal gas, the electric chair, hanging, and shooting, are different significantly, being different ways of causing death, and are simply ways of causing death. Furthermore, in our culture, we seem to want to reduce the death penalty, if we have it at all, to the most gentle and efficient way of killing someone. Some would say that the bad thing about methods of killing people is that they wind up dead, and that the different values of the different methods of killing are unrelated to the value of the death penalty. The methods of killing are inessential to the nature of the death penalty. It seems that the only remaining candidate is the state of being dead, and that that state is what constitutes the death penalty. But what is bad, Epicurus would ask, about being dead, for the person who is dead? The power of Caesar's implicit thinking should be becoming apparent.

The argument is relatively simple and straightforward, and I hope I have not obscured its simple strength. Very crudely, for the sake of clarity, it consists in the following three ideas, simplified for the sake of clarity: (1) Punishments are appropriately administered effects on people which are bad for them, and an effect on someone is not a punishment if it is not bad for him or her. (2) The death penalty (capital punishment) is death, in the sense of being dead. This is to describe it in terms of the effects which constitute the punishment, rather than the causes of those effects. One might characterize the death penalty generically as the action which brings about the effect of death on someone, but that is just to focus on the killing action rather than the effect. Finally, (3) death, in the sense of being dead, is not bad for the people who are dead—the Epicurean view. It seems to follow that death is not a punishment, and that the death penalty will be bad for someone depending only on effects that are extraneous to the nature of the penalty. Then, how severe the penalty will be will depend on the severity of those effects.

Even including effects extraneous to, or logically separate from, the death penalty, such as psychological distress and anxiety, which would obtain while waiting for execution, it might well be that imprisonment in many cases would be worse than the death penalty (remembering that the badness would attach only to elements of the situation logically unrelated to the penalty). If the penalty is death, then the psychological effect of knowing that that penalty will be administered might perhaps be great, depending on the person. It strikes me that if one estimates the effect on someone who is imprisoned for, say, ten years, the punishment of imprisonment might well be worse than the possible effects of believing that the death penalty will be administered. Depending on how one were treated, the bad effects of imprisonment could easily be very much greater than those affiliated with the death penalty. One might in prison be unable to exercise, to read, to talk with friends, to eat properly nourishing food, to feel personally safe, and to be unable to do much of interest. Additionally, the psychological effects of incarceration might be almost as bad as the effect of knowing one will soon die. It seems that imprisonment could very often be worse than the death penalty.

One might try to rebut that point about the relative bad of imprisonment in relation to the side effects of the death penalty by exploring what people actually prefer. One might propose to ask people whether they would prefer imprisonment, even life imprisonment, to the death penalty. Supposing that all respondents claimed to prefer imprisonment to death, we might be invited to conclude that death is the greater harm. The logic of the effort would be faulty, however. That people prefer one thing, a, to another, b, does not show either that b is harmful or (assuming that a and b are both harmful) that b is more harmful than or worse than a. Hamlet's reservations about death seem psychologically realistic, but show nothing whatsoever about whether death is more harmful or worse than being alive under difficult conditions. Such preferences might be based on beliefs which are not grounded in facts about harm or what is bad, but might be based on cultural beliefs that death is bad and that the death penalty is the worst penalty. If so, such a procedure would be question-begging in the sense that, as evidence, it is based on acceptance of the negation of the conclusion of the argument. Basically, such evidence would amount to using the belief that death is worse than imprisonment, embedded as it were in the framework by which people construct preferences, to argue that death is worse than imprisonment. Without acceptance of the proposition that death is worse than imprisonment, there would be no reason to accept the conclusion that death is worse. One would need to supplement the argument with an account of how people form such preferences independently of their beliefs about the badness of death in relation to imprisonment, and I do not readily see how this could be done.

The point of affiliating the death penalty with psychologically negative effects is to include psychological harm in the punishment, in order to compare it in severity to other common punishments. Of course, there is something artificial about this, if the penalty is death, because one's being dead is not associated with psychological effects. Nevertheless, so including psychological harm, it seems not very plausible that the death penalty would be worse than other punishments that are commonly regarded as less severe than the death penalty. It is quite easy to imagine that ten years of imprisonment would be at least just as harmful or bad as the time between the realization that one will be executed and one's being killed. The psychological effects of the punishments might be quite similar, the belief that one could not achieve one's important aims, the depression, the regrets, the blind fear, etc. If one suggested that a person could adapt oneself psychologically to ten years in prison, it is worth suggesting, too, plausibly I think, that one could also adapt psychologically to the prospect of death. It seems to me that the death penalty, including the psychological harm of expecting to be killed, would not be worse, or more severe than many other common punishments, and it strikes me that other common punishments would be much worse in many cases.

It is worth recalling that the death penalty does not really include the psychological accompaniments of knowing that one has been sentenced to death, if my earlier comments are correct. It is death, being dead. If it were not death, but merely the psychological effects, it is important to note that it would be possible to administer all the bad or harm of the death penalty without killing. Sentence people to death, convince them that they were to be executed on May 1, let them worry themselves sick, bring them to the point of execution, and then let them go free. One would have accomplished all the harm of doing all that and then actually killing the persons. Of course, for this to work generally, there would need to be special arrangements to prevent the punished from knowing that they would not be killed. There is reason not to associate the psychological effects of the death penalty with the penalty itself.

Some might be concerned that if the death penalty is not really a penalty, or much of a penalty at all, on the grounds that it is death and being dead is not bad for the person who dies, then it would become theoretically questionable whether killing someone could be morally wrong. Thus, one would question the Epicurean view on the ground that it would imply an absurdity. Those who think this way believe that somehow the badness of death for the person who dies is the basis, and perhaps the only basis, for killing's being generally morally wrong. Perhaps this derives in some way from the modern utilitarian tradition, which bases morality on value. In any case, it is possible to conceive of moral ideals—Epicurus's ideal is one of them—which do not treat morality in this way. In Epicurean thinking, justice (what we would call morality) had a contractarian basis. Justice for Epicurus came from a *syntheke*, a compact, which included prohibitions about killing. However, the prohibitions were not based directly on the value of experiences or conditions of people but rather on the nature of the compact. For Epicureans, the rule forbidding murder and perhaps generally killing came from the fact that murder or killing "is not useful to the general structure of human life," as Hermarchus thought.[9] However the details of this should be understood, or might be developed, the point is that there are conceptual ways of providing for the wrongness of killing that are compatible with the death penalty not being a penalty because it is just the condition of being dead. The general wrongness of killing need not be based on the badness of death.[10]

The basic premises of the argument might be questioned to generate further possible objections to my argument. Someone might object to what I have described as the classical conception of punishment, and urge that punishments need not generally be harms or bad effects on people. Suppose that being harmful is not necessary for something to be a punishment. Then treatments of persons could be punishments even if they did not harm those persons. So the death penalty could be a punishment even if it did not harm, or did not consist in a bad effect on someone. But what theoretical conception of punishment could yield this result? It is interesting to spin fanciful principles out of one's philosophical imagination, but how could these ideas be grounded theoretically, and could the theoretical basis be plausible? I do not have time now to describe a completely different conception of punishment, nor am I now in a position to defend a rather different theory of punishment. However, I want to sketch a notion of punishment that could possibly accommodate the idea, a conception of punishment inspired by the ideas of Adam Smith in *The Theory of Moral Sentiments*.[11]

Suppose that punishment is essentially the expression of a kind of resentment, and that its function is to satisfy the feelings of resentment felt by the members of a society when the important rules of behavior in the society are known to have been violated. The state would be the agent which acted for the members of society, and the members of society would have their feelings for resentment appeased by knowing that the state acted against those who violate the rules. One could herewith account for the different degrees of severity for punishments, by observing that there are different grades of action that would satisfy differing grades of resentment. One could also account for the fact that punishments are commonly harms or bad effects on people, by noting that persons would seek to inflict what they regard as harm on those against whom they feel resentment of the kind on which state punishments are predicated.

---

9 Porphyry, *On Abstinence*, 1.7.1–9.4 (quoting Hermarchus), in A. A. Long and D. N. Sedley, *The Hellenistic Philosophers* (Cambridge: Cambridge University Press, 1987), p. 129.

10 For an account of Epicurus's moral prohibition against killing, see my "Epicurean Moral Theory", *History of Philosophy Quarterly* 13 (1996), pp. 389–410.

11 Adam Smith, *The Theory of Moral Sentiments* (Oxford: Clarendon Press, 1976), pp. 67–77.

One could further account for the fact that capital punishment is regarded as the most severe punishment, by observing that feelings of resentment are assuaged by what persons believe is harmful, and that, in some societies, people believe that killing a person is the most harmful thing that could be done to the person. There are of course other things to be said about this idea. It is obviously inchoate and incomplete. The point, however, is not here to display plausibly the beginnings of a very different theory of the nature of punishment. The point rather is simply to suggest a way of grounding theoretically the idea that something could be a punishment without being harmful, and to show a way of believing that the death penalty really is a punishment, in spite of Epicurus's view that death is not bad for people. If death is not bad for those who die, the death penalty still could be a punishment. This is clear from the logic of the argument.

Perhaps some would regard the premise that the death penalty is death (being dead) as questionable. Coupling this with the theory of abstract propositional value I mentioned earlier when I described Aristotle's view, one might argue both that the death penalty is bad for people and that the real death penalty is not being dead or the condition of nonexistence, but rather the fact that one dies at a certain time. To recall Aristotle's idea, some things can be bad for people even without having negative effects on them. Specifically, propositions can have value for them—be bad for them or good for them—even if those propositions do not entail the occurrence of effects on people. Thus, it is in an important sense proper to call them abstract. What proposition might be bad for a person, where the proposition is associated with the person's dying at a particular time, but does not entail the existence of effects on the person of which the person could be aware? I do not think it would be proper to insist that there would be only one proper answer, but an illustration would be helpful. Suppose that the proposition in question would be this: "that the person killed was caused to die, to stop living, prematurely by the state, enforcing a statute." One might say that this proposition was bad for the person, but need not entail any concrete effects of which the person could be aware. This proposition would be true of the person, specified properly, but, like the proposition that his or her descendents suffered terrible reverses after his or her life had ended, it would not be related to effects on the person of which he or she might be aware. With this idea that bad need not be concrete, but might rather be abstract in the sense explained, one could think that the death penalty is a severe punishment, or, perhaps, one of the most severe punishments. According to this idea, the death penalty would *not* be death (being dead), but would rather be a fact about the person's life, or perhaps better said, the person's history.

I think we should make several observations about this notion of the death penalty. This conception of the death penalty makes the punishment literally a kind of non-affecting abstraction. As such it is very different from other punishments, and perhaps so different in kind that it would be incommensurable with other kinds of punishments. In fact, it seems so different that one might question whether it would make sense to think of it as a real punishment. Other punishments consist in concrete effects on those who are punished. Imprisonments and fines are real deprivations, which affect people greatly. Embarrassment, social ostracism, and the long term effects of a prison record are effects which somehow define the quality of a person's life, and people suffer concretely more or less depending on their psychological constitutions. The death penalty would not be anything like this, but would be very different in kind. As such, I do not see how one could estimate its severity in relation to other common punishments. Would it be worse than life imprisonment? Would it be worse than a shorter imprisonment? How about a fine? Would it be worse than a fine? Of course we do think the death penalty is worse than a fine, but I don't see how one could justify that idea, on the assumption that it is abstract in the way suggested, and so different in kind from other punishments. Because I would have a difficult time comparing it to concrete punishments, so conceived, I am inclined to believe that thinking of the death penalty in such an abstract way would make it incommensurable with other punishments. I believe that there are serious theoretical problems with the conception of making the punishment of death as making a fact, a proposition, true of someone.

Moreover, if the death penalty were really conceived in such an abstract way, and if people reflected carefully on the basic nature of the penalty, assimilating the idea fully, I do not think the penalty would commonly be thought to be very severe. If the penalty is an abstraction, without effects on the person punished, is it something people would mind, *so conceived*? Of course, people look to avoid dying and the death penalty, but I doubt that we can attribute it to any very clear and penetrating reconstruction of what is bad about it. The desire to avoid it seems to me based on the desire, or, perhaps better said, the drive to continue living, but I don't easily see how to explain this desire or drive rationally, by citing something about death which might be bad. I do not think capital punishment would be seen as severe as concrete bad, conceived in this way, as an abstract propositional bad.

Especially if one tries to compare a very severe concrete bad to an abstract propositional bad, I believe one will see a difficulty with the commensurability of the two types of bad and with a traditional idea that the death penalty, for example, is worse than life imprisonment. Suppose one compared the abstract bad of it being true of one that one is made by the state to die prematurely (where one should assume, clearly recognize and accept that there is no concrete bad entailed by the proposition) to the concrete bad of being in prison for the rest of one's life. So described, it does not seem clear to me that people would prefer to avoid the abstract in favor of accepting the concrete bad, provided they were basing their preferences on the nature of the concepts involved and not their barely conscious or subconscious drive to survive. So I am not sure that the conception of the death penalty as something other than death—being dead—will achieve the result of laying the basis for thinking of the death penalty as a particularly severe punishment.

What I have argued thus far suggests that the very conception of punishment and the death penalty is fundamentally important for thinking about whether killing someone is a penalty and how much of a penalty it is. An alternative conception of punishment may well enable one to think that death is a severe penalty. Realizing that people basically do not want to be killed because they want to continue living, one might perhaps think of punishments as forcing people to have what they do not want, or forcing them not to have what they do want. This idea need not regard whether what they want or what they do not want is rational, in some sense of the term, and it need not explain what they want in terms of what has value, is good or bad. Suppose punishing people involves simply depriving them of what they want. Then one could argue simply that death is a penalty because it is a condition in which people do not have what they want—continued existence—and that the penalty is severe, relative to other penalties, because of the relative strength of the desire or drive to continue living. So conceived, the death penalty would be a penalty only for those people who want to continue living. For those whose continued existence is a matter of indifference to them, there could be no death penalty, at least on this conception. If people on average, as it were, desire to continue living more than they desire to have money or freedom of movement, then one might be able to say that the death penalty is more severe, on average anyhow. The basis for this would be that people want to continue living more than they want not to be incarcerated and more than they want not to be deprived of their money by fines.

This conception of punishment and the severity of the death penalty, however, is not dependent on the idea that punishments generally are bad effects on people. One cannot simply identify what is bad with what is contrary to someone's desires, even if one makes those desires especially important to the person, just as one cannot identify what is good, or good for someone, with what accords with someone's desires. Nevertheless, this conception allows the conceptual possibility that the death penalty is a punishment and is perhaps relatively severe, because it does not depend on the idea that death is bad for people. It would not be inconsistent with the Epicurean view of the value of death for people.

Many of the points I have made in this paper are likely to strike people as at least somewhat controversial and perhaps deeply disagreeable. In any case, I feel persuaded by my reflections that if the death penalty is a punishment at all, then the death penalty is not death—being dead—or else punishments are not harms as traditionally conceived. If the death penalty is not death, then it is either at bottom a kind of unaffecting, or minimally affecting, abstraction (the fact about one's history that one's life was ended prematurely by government officials) or it is preventing people from having what they want, namely to continue living. In either case, it is not bad for the person being punished, because it does not affect them. If punishments are not harms to people, then they are perhaps socially accepted forms of vengeance, constructed to satisfy feelings of resentment, or alternatively they are simply events which prevent people from having what they desire. In either case, they need not be bad for the people punished in any important sense of the term.

For reasons sketched in this paper, it is apparent to me that the whole issue of the nature and justifiability of the death penalty deserves a fresher and much closer look, since the penalty is, if a harm at all, not the great harm it is commonly thought to be. Such an examination should consider the basic nature of punishments generally and how to assess and compare the severity of different punishments.

WORKS CITED

Aristotle, *The Complete Works of Aristotle*, vol. 2, ed. Jonathan Barnes (Princeton: Princeton University Press, 1984).

Bentham, Jeremy, *An Introduction to the Principles of Morals and Legislation* (London: The Athalone Press, 1970).

Diogenes Laertius, *Lives of the Eminent Philosophers*, X.125.

Hart, H. L. A., *Punishment and Responsibility: Essays in the Philosophy of Law* (Oxford: Oxford University Press, 1968).

Mill, John Stuart, *Utilitarianism* (Indianapolis: The Bobbs-Merrill Co., Inc., 1957).

Porphyry, *On Abstinence*, in A. A. Long and D. N. Sedley, *The Hellenistic Philosophers* (Cambridge: Cambridge University Press, 1987).

Rosenbaum, Stephen, "Epicurean Moral Theory", *History of Philosophy Quarterly* 13 (1996), pp. 389–410.

———, "Appraising Death in Human Life: Two Modes of Valuation", *Midwest Studies in Philosophy* 24 (*Life and Death: Metaphysics and Ethics*), ed. Peter French and Howard K. Wettstein (Oxford: Blackwell Publishers, 2000), pp. 151–171.

Sallust, *The Cataline Conspiracy*, trans. S. A. Handford (Baltimore: Penguin, 1967).

Sidgwick, Henry, *The Methods of Ethics* (Chicago: University of Chicago Press, 1907).

Smith, Adam, *The Theory of Moral Sentiments* (Oxford: Clarendon Press, 1976).

Wasserstrom, Richard, "Capital Punishment as Punishment: Some Theoretical Issues and Objections", *Midwest Studies in Philosophy*, ed. Peter French, et al. (Minneapolis: University of Minnesota Press, 1982), pp. 476–478.

DIOGENES'S INSCRIPTION AT OENOANDA

Andrew M. T. Moore

The philosophy of Epicurus was influential over a wide area of the ancient world. From Greece his thoughts and sayings spread west to Italy and eastward around the Mediterranean to Egypt, Syria, and Asia Minor. They were enthusiastically adopted by the people of Lycia in Southwest Turkey and, especially, by the inhabitants of the inland town of Oenoanda (Figure 1). Here, probably in the early years of the second century A. D., one Diogenes, a citizen of the town, in his words "Having already reached the sunset of my life (being almost on the verge of departure from the world on account of old age), I wanted, before being overtaken by death, to compose a fine anthem to celebrate the fullness of pleasure and to help now those who are well-constituted."[1] He caused significant elements of Epicurus's ideas and writings to be recorded in a massive inscription chiseled in stone on a wall, possibly at the back of a stoa or arcade, in the center of the city.

Oenoanda lies high in rugged mountains (Figure 2) northeast of the little port, now a modern resort town, of Fethiye, the ancient Telmessus.[2] The city was probably founded soon after 200 B. C. by colonists from Termessos, a town that lay to the northeast, inland from the head of the Gulf of Antalya. Despite its mountainous setting, Oenoanda seems to have flourished at a time of growing prosperity in the years before and after its incorporation in the Roman Empire, on the evidence of the remains of its numerous public buildings, theatres, baths, fora, and also its considerable extent (Figure 3).

The site was discovered by a British naval officer, R. Hoskyn, and a friend, Edward Forbes, in 1841 while on shore leave from charting the bay of Fethiye.[3] It was mapped by a second group led by another naval officer, Lieutenant T. A. B. Spratt, two years later. Oenoanda remained unfrequented for some time thereafter but in the last two decades of the nineteenth century the site was visited by French, Austrian, and other epigraphers who discovered fragments of the Diogenes inscription, 88 pieces in all, lying on the surface.

1   Martin Ferguson Smith, *Diogenes of Oinoanda: The Epicurean Inscription* (Naples: Bibliopolis, 1993).

2   J. J. Coulton, "Highland Cities in South-West Turkey: The Oinoanda and Balboura Surveys", in *Ancient Anatolia*, ed. R. Matthews (London: British Institute of Archaeology at Ankara, 1998), pp. 225–236, at p. 226.

3   Ibid., p. 227; A. Hall, "The Oenoanda Survey: 1974–76", *Anatolian Studies* 26 (1976), pp. 191–197, at p. 191.

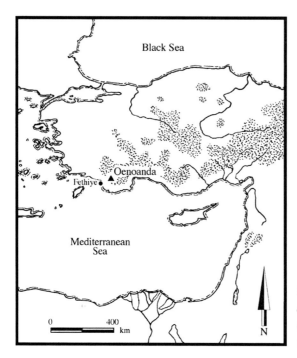

FIGURE 1: *The location of the ancient city of Oenoanda in Southwest Turkey.*

There matters rested although other classical scholars did visit the site on occasion during the mid-twentieth century. Martin Ferguson Smith, then a young British student of philosophy, came to Oenoanda in 1968 with the intention of documenting the remains of Diogenes's inscription more thoroughly. In the next five years he relocated most of the pieces of the inscription that had been noted during the nineteenth century and found an additional 38 fragments.[4] This prompted Alan Hall to undertake a surface survey of the site to determine its configuration and history in more detail and to enlarge the collection of fragments of the inscription, a program of research that continued from 1974 to 1983. The survey yielded a substantial increase in knowledge of the layout of the city and the inscription itself. The site was mapped in considerable detail, several major buildings were studied, and another 86 fragments of the inscription were located.[5] Pieces of the inscription were found scattered across the site and even in villages and farmyards some distance away.[6] The find spots of the fragments of the inscription were marked on the site map to determine their distribution. The concentration of pieces near the so-called esplanade, probably an ancient agora, gave a good indication of the likely location of the wall on which

---

4   Hall, "The Oenoanda Survey", p. 193.

5   Coulton, "Highland Cities", p. 228.

6   Martin Ferguson Smith, "Diogenes of Oenoanda, New Fragments 122–124",
    Anatolian Studies 34 (1984), pp. 43–57, at p. 43.

FIGURE 2, ABOVE: *Wall-walk, curtain and tower entrance in the Hellenistic fortifications. (Photo by S. Mitchell.)*
FIGURE 3, LEFT: *The lower agora of the city. (Photo by S. Mitchell.)*

Diogenes's inscription had once been carved.[7] The Turkish authorities under the dictates of their antiquities' legislation were not inclined to allow pieces of the inscription to be removed from the site and the surveying team was unable to raise the money to conduct a proper excavation. The project was eventually suspended on the untimely death of Hall himself.

The most recent phase of research at Oenoanda began in 1994 when Stephen Mitchell returned to the site to assess the possibility of mounting an

---

7   Hall, "The Oenoanda Survey", p. 196.

FIGURE 4: *Diogenes of Oenoanda fr. 3 (Smith) from the* Physics. *Here Diogenes explains the purpose of his inscription (excerpt quoted on page 209). (Photo by S. Mitchell.)*

excavation there.[8] A small excavation took place in 1997[9] and further work is contemplated at the site. The 1997 excavation was largely confined to the south side of the esplanade because it was thought Diogenes's stoa may have been located there. This effort was most productive. Ten large pieces of the inscription were found on blocks of stone reused in later buildings. These added some 500 words to those known already, bringing the total up to 6,500. The total number of fragments known now stands at 223.[10] We may expect that many more will be found as research proceeds (Figure 4).

What is the significance of all this? It now appears that the inscription was probably even more massive than hitherto thought, perhaps some 25,000 words in all (Diogenes was a prolix writer), and may have covered 260 square meters of wall.[11] Much more is known about the content of the inscription, treatises on old age, physics, and ethics, as well as the texts of at least two letters. The latter highlight Diogenes's tendency to expound at considerable length in the inscription. Writing to Antipater in Greece he says:

---

8   Stephen Mitchell, "Oenoanda and Western Pisidia", *Anatolian Studies* 45 (1995), pp. 14–16.

9   Smith, "Excavations at Oinoanda 1997: The New Epicurean Texts", *Anatolian Studies* 48 (1998), pp. 125–170.

10 Martin Ferguson Smith, "Elementary, My Dear Lycians: A Pronouncement on Physics from Diogenes of Oinoanda", *Anatolian Studies* 50 (2000), pp. 133–137, at p. 133.

11 Smith, "Excavations", p. 125.

My dear Antipater,

Of goodwill you have often given me indications already, Antipater, both in the letter which you sent us recently and earlier when I was ardently trying to persuade you in person to turn to philosophy, in which you, if anyone, live the most pleasant life through employing excellent principles.

Accordingly, I assure you, I am most eager to go and meet again both you yourself and the other friends in Athens and in Chalcis and Thebes, and I assume that all of you have the same feeling.

These words of this letter I am now writing to you from Rhodes, where I have recently moved from my own country at the beginning of winter ... our own land being hit by snow.[12]

As we read the inscriptions we are struck by their philosophical insights, combined with commonplace observations. It is all the more remarkable when we remember that every word, including Diogenes's comments about the winter weather in his home town of Oenoanda, were chiseled out by a stonemason on the famous wall. This was a work not of days or even weeks but months and possibly years, laborious and painstaking, truly a work for the ages. It is even more remarkable that the inscription, or at least its many fragments, have survived almost two thousand years down to the present day to be recovered by archaeologists. It provides one of those rare moments when the past speaks to us directly, or at least appears to do so.

And finally, who was Diogenes? We do not know for certain, and this is perhaps a surprise given the prominent place his inscription occupied in the town. He was obviously wealthy and presumably held a position of some note. One possibility is that he was a kinsman of one Licinnia Flavilla who built a mausoleum at Oenoanda in the third century A. D. on which was inscribed a genealogy of her family going back many generations.[13] The name Flavianus Diogenes is included in the list of names. A second possibility favored by some is that our Diogenes was Marcus Aurelius Diogenes known from an inscription on a statue base who was also evidently a prominent citizen of Oenoanda. Or perhaps Diogenes is known to us only through his inscription. However that may be, his inscription with all its idiosyncrasies is one of the more remarkable documents that has come down to us from ancient times. The authors of the

---

12 Smith, *Diogenes of Oinoanda,* p. 397.

13 A. S. Hall, N. P. Milner, and J. J. Coulton, "The Mausoleum of Licinnia Flavilla and Flavianus Diogenes of Oinoanda: Epigraphy and Architecture", *Anatolian Studies* 46 (1996), pp. 111–144.

---

papers in this volume on Epicurus will be among those who eagerly await further discoveries of fragments of Diogenes's inscription in the years to come.[14]

WORKS CITED

Coulton, J. J., "Highland Cities in South-West Turkey: The Oinoanda and Balboura Surveys", in *Ancient Anatolia*, ed. R. Matthews (London: British Institute of Archaeology at Ankara, 1998), pp. 225–236.

Hall, A., "The Oenoanda Survey: 1974–76", *Anatolian Studies* 26 (1976), pp. 191–197.

Hall, A. S., N. P. Milner, and J. J. Coulton, "The Mausoleum of Licinnia Flavilla and Flavianus Diogenes of Oinoanda: Epigraphy and Architecture", *Anatolian Studies* 46 (1996), pp. 111–144.

Mitchell, Steven, "Oenoanda and Western Pisidia", *Anatolian Studies* 45 (1995), pp. 14–16.

Smith, Martin Ferguson, "Diogenes of Oenoanda, New Fragments 122–124", *Anatolian Studies* 34 (1984), pp. 43–57.

——, *Diogenes of Oinoanda: The Epicurean Inscription* (Naples: Bibliopolis, 1993).

——, "Excavations at Oinoanda 1997: The New Epicurean Texts", *Anatolian Studies* 48 (1998), pp. 125–170.

——, "Elementary, My Dear Lycians: A Pronouncement on Physics from Diogenes of Oinoanda", *Anatolian Studies* 50 (2000), pp. 133–137.

Stenton, E. C., and J. J. Coulton, "Oenoanda: The Water Supply and Aqueduct", *Anatolian Studies* 36 (1986), pp. 15–59.

---

14 I wish to express my thanks to Stephen Mitchell who allowed his illustrations to be reproduced here.

God(s), 7f, 13, 29, 30 n.29, 31, 45–63, 82–86, 92–98, 115, 121f, 144, 148, 153, 159–163, 190
Gow, A. S. F., 26
Grant, Michael, 7f
Gregory of Nazianzus, 158
Gregory of Nissa, 158

H
habit, 140, 143ff, 147
Hall, Alan, 210f
Hamartols, George, 157
Hamilton, Emma, 21
Hamlet, 200
happiness, 113–119, 124f, 171 n.8, 172, 173 n.17, 178ff, 183, 184 n.7, 190, 193
harsh speaking, 27, 29
Hart, H. L. A., 198
Hayter, George, 21f, 26
hedonism, 117ff, 139, 144, 173–180, 183f, 188, 190f
Hegel, G. W. F., 127–129, 134f
Hellenistic, 6, 7, 11, 163
Herculaneum, 17–39
Hermarchus, 202
Herodotus, 158
Hesiod, 158
Hinduism, 14
Hirtzel, Rudolf, 161
Hobbes, Thomas, 114
Homer, 158
Horace, 17, 20, 24, 26, 27
Hoskyn, R., 209
human nature, 117f
Hume, David, 128

I
immortality, 11f, 92–96
incorporeality, 92–98, 104
Indelli, Giovanni, 24
inertia, 87, 104
Institute for the Study and

Preservation of Ancient Religious Texts (ISPART), 18
Institute of Religion in the Age of Science, 14
instrumental value, 169 n.4, 184 n.7, 188f
intrinsic value, 150, 176, 183, 184 n.7, 189ff
Iphigenia, 7
Irenaeus, 158
Isis, 11
Isocrates, 158
isonomia, 161f

J
James, William, 8f
Janko, Richard, 17
Jaspers, Karl, 163
Jefferson, Thomas, 163
Jensen, Christian, 23
Jerome, St., 159
Jesus Christ, 15, 49, 53–55, 61, 63
John of Damascus, 158
Jungkuntz, Richard, 47
just-war theory, 61

K
Kant, Immanuel, 135 n.15
katastematic pleasure, 142–152, 174–178, 183–191, 194
Kilpatrick, Thomas B., 62
kinetic pleasure, 142–147, 174–178, 183 n.1, 186f, 190
Kleve, Knut, 161
knowledge, 69–80, 91 n.20, 128
Koerte, Alfred, 24
Krokevich, Adam, 162
Kuiper, Taco, 23, 25

L
Lactantius, 45–63, 121, 160
Lemke, Dietrich, 162

David Armstrong is Professor of Classics at the University of Texas at Austin. Expert in many areas of Greek and Roman literature and culture, he is the author of *Horace* (Yale, 1989) and numerous articles on Greek and Latin poetry, ancient literary criticism, and Epicureanism. His recent research centers on the Epicurean Philodemus and he has been active in the Philodemus Translation Project since 1993. He is currently preparing editions and translations of Philodemus's *On Anger* and *On Death*, and, with Jeffrey Fish, of Philodemus's *On Poetry* Book 5. He is also editing *Vergil, Philodemus, and the Augustans: Proceedings of the Cumae Conference, 2000* (University of Texas, forthcoming).

James I. Campbell is Professor Emeritus (Philosophy), Rochester Institute of Technology. The author of *Language of Religion*, he is actively involved in volunteer work for not-for-profit agencies in Rochester, NY, while continuing research on Buddhism and on the development of Western "just war" theory in the fourth and fifth centuries.

Lloyd P. Gerson is Professor of Philosophy at the University of Toronto. He is the author of books and articles on ancient philosophy. Among his books are: *Aristotle's Platonism* (Cornell University Press, 2004), *Readings in Neoplatonism* (with John Dillon) (Hackett, 2003), *Knowing Persons: A Study in Plato* (Oxford University Press, 2003), *The Cambridge Companion to Plotinus* (Cambridge University Press, 1996), *Plotinus: Arguments of the Philosophers* (Routledge, 1994), *Readings in Hellenistic Philosophy* (with Brad Inwood) (Hackett, 1988; second edition 1997).

Dane R. Gordon is Professor Emeritus in Philosophy at Rochester Institute of Technology. His books include: *A Feeling Intellect and a Thinking Heart* (University Press of America, 2002), *Philosophy and Vision* (Rodopi, 1998, first published in Polish in 1995), *The Old Testament in its Theological, Cultural and Historical Context* (Prentice-Hall, 1985, and UPS, 1994), and *Thinking and Reading in Philosophy of Religion* (Haven, 1994). He is currently bringing up to date the history of Rochester Institute of Technology (Edwin Mellen, 1983), and co-editing with David Durst *Philosophical Issues in South East Europe* (Rodopi, forthcoming). Professor Gordon is a Presbyterian Minister.

Veronica Gventsadze holds a PH.D. in Social Thought from the University of Chicago. Her research interests include Hellenistic philosophy, Early Modern philosophy and the Scientific Revolution, and the history and philosophy of science. She teaches philosophy at Lakehead University in Thunder Bay, Ontario.

Andrew M. T. Moore is an archaeologist who was born and educated in England. For the last two decades he has lived and worked in the U.S.A. The principal aim of his research has been to elucidate the transition from foraging to farming in Western Asia and to examine the spread of this new way of life to the rest of Asia, Europe and Africa. Moore has documented the inception of farming at the early settlement of Abu Hureyra in Syria, research that has recently been published (with G.C. Hillman and A.J. Legge) in *Village on the Euphrates* (Oxford University Press, 2000). In his current project Moore is investigating the economy of Neolithic villages on the Dalmatian coast in Croatia. Moore is a Professor of Anthropology and Dean of the College of Liberal Arts at the Rochester Institute of Technology.

Stephen E. Rosenbaum is Professor of Philosophy and Dean of the Honors College at University of Nevada, Las Vegas. He has published a number of papers and reviews on Epicurean theories about death and ethics, and continues scholarship designed to reveal the virtues of ancient Greek ethical ideals. Currently he is revising work on Epicurus's ideas about death and ethics for a book titled *Life in the Unwalled City: The Epicurean Way of Death*.

Daniel C. Russell is Assistant Professor of Philosophy at Wichita State University in Wichita, Kansas. His primary research interests include ancient moral theory, ancient moral psychology, and ancient theories of practical reasoning. His manuscript on pleasure, psychology, and value theory in Plato's ethics, titled *Plato on Pleasure and the Good Life*, is currently under review.

Paul M. Schafer is Assistant Professor of Philosophy at Xavier University of Louisiana. His PH.D. is from DePaul University and he maintains an active interest in the History of Philosophy, in particular in the area of Post-Kantian European thought. Schafer has published reviews of works on Hegel and Marx, and is editor of a forthcoming volume on the Doctoral Dissertation of Karl Marx.

Marianna Shakhnovich is Professor and Head of the Department of Philosophy of Religion and Religious Studies, Faculty of Philosophy, St. Petersburg State University, Russia. Her research interests in the sphere of philosophy of religion are reflected in her recent books: *Epicurus's Garden: Epicurus's Philosophy of Religion and Epicurean Tradition in Russian and West European Culture* (St. Petersburg State University, 2002), and *The Paradoxes of Epicurus's Theology* (St. Petersburg Philosophical Society, 2000) (in Russian).

David B. Suits is Professor of Philosophy at Rochester Institute of Technology. His current research interests include the philosophy of death, the philosophy of mind, artificial intelligence, and the nature of empathy. He is finishing a book, *The Singularity of Death: An Epicurean Perspective*.

M. R. Wheeler teaches philosophy at San Diego State University in San Diego, California. He has published papers on Aristotle's philosophy of language and Kant's theory of causality. His principal academic interests are ancient Greek philosophy, Kant studies, and contemporary metaphysics.

David E. White is Associate Professor of Philosophy at St. John Fisher College, Rochester, New York. A graduate of the Sage School of Philosophy at Cornell University, he has published mainly in the philosophy of religion and is currently editing the papers of the Creighton Club (New York State Philosophical Association) and working on a new, critical edition of the works of Bishop Butler.

C O L O P H O N

DESIGN   Bruce Ian Meader
PRODUCTION   Amelia Hugill-Fontanel, Marnie Soom
TYPEFACE   Adobe Minion Pro
PRINTING   Lightning Source USA

CPSIA information can be obtained at www.ICGtesting.com
Printed in the USA
BVOW080410120712

294964BV00002B/8/A

9 780971 345966